"Gerard S. Sloyan is one of those rare scholars who can claim an expertise in both Bible and theology that enables him to bridge the gap between exegesis and systematic theology. In this volume, he first explains how the writers of the New Testament understood the person of Jesus. Then he considers how some of the most significant figures of the Apostolic and Patristic periods dealt with the theological issues raised by the biblical material. Compact and elegantly written, this volume will be of special interest to those who seek a comprehensive portrait of Jesus."

Frank J. Matera
The Andrews-Kelly-Ryan Professor of Biblical Studies
The Catholic University of America, Washington, DC

"Father Sloyan here explores the story of the true Jesus of history—the Jesus whose influence redirected the course of history. His usual precise and accurate prose shows his easy command of the historic sources and of two centuries and more of debate about their interpretation. Jesus exemplifies how a man of faith can use historical work and how a historian can show his faith in his work. For someone smart enough to be perplexed by the differences in the gospels and the offerings of the 'Historical-Jesus of the Month' club, here is the book to study and contemplate."

Terrence W. Tilley
President-elect, Catholic Theological Society of America
Professor of Theology and Chair of the Department
Fordham University, Bronx, NY

Engaging Theology: Catholic Perspectives

Jesus

Word Made Flesh

Gerard S. Sloyan

Tatha Wiley, Series Editor

A Michael Glazier Book

LITURGICAL PRESS
Collegeville, Minnesota

www.litpress.org

A Michael Glazier Book published by Liturgical Press

Cover design by Ann Blattner.

1	2	3	4	5	6	7	8	9

Library of Congress Cataloging-in-Publication Data

Sloyan, Gerard Stephen, 1919–
   Jesus : Word made flesh / Gerard S. Sloyan.
      p.   cm. — (Engaging theology : Catholic perspectives)
   Includes bibliographical references and index.
   ISBN 978-0-8146-5991-5
   1. Jesus Christ—History of doctrines.   I. Title.

BT198.S595 2008
232—dc22

2007052136

Contents

Editor's Preface

In calling the Second Vatican Council, Pope John XXIII challenged those he gathered to take a bold leap forward. Their boldness would bring a church still reluctant to accept modernity into full dialogue with it. The challenge was not for modernity to account for itself, nor for the church to change its faith, but for the church to transform its conception of faith in order to speak to a new and different situation.

Today we stand in a postmodern world. The assumptions of modernity are steeply challenged, while the features of postmodernity are not yet fully understood. Now another world invites reflection and dialogue, and the challenge is to discover how the meanings and values of Christian faith speak effectively to this new situation.

This series takes up the challenge. Central concerns of the tradition—God, Jesus, Scripture, Anthropology, Church, and Discipleship—here are lifted up. In brief but comprehensive volumes, leading Catholic thinkers lay out these topics with a historically conscious eye and a desire to discern their meaning and value for today.

Designed as a complete set for an introductory course in theology, individual volumes are also appropriate for specialized courses. Engaging Theology responds to the need for teaching resources alive to contemporary scholarly developments, to the current issues in theology, and to the real questions about religious beliefs and values that people raise today.

Tatha Wiley
Series Editor

Author's Preface

As a college freshman I bought a Greek grammar at second hand and found it richly commented on and illustrated by the previous owner. The class in the accidence of an ancient tongue was a thrice-weekly hour of charm conducive to doodling to stave off narcolepsy. My "pre-owned" grammar (there are no more used cars) carried on a conversation with the author. When an empty space denoted that a form of a verb did not exist it was identified as "Wanting." A marginal note asked, "Who wants it?" There was a sketch in the end pages of an indigenous American with a tepee in a balloon over his head that contained the thought "Mental Reservation." That sketch must have been done in an ethics class whose dullness invited artistry.

Is the book the student now holds in hand a guaranteed substitute for No-Doz? Hardly. Let it only be said that the textbook that guarantees wakefulness has yet to be written.

There are many hundreds of books about Jesus, good, bad, and different. Few are written with style. Jesus had style, a style so high it is impossible to convey it in a book of words. The four evangelists did a reasonably good job but, even with the help of the Holy Spirit, it was not easy. The magnitude of the man outruns the power of words. There is evidently a convention in textbook writing that the author should not attempt to amuse, entertain, or emotionally engage the reader. An interesting paragraph is at times admissible, perhaps an occasional sentence with color, but nothing more. There is a fabled directive on a piece of sheet music for orchestra and choir that reads, *Religioso, ma non troppo.* Doleful, but not overly. Dr. Johnson told Boswell of a young friend who once considered studying for the ministry but had to abandon the idea because cheerfulness kept breaking in. A character in Evelyn Waugh's *The Loved One*, a novel about the burial industry in California, is named Mr. Joyboy. That was Jesus. He would eat and drink with anybody.

The only way to pump a little life into a textbook about him is to get a class discussion going about him, better still, an argument about whether this or that statement in the book has got it right.

I have written about Jesus at book length before. The first time was in 1960 when a journalist friend who had invented a paper for high schoolers she dubbed *Hi-Time* asked me to do a series about him over the course of the school year. Two years later it appeared as a hardcover book titled *Christ the Lord*. Another publisher made a paperback of it when that industry was young. I had another go at our Savior in 1975 with *Jesus on Trial* and again three years later with *Is Christ the End of the Law?* Still another book appeared in 1983, *Jesus in Focus: A Life in Its Setting* and, in 1986, *The Jesus Tradition: Images of Jesus in the West*. The last two were a bit of an improvement on the first try of twenty-odd years before. In four of those cases the impetus came from a woman editor, normally of books in a series, each who loved Jesus deeply and knew what she wanted a book about him to say. Those women are Henriette Mackin, Patricia Kluepfel, Monika Hellwig, and now Tatha Wiley. Two others who said that such and such a book could well exist were Jesus scholars whom I revere as my teachers, John Reumann and Howard Clark Kee.

My long-term colleague at Temple University, Leonard Swidler, wrote a book concerned with the disputed writings and censure of Hans Küng, a priest of Luzern, and the admonition of Edward Schillebeeckx, OP, with a fresh contribution from each. Swidler did the English translation of Küng's essay and asked me to do the same with that of Schillebeeckx, which arrived on a tape of spoken, idiomatic French. Two years after the book appeared I met Schillebeeckx on an open railroad platform in this country, and instead of the customary warm greeting I expected, he said without introduction: "You got an important sentence wrong in your translation of my piece." Guilty as charged.

I fully expect to be told by our Lord at the judgment something similar, delivered in the gentlest of tones. It will be easier to take it from him than from some secretary at the Congregation for the Doctrine of the Faith, a body from which happily I have never heard.

The real business of a preface such as this is to acknowledge gratefully those who assisted in the preparation and production of the book. The humorist Robert Benchley skewered the genre by thanking the inventors of the Bessemer Open Hearth Process, without which his book could not have been written. Another courageous author thanked his beloved wife and small children, without whom his book would have been completed in half the time. Bereft of such welcome interruptions by Pope Damasus I, who enjoyed better quarters while depriving the Western clergy of their better halves, I have managed to produce this manuscript only with help of another sort. My auxiliaries in the spread of the Gospel through writing are Dr. Nicholas Rademacher of Cabrini College, Radnor, Pennsylvania; Mary Dancy and Grace Ann Lewis, both of deans' staffs at The Catholic University of America; and Angela Howell of Mayfield Senior School in Pasadena, California. All of these friends are associates in a skill I do not possess. They process words. So do I but in a different sense. But theirs is a skill that, at minimum, requires theological sophistication. Without them this book would not exist. Nor would it exist without the cheerful support of colleagues on the faculty of The Catholic University of America and Georgetown University, where a kind Providence has situated me after retirement from Temple University. There I was privileged over twenty-five years to make sense of Christianity in words in the company of American Jews, Muslims from around the world, and Korean Buddhists, not to speak of some East Coast Protestants and Catholics. Speak of a support system! I have known it over many days and hours as this book was being prepared for in thought and written in fact.

Hyattsville, Maryland   Gerard S. Sloyan
July 2007

Chapter One

Who Jesus Was in the Religion of Israel

The religion known as Christianity is widely supposed to have Jesus at its center, the Galilean Jew venerated after his resurrection from the dead and ascension into heaven as the Christ and Lord, now intercessor with his Father in the power of the Holy Spirit on behalf of all humanity.

People who are not Christians and who do not explore the matter in any depth tend to think that Jesus holds the same place in that faith as Moses does in Judaism, the prophet Muhammad in Islam, and Gautama the Enlightened in Buddhism—or that for Christians Jesus has replaced the one God.

None of these analogies or errors is close to the fact.

The heart and center of Christianity is God—the Infinite, the Eternal, the Indescribable in any words even remotely adequate to the task.

If this is so, how is it that occasional media reports on the activities of some Christians (who tend to deny the title to any but themselves) can be thought by outsiders to be Jesus worshipers as their primary religious identity? The press and television coverage of such groups gives the impression that Jesus has dislodged God from his throne in the heavens and is himself seated on it in solitary glory. It is no wonder that some Jews and most Muslims take this to be the basic Christian position, namely, idolatry, worshiping a man as God.

This book means to explore who Jesus was, is, and is to come, and by what series of events this man of Jewish history came to be viewed by millions as a man of Godlike powers in their present lives and their hoped-for future.

But first it must be declared as loudly and clearly as possible that God is at the center of Christianity, not Jesus, or that Jesus is the center

1

of Christianity only insofar as God dwells in him and dwelled in him from the moment of his earthly beginnings. Moreover, it must be stated strongly that it is a flawed proclamation of the Gospel that Jesus is central to Christianity and God is not, or that the only way God's love for the human race can be known is through the love Jesus bears for it. A confused preaching of the Gospel is bound to result in a confused perception of it, both by believers and interested or even casual onlookers. There can be no denying that there has been much of such preaching. Television evangelism and the internet are full of it.

The Actual or Real Jesus

Who, then, is this Jesus about whom some people are right and others woefully wrong—in both cases many millions of people? The short answer is that he was a Jew of Galilee, the northern province of Roman Palestine, in the early years of the first millennium of our era, whom the Roman Empire executed by crucifixion and who, although dead and buried, was experienced alive by many after three days.

Jesus is a towering figure in human life in many quarters of the globe, but little is known of his early life apart from his having been a village craftsman in wood, in association with his mother's husband who was his father at Law. What we know of his brief public career is largely confined to his teaching and the events of the last week of his life. There is a fairly lengthy account of his last days and hours in the four gospels, which are also the source of what he taught publicly. There is almost as much again about him in another source, the letters and treatises from the mid- to late first century, which is reckoned by the presumed date of his birth in the Christian calendar. In these writings he is venerated under the titles of Christ and Lord (not the LORD, who is the God of Israel). Important in all that is written about him is the fact that his upraising from the dead was witnessed by those who knew him well in life and had witnessed his bloody execution only days before. In one recorded instance he appeared in his risen state to a Jew named Saul who was not of Roman Palestine and who had not known him, and in the same report to "more than five hundred believers at once, most of whom are still living, although some have died" (1 Cor 15:6).[1]

---

[1] Scripture here and following is either the author's own translation or from the Revised English Bible © 1989 Oxford University Press and Cambridge University Press. Used with permission.

That is certainly the most important thing that can be said of Jesus: that he was raised up from the dead to live again, however briefly, in the company of his friends. If it were not for this claimed resurrection by the power of God (not a resuscitation or return to a former life), the Jewish and non-Jewish worlds would probably never have heard of Jesus. This is very important. Some who are not Christians think he would be remembered for the sublimity of his teaching and the way he faced death, but there is no sufficient reason to think so. His disciples record that they knew what to make of him only after he had risen from the dead. Several times the reminiscences of his life and teachings called gospels (Anglo-Saxon *gōd-spel*, rendering the Greek *eù-aggélion*, good tidings) say that those who were associated with him as *talmidim* (learners) did not comprehend his teaching until he had been raised up in the glory of the Father. That is totally understandable. How could anyone look back on every word, gesture, and action of a person one knew well—and to whom this had happened—other than differently from the way one would remember the life of any other human being who had died? If the occurrence was unique in human history, which is the claim, the person concerned would have to have been remembered as unique. This deed of God with respect to the man Jesus is basic to all else that has been said or can be said of him.

Being Raised Up from the Dead to a New Life— Fact or Fancy?

The basic question posed by the Church's faith in the resurrected Jesus is, did it actually happen? The only satisfactory answer is that persons in great numbers, all of them Palestinian Jews, were convinced that it did. No one answer testifies to a group delusion or fantasy. The price of given testimony was too high. Many witnesses devoted their lives to spreading the word of the resurrection of this man they had known, calling it a fact of their experience. An exception, and an important one mentioned above, was the Tarsus-born Saul/Paul (a man who would have had a Jewish and a gentile name from birth). He acknowledged with regret more than once his early disbelief in what was being claimed for Jesus by the movement that professed faith in him. Paul did more than disbelieve. He claimed to have harassed—his word is persecuted—followers of the man of Nazareth who had this belief. His skepticism came to an abrupt halt when Jesus appeared to him in circumstances he did not record in any extant communication. All we have is the rhetorical question in one of his letters: "Have I not seen Jesus our Lord?"

(1 Cor 9:1). In that piece of correspondence to friends in the port city of southern Greece among whom he had lived he went on to say, "I handed on to you as of first importance what I had in turn received, that Christ died for our sins . . . that he was buried; that he was raised on the third day . . . that he appeared to Cephas, then to the Twelve." Next, Paul lists the appearances of Jesus to more than five hundred at once, to James, then to all the apostles. "Last of all . . . he appeared to me. I am the least of the apostles, not fit to be called an apostle, because I persecuted the church of God" (1 Cor 15:3-9).

The company of believers that Saul of the tribe of Benjamin calls the churches had not only believed in the risen Jesus before him; they were spreading this belief in the area of Damascus, the Syrian capital. Was Paul's violent antipathy triggered by the claim that Jesus lived again after death, so little did that claim accord with Pharisee faith in the resurrection of the just on the Last Day? What wild tale was this group propagating, instead of teaching utter fidelity to the oral and written Law of Moses? That fidelity is what anyone who attracted crowds by the thousands should have been about. The response of Paul to the early Church's faith in Jesus' upraising by the power of God—before he came to share that faith—is an important one.

The question has legitimately been asked, does history record Jesus' resurrection only as claimed by a company of devotees prone to believe in it? The testimony of Paul is especially important because he was at first a violent disbeliever in it, as hundreds must have been who first heard the claim. Experiencing the reality behind the claim, and it alone, made Paul think otherwise. In other words, not faith alone but faith based on sight, on the experience of the senses.

Belief in what God had done in Jesus spread rapidly throughout the Jewish Diaspora, and through Jews to some non-Jews. But basically it was a Jewish faith and movement. The testimony of those who had known Jesus Christ risen was evidently widely accepted. There must have been appearances too, to other Diaspora Jews aside from the one to Saul of which we know. At the very least, it is folly to suppose that word of a man upraised from the dead was brought to the gentile Mediterranean world by one disciple only. Saul writes of a couple in Rome named Andronicus and Junia, "who were in Christ before me," calling them his kin and therefore Jews (Rom 16:7). Had they come to belief in the capital, or emigrated to it from the Middle East, as already believers? There is no way to know. Paul's letters to six of the communities or groups of communities to which he had brought the Gospel have by providence or chance been saved. That correspondence must have been but fragmentary evidence in a much larger picture in the lives of many others.

The question is often raised, "If Jesus did and said all these memorable things, why is there no evidence of it from outside Christian circles?" Some have even asked, "Given his immense popularity with the crowds, why was there no correspondence between Pilate and Rome on his execution?" The answer to the second question is that an imperial functionary in the provinces had no need whatever to report doing rough justice in putting down potential uprisings led by individuals. As to the first question, there is extra-Christian evidence from the pen of a Jewish historian Flavius Josephus, a court employee of the Caesar in Rome writing toward the year 90:

> At this time there appeared Jesus, a wise man [or sage]. He was a doer of remarkable deeds, a teacher of those who received the truth willingly. He had a following from among many Jews and Greeks [i.e., gentiles]. And when Pilate, because of an accusation made by the leading men among us, condemned him to the cross, those who had loved him in life did not cease to do so. Up until this very day the people called Christians have not died out. (*Antiquities*, book XVIII, 63–64)

That sounds like the kind of factual report a fellow Galilean might have made sixty-odd years after the event, assuming Jesus' life and death had survived in memory in Roman Palestine both North and South. As to his resurrection—mention of which along with other claims, such as that he was the Messiah, as a later Christian hand inserted—Josephus might never have had word of that marvel transmitted by his Judean informants. Or else he may have heard "was resurrected" and rejected it as a fanciful tale. Josephus was writing a history of his people for the most important non-Jewish readership conceivable, the imperial court. Hence he may not have wished to feature the execution of a much-revered figure by an official known for his brutal behavior. At the same time, Josephus had no scruple in reporting on the death of "John surnamed the Baptist" at the hands of the tetrarch (ruler of a fourth part) Herod Antipas, a preemptive strike lest John's great popularity lead to "some form of sedition" (*Antiquities*, book XVIII, 116–19). Josephus's mention of Jesus and John is only a little of the light he sheds on the events of the 20s and 30s. Without his *Antiquities of the Jews* and *The Jewish War*, of events of a later decade, plus the four gospels, we would be largely in the dark about

Jewish life in that corner of the empire. Only Philo, an Egyptian Jew who was born before Jesus and died after him, left a record of a similar Roman-Jewish clash in his *Legation to Gaius*. His other writings were treatises on how Jewish worship practices might be made comprehensible to non-Jews, namely, by way of allegory.

This is a way of saying how little we know of a period in the life of a particular people in their homeland and the Diaspora, from a record that is fragmentary at best. The *Mishnah* compiled by Judah the Patriarch around 180 does it for a later period, at least in learned circles, in the land of Israel. Besides the letters of Paul and a few others attributed to him and to other disciples of Jesus, which provide information on the spread of the Gospel in different locales, there are three writings from the second half of the first century that report on the movement from within. These are titled The Acts of the Apostles (by the author of the Gospel according to Luke), In Times Past (erroneously named Hebrews), and Apocalypse (Revelation), the latter two names deriving from their first words.

Witnesses to the Movement Rather Than to the Man

From outside the circle of believers in Jesus' resurrection come the testimonies of three pagan Roman writers who speak of a movement they have heard of, known by the name—or, rather, title—of its central figure, *Christiani*. Publius Cornelius Tacitus (d. 120), one of whose two works of Roman history is the *Annals*, writes that "Christus suffered the extreme penalty (*supplicium*) under Tiberius" (15.24). He also repeats the rumor that Nero's response to that "pernicious superstition" was to blame Jesus' devotees for setting fire to a deteriorated Roman neighborhood. Gaius Suetonius Tranquillus (d. after 122), the son of a military man, who ended his career as a biographer and man of letters as the emperor Hadrian's secretary, wrote *On the Life of the Caesars*, twelve of them. It contains two references to the Christians, one under Claudius (41–54) and the other in Nero's reign (54–68). The former charges that, "Because the Jews at Rome caused continuous disturbances at the instigation of *Christus* Claudius expelled them from the city" (25.4). It is from this act of expulsion that Paul came to know the Jewish couple of Pontus on the Black Sea, Aquila and Priscilla, to whom he extends a greeting at the end of Romans and 1 Corinthians. Their fate at the emperor's hands is mentioned in the book of Acts at 18:2, as is their sailing with Paul from Corinth to Ephesus where he left them (vv. 18-19, 26).

Nero's torching of the drab old buildings in the winding streets of Rome is described at length in Suetonius's account of that emperor's career (38). An earlier section mentions without introduction the great fire at Rome and Nero's architectural innovations that followed it; then, a series of restrictive laws that the ruler enacted in his youth to achieve public order (16). These were followed immediately by the phrase: "Punishments were also inflicted on the Christians, a sect professing a new and mischievous religious belief." This conjunction of Nero's action with his punishment of the Christians for no specified reason may be Suetonius's oblique way of describing the scapegoating of the Christians that both he and Tacitus accuse Nero of directly.

Suetonius had a close friend in Pliny the Younger (d. ca. 113), a collection of whose letters has survived.[2] The emperor Trajan at some point in his seventeen-year reign in the early second century had sent Pliny on an embassy to the extensive province of Pontus and Bithynia where he encountered a colony of Christians. A few had already been brought up on trial, but Pliny writes sometime around the year 112 that he has not been present at any of these cases. He evidently has the power of empire to execute them on the charge of being Christians but is uncertain how he should proceed against them. To gain the emperor's help in resolving the dilemma he asks what the customary penalties or investigations and the limits are in such matters. He writes that he has questioned some of them three times as to whether they are Christians, threatening capital punishment for their obstinacy in continuing to maintain that they are. Any who are Roman citizens he has ordered to be sent to the capital for judgment. The number of cases brought before him, however, has grown. A pamphlet was circulated delating by name those who were to be acted against. On repeated interrogation, some said they had belonged to the group but had recanted years ago. His practice has been to release any who reverence the gods with incense and wine, and worship the emperor's image. A few have even cursed Christ, something he has heard genuine Christians would never do.

In light of all this, why Pliny's uncertainty as to how to proceed? Perhaps because he has heard some

> declare that the sum of their guilt or error has amounted only to this, that on an appointed day they have been accustomed to meet before daybreak and to recite a hymn antiphonally to Christ as to a god

[2] A. N. Sherwin-White, *The Letters of Pliny* (Oxford: Clarendon Press, 1966).

and to bind themselves by an oath, not for the commission of any
crime but to abstain from theft, robbery, adultery and breach of
faith. . . . After . . . this ceremony it was their custom to depart
and meet again to take food; but it was ordinary and harmless
food. . . . In accordance with your orders, I had forbidden secret
societies. . . . I thought it necessary . . . to find what truth there
was in this by applying torture to two servant girls who were called
deaconesses. But I found nothing but a depraved and extravagant
superstition.[3]

Trajan's reply was calm and judicious, given the cruelties sanctioned
by the empire at the time. The Christians are not to be sought out. If identified they are to be punished. The one who denies he is a Christian and can
prove it is to be pardoned. "Pay no attention to anonymous pamphlets.
They are out of keeping with our age." If there were any gods of Rome,
they surely would have approved the twofold defense of their cult.

The Little Known of Jesus' Infancy and Early Years

Who was this man Jesus to whom people were paying divine honors
under the name of Christ? This was being done, not by a fraudulent
demand for obeisance to a human, lodged by the weakest of human clay,
but was an act based on the conviction that Jesus had ascended in glory
to the right hand of the one God and Father. The only reasonable explanation for this belief is the remembrances of Jesus by some still living
that had been transmitted first orally and then in writing by disciples of
his disciples. Only the details that do not stand the test of critical examination are to be discarded. Such would be the tale of discovery of the
infant Moses by the pharaoh's daughter, then to be handed over to his
mother to wet-nurse him while the younger woman adopted him as her
son. The obvious place to start with the Jesus narrative is the gospel affirmation that he was of the tribe of Judah and the house of David. There
is every reason to accept this as remembered fact. Semitic peoples tend
to know something of their genealogical origins, at least in the case of
Jews, of their tribe and family. The Matthean list of fourteen ancestors
from Abraham to David and another fourteen from David to the Babylonian exile is derived from the Bible. The same is true of the thirty-five
names from Nathan, son of David, back to Adam in Luke's list of seventy-

---

[3] Plin. Epp. X (ad Traj.), xcvi., in Henry Bettenson and Chris Maunder, *Documents of the Christian Church* (New Edition, Oxford, 1999), 3–4; Sherwin-White, 691–710.

seven names. The source of Matthew's genealogy from Abiud on is unknown, just as Luke's source for the names down to Heli, father of Joseph, defies research. That both lists are multiples of the sacred number seven is clear. It is equally clear that what is called a generation may be a matter of many decades. The two lists of ancestors of Joseph are constructs like the many found in the Hebrew Scriptures. Where the two evangelists got the nonbiblical lists is beyond us. A compilation of characteristic names of men of Judah might have been composed by believers in Jesus in the Galilee, then become available to Matthew and Luke writing in Greek in the near Diaspora. This is not a matter of great moment, however, since simply establishing Jesus' Davidic origins was the main concern of both.

In Jewish thought membership in the Jewish people was matrilineal, while the passing on of name and property was through the father. Luke's account of Mary's virginal motherhood, therefore, and Matthew's strong indication of remembrance of it, means that accepting a tradition already in place caused no conflict for either evangelist, with Joseph as Jesus' father. The same is true of the nonproblematic character of Jesus' birth in Bethlehem, David's city, when Nazareth was well known as his growing up place. Although each evangelist dealt with his birth midrashically (that is, in homiletic elaboration) as the Exodus author did with Moses' infancy, it is unlikely that the tradition they received about Jesus' birth was composed out of whole cloth to make a point of his Davidic lineage. In the nature of the case, many Judahites would have had to be of royal blood because the hero king had sired so many sons. No tale had to be invented to establish Jesus' descent from him. The family of Joseph, whose forebear is called Jacob by Matthew and Heli by Luke, would have been well aware of it. Acknowledging the literary skill of each evangelist does not mean that they were ignorant of the rigid rules in tracing Semitic family lines. Since, however, the sources for Jesus' birth and infancy are two of the gospels, and neither of these sources is accessible to modern historical research, it may suffice to indicate the sources that they in turn drew on. There is no literary evidence that the author of Matthew was familiar with the Gospel of Luke or vice versa. The following eleven matters are shared in the two accounts of Jesus' human origins:

- Mary and Joseph were committed to each other by their families in the first stage of Jewish marriage (the modern written agreement is called *ketuvah*) but not the second stage, consummation (Matt 1:18; Luke 1:27, 34).

- Joseph is of Davidic descent (Matt 1:16, 20; Luke 1:27, 32; 2:4).

- An angel announces the forthcoming birth of the child (Matt 1:20-23, in a dream; Luke 1:30-35, in Gabriel's message, 19).

- Mary's conception of the child is not through intercourse with her husband (Matt 1:20, 23, 25; Luke 1:34).

- The conception is through the Holy Spirit (Matt 1:18, 20; Luke 1:35).

- The angel directs that the child be named Jesus (Matt 1:21, to Joseph; Luke 1:31, to Mary).

- An angel states that Jesus will save people from their sins (Matt 1:21; be a savior, Luke 2:11).

- The child is born after the parents have come to live together (Matt 1:24-25; Luke 2:5-6).

- The birth takes place in Bethlehem (Matt 2:1; Luke 2:4-6).

- The birth is related in time to the reign (days) of the still-living Herod the Great (Matt 2:1; Luke 1:5).

- The boy is reared in Nazareth (Matt 2:23; Luke 2:39).

It has been argued, and not only by those who refuse to credit a miraculous occurrence such as a virginal conception, that the tradition on which the two gospel writers drew view Mary as a type or exemplar of the people Israel, whom the Scriptures often refer to as the virgin daughter of the LORD. A rationalist mentality may require that there be no such thing as miracle, but this is not what lies behind the view of believers in the possibility, who think something else may be going on here. Typology of this sort, a person standing for a whole people or a segment of the people, is a biblical commonplace. Its presence in the tradition that lies behind the two gospels, some believers in the limitless power of God think, must be allowed. In that case the origin of the tradition would be marvel and wonder at the uniqueness of the child who had come to birth, presented as the mode of birth itself. This bears no relation to theories that Jesus was the fruit of the rape of an innocent Mary or was thought to be illegitimate, theories about his origins drawn from wisps of phrases in the gospels.

Similarly, questions have been raised over the authenticity of the one story of Jesus' growing-up years, Luke's narrative of Jesus' parents' having discovered him missing from the caravan after early days of pilgrimage north from the Passover feast. Luke has written in an introduction to his first book, addressed to a certain Theophilus (who may be his literary patron), that after investigating in detail once again the events recently come to pass among them, he has decided to write down the record "in an orderly sequence so that your excellence may know how dependable was the teaching you received" (Luke 1:3-4). This indicates that Luke intends to conduct himself as a historian in the manner of those times. In that literary genre pure fiction was outlawed. Elaboration upon a core reminiscence or valid supposition, however, was at the same time in order. Such was the method employed centuries later by biblical chroniclers of the days of Samuel, Saul, and David and even more recently of the Maccabean revolt. Greek historians like Herodotus and such Latin writers as the author of *Caesar's Gallic Wars* were familiar with the technique: seize upon a remembered fact and work it up in a colorful story. This literary convention may or may not have been the origin of Luke's narrative of Jesus' distraught parents having found him, "sitting in the midst of the teachers in the temple, listening to them and asking them questions" (Luke 2:46). The foundation of the tale may simply have been the well-remembered fact of his skill as a teacher that in another much later setting brought the angry query, "How does this man have such learning when he has never been taught?" (John 7:15), meaning formed under the tutelage of a rabbinic teacher. His precociousness in learning as a twelve-year-old in light of his later familiarity with the Scriptures could have been presumed. To this was added the charming tale of a little boy lost. "Son, why have you done this to us? You see that your father and I have been looking for you anxiously" (Luke 2:48). The nub of the tale lies in his response: "Do you not know that I must be about my Father's business?" (Luke 2:49). The Greek, characteristically, has no noun at that place, only a plural definite article, so "in my Father's house" might just as well be the meaning. If so, Luke is situating the boy in the Temple precincts where he would later do so much of his memorable teaching.

There is another instance of the work of the master storyteller Luke in which he employs an incident early in Jesus' career to indicate what lies ahead for him. Conscious of a lively reminiscence among Jesus' Nazareth townsfolk that his extended family was embarrassed by the forthrightness of his teaching, and perhaps fearful that it might bring reprisals from the acknowledged scholar or two in the community, Luke narrates what he means to be Jesus' earliest rebuff. Luke is bent on showing that coming events cast their shadows before and so begins what will be his presentation throughout of a Jesus who taught God's concern for those outside the confines of the people Israel. The religion of this people had always been ethnic centered. The dealings of their God, the LORD, with them and not with the pagans around them had been their centuries-long main concern. The author of the book of Jonah, that clever bit of irony in fiction, had had the courage to present Nineveh, the fabled capital of Assyria, as accepting the unwilling prophet's call to repentance when Israel would not. The cautionary tale that had Job as its main character challenged head-on the received wisdom that God rewards the good and punishes the wicked in this life. Its author had the good sense to make the challenger a resident of the land of Uz, an undisclosed location to the east. The Bible is filled with what we could call fictitious tales, but its authors would not refer to them as such; rather, they saw them as interesting stories that made a serious religious point.

The third portion of the book of Isaiah predicts outright that the foreigner would in the future not be excluded from the worship of the LORD but would minister to him in the Temple (see Isa 56:6-8). The vision of a distant day was even bolder: "[A]ll the nations and tongues shall come [to the temple] and behold my glory . . . And out of all the nations, said the LORD, they shall bring all your brothers . . . to Jerusalem My holy mountain as an offering to the LORD—just as the Israelites bring an offering in a pure vessel to the House of the LORD" (Isa 66:18b-21; *Tanakh, The Holy Scriptures* translation). As if calling the despised pagans coming on horses, mules, and dromedaries "your brothers" were not enough, the passage continues: "And from them likewise I will take some to be levitical priests, said the LORD." The prophet's vision was of a far-off day when everything would come around right for Israel by the LORD's power. Jesus, however, in reminding his fellow Nazarenes of what God had done for the gentile widow of Zarephath and the Syrian general Naaman, is described as arousing their fury. Luke makes this narrative the introduction to all of Jesus' public teaching. His rejection as a prophet in his native place sets the tone for what is to follow (Luke 4:24). The punishment of threatening to throw him headlong off the brow of a hill does not seem to fit the crime. But Luke's purpose is clearly to show that the LORD's concern for the pagan world, identical with that for Israel as Jesus would teach it, was to be part of Jesus' downfall. This gospel, like that of Mark, Matthew, and, to a lesser degree, John, contains echoes of the admission of gentiles into the religion of Israel by the infant Church at the time of the later first-century writing.

A minor point in the Nazareth synagogue story is that Jesus is called the son of Joseph without the qualification "as was thought" found earlier (Luke 4:22; cf. 3:23). When John refers to him as the son of Joseph it bespeaks nothing of that gospel's ignorance of the tradition of a virginal conception (John 1:45; 6:42). In all those instances the designation of a person by naming his father was normal. Calling Jesus the son of Mary as a way to identify him would not have occurred to a Semitic writer. When a certain Mary who witnessed Jesus' crucifixion is called the mother of James and Joseph, it is to distinguish her from the Mary just named (Matt 27:56).

Jesus Grown to Adulthood

All that is known of Jesus' young manhood before he left his Nazareth home to recruit associates on an itinerant preaching mission is that his craft was that of a worker in wood. Once he is called "the woodworker" (Mark 6:3) and again "the son of the woodworker," in a passage where Matthew copies Mark verbatim (Matt 13:55). It is probably a mistake to render the Greek word as a carpenter because of the limits of its connotation in English. Extra-biblical sources use the word to describe variously a maker of plows, a worker in stone, and even a builder, but usually to distinguish this type of artisan from a worker in bronze. Surely Jesus, along with his legal father Joseph, made many a coffin, plow, doorjamb, and door. Of his decision to abandon his source of income and go on the road, the first three gospels tell us nothing, any more than they inform us of his mental or emotional states. The exceptions, if they are that, would be Mark and Matthew's disclosing him as moved with compassion (Matt 20:34) or with pity (Mark 1:41) before performing a miracle of healing, and John's frequent, confident assertion of what Jesus knew at a distance or even of what was going on in the human heart (John 2:24f; 6:64; 13:11). The gospel narratives about him are phenomenological rather than psychological, probing no deeper into his inner life than could be deduced from his words and acts. From these it can be concluded that in response to a divine call he set out to proclaim the future reign or kingship of God and human readiness for it. Nothing can be said of his motivations. That is simply to say that what we know of Jesus is known from his recorded utterances and the way he died, nothing more. But that is already quite a lot.

Jesus as Teacher: Debates over Law Observance

What did Jesus teach and in what circumstances? The first will take some time to discuss. The second is an easier matter to summarize.

Out-of-doors in his homeland Galilee was his favored site and often near the lake because of the amplification of the human voice over water. When he is described as having taught in the Temple it would have been in its vast outer courtyard for men or in its porticoes if there was access to them. The gospels suggest that he addressed great crowds of the landless poor on the shores of the low-lying lake, and there is nothing to make us think otherwise. Public discourse and teaching was, after all, the education of the unlettered. It was their entertainment as well. This means that Jesus would have spoken uninterruptedly for two hours or perhaps three. And he would had to have employed rhetorical devices—clever wordplay, lively images and examples, current happenings in their lives as oppressed by the rich landowners and the occupying Roman army—to keep the attention of the crowd. Numerous situations are described in which he was engaged in heated and bitter exchange with other teachers. These would be members of two groups that were not mutually exclusive: the scribes, or men of letters, meaning the letter of Mosaic law (Luke usually calls them "men of the Law"); and the hyper-observants of written Torah, the Pharisees, or Separated, although from what or from whom they separated themselves we are not quite sure. These groups are the familiar coupling "the scribes and Pharisees." Both sought to find contemporary meaning in the centuries-old legal corpus, actually several collections of laws, of the Mosaic books. Some of it was already incomprehensible in Jesus' increasingly town-centered and no longer exclusively rural or nomadic day, but these scholars succeeded in promulgating laws called "the oral law" that could be teased out of the archaic legislation that had had meaning in the people's tribal and desert past.

One thing that is by no means sure is whether Jesus had the exact differences with the learned that the gospels report. The latter accounts were almost certainly colored by the rapid developments in both the synagogue and emerging Church of four and five decades after Jesus' lifetime. It is safe to assume that they were thus edited, since the disciples by then were convinced of Jesus' absolutely authoritative stance. At the same time, the rabbinic teaching of Torah that became Judaism was gaining momentum. This much, at least, is sure. However heated the actual argumentation of Jesus' day might have been, it would never have led to the threats of death that the Gospel of John reports, or the Matthean charge that Jesus' utterances constituted blasphemy. Jews love to debate, and over the demands of their religion above all. The arguments Jesus engaged in may have been many and vigorous, but they would have had nothing to do with the tightening of the net that culminated in his death. Lethal opposition to him came from another quarter.

The gospels tell us much of the mode of Jesus' teaching but not all. We know that he taught at times in short, tight proverbial expressions. Some of these were doubtless ancient and others he would have coined. He told many short stories based on the lives of his listeners that placed in parallel their familiar activities with the way God acted regarding them or would have them act with each other. He taught by contrast as the Scriptures of his people so often did: such was the way this character in a story conducted himself, the other character in quite another way. Or, the outcome of this situation is thus, of that situation is so. Jesus never explained his tales. His technique was "give and go." Even when a story was in essence thoroughly paradoxical he would stop at a point where people would have to argue his meaning. Often they did so far into the night.

That was the case in his developed short stories. At other times he employed metaphors that went undeveloped at narrative length: this stands for this, that stands for that, no need to work it out. The gospel writers, not being as clever teachers as the Master, at times did not trust their hearers (very few learned the written gospels by reading) to get the point of his parables. Not leaving well enough alone, they allegorized them. The parable of the sower (Mark 4:3-8) is perhaps the best example: "Now the seed is the word of God," and so on, a moralistic application— of a certain worth, perhaps, but not what Jesus intended by telling the story. The seed in the spring sowing might have all sorts of adventures: the wind, the birds, stony ground, thistles along the path; but a crop came up all the same. It was inevitable. And so would God's rule, his reign over Israel, be over the minds and hearts of all its people. The seed of God's word is sown. It encounters every obstacle. The sowing and the harvest alike are God's doing, not humanity's. And it will happen. God's reign will come to fruition.

In puzzling out the parables two things must be kept in mind. The main figure is usually not God. And Mark and Matthew favor God's kingship parables, while Luke favors the conduct that will make the hearer ready to receive it. John has no parables, strictly speaking, but many powerful similes.

The above are the two chief methods of Jesus' teaching: the pithy saying packed with wisdom and the short, short story, which sometimes is so brief as not to be a story at all. The third didactic method is the developed discourse. John's gospel provides the best examples of these, although as Jesus spoke them they would not have had the same content as in John. More of that later. For now, the homily was a teaching technique of Jesus that by definition meant the development of a biblical theme. The clearest example of this in the first three gospels is what has come to be known as Jesus' apocalyptic, or end-time, discourse. Mark is the first to provide one (13:5-36), while Matthew (24:4-44) and Luke (21:8-36) edit it, adding and subtracting certain details. A few of the details are so similar to what we know from Josephus of all that occurred in the Roman army's sack of Jerusalem that they seem to have been incorporated into what is presented as a prediction. This grim narrative was meant to describe how things would be with God as self-*revealed* (hence *apokálypsis*) as judge at the end of days. The chaos of the final days was the downside of the life of the just under God's kingship on earth, to be as it is in heaven. The biblical record of human life, both for Israel and for the peoples around them who did not know the one God, was one of recurring sin and evil. The LORD who is infinitely just would have to punish the wicked in a way known to God alone. He could not *not* do so and be true to his nature as perfect justice. The LORD would at the same time have to reward the upright, not solely out of merciful forgiveness for their sins but for their perseverance in lives of justice. All of God's promises would have to be fulfilled both in respect to the good and to the evil.

That is the subject of Matthew's discourse on the separation of the sheep and the goats (25:31-46) at the traditional right hand and the left hand of the Son of Man. The daily reality among this pastorally oriented people was that sheep and goats by and large grazed peacefully together. They did not need to be separated into aggressors and the meek object of the aggression. But, aside from an occasional old battering ram, the sheep were a peaceful species, while the goats showed a tendency toward domination in the flock. Hence, the parable of contrast. Briefly developed as that discourse of Jesus is, and with its repetitious wording that is good ancient Semitic style but not modern Western, the judgment scene is a good example of what must have been Jesus' lengthy development of a single theme. Important to remember is that the religion of Israel has but a single doctrine or dogma: there is but one God who is all-powerful, all-merciful, and all-just. Everything else is a matter of how God acts in Israel's regard, how God is sure to act with respect to sinners and the just, and how the human creature responds fittingly to God in the prayer of praise, petition, and active obedience to God's will. These simple truths about Creator and creature are what the three modes of Jesus' teaching are necessarily devoted to: the proverb, the parable, and the discourse bringing to light the incredible love God has for God's people and the love God expects in return. Like the familiar figure of the shepherd who would desert a flock of ninety-nine to rescue the unintelligent wanderer from death on a high crag or in a crevice it could not negotiate, Israel's LORD was forever faithful to Israel's least. Jesus lost no opportunity to drive that home.

Jesus was remembered to have done much more than teach in his brief public career. He was gifted with not only the power of words but also of healing. Matthew, Mark, and Luke call these deeds "powers" (*dynmaeîs*). John favors the term "signs" and sometimes "works." These were largely cures of physical illness but sometimes of violent mental or emotional disturbance. The concept of possession by demons— "unclean spirits," as the gospels call them—is totally ambiguous. What we know is that Jesus was given the power by God to adjure them to be gone. The archaic English phrase for exorcism is "casting them out," but there is no ambiguity as to its meaning. Profoundly troubled people were returned to instant calm by Jesus' word. They may in fact have been victims of diabolic possession but just as well of paranoid schizophrenia or *grand mal* epileptic seizures or God knows what other psychic disturbances.

Three instances of Jesus restoring the dead to life were well remembered. Three others of control over nature were equally fixed in memory: his stilling of a storm, his walking on the Sea, and his multiplying bread and fish to feed a hungry crowd.

When we read of Jesus' public teaching or his deeds of power we know that the gospel writers are transmitting to their circle of believers the collections of stories and sayings or miraculous deeds that they have access to. They have no interest in where these things actually took place or the exact circumstances that occasioned them. The only exception to this is their naming Galilee with its lake as the setting of some, Judaea and specifically Jerusalem and its Temple area of others. Similarly, they had no interest in historical context. That is why some sayings will be delivered in a certain location in one gospel and in a quite different place and circumstance in another. A literary device that occurs in the first three gospels is the culmination of a parable in an appended proverbial utterance—once, in Luke, as many as three—meant as comment on what has gone before. One thing that must be noted about Mark in particular is that he will speak of Jesus' teachings, preparing his hearers for more of them; then instead he will recount another deed of power.

The two features that all the gospels have in common are the opening scene of Jesus' accepting from John the ritual of baptism in the waters of the Jordan and the closing scene of his arrest, torture, and grisly execution.

This "passion," as it is called, is preliminary to the climax of each gospel, which is his death and resurrection understood as a single act of God— proclaimed in Mark by a young man clothed in white, saying that the entombed victim is not here but is risen, in Luke and John by various friends of Jesus in his not immediately recognized risen state.

The Distinctive Purpose of Each Evangelist

Each of the gospels has the purpose, in recalling in summary the account of Jesus' life, death, and resurrection that the writers have delivered orally many times, of confirming believers in the faith they already hold. Their authors' main concern was to help their contemporaries live their lives in Christ. They employed the recall as a means to that end. Each went about his task in a different way. Mark presented Jesus as a man endowed by God with the power to restore a measure of order in the cosmos and in the chaotic lives of humans but who had to undergo the sufferings and death that are the lot of all. So too would Mark's believers if they were to live again in the body with him. Matthew also knew that he had to renew the commitment of his church to the one in whom they believed. He chose for the purpose Jesus' teaching on how the Law was to be lived in contrast to the emerging literalist way of the Pharisee teachers. Luke, like Matthew, took much from Mark and added much not to be found there. In his case it was a succession of narratives in which the divine compassion and willingness to forgive was the paradigm for a like human response. John retained only a few major accounts from the Markan tradition: the multiplication of loaves and fish followed by Jesus walking on the Sea and a number of Lukan more than Markan-Matthean details from Jesus' last days and hours. For the rest, John opted to put the faith of his church on Jesus' lips, faith about who Jesus was and what he had come to do and to be, as the townsfolk of Sychar in Samaria put it upon experiencing him, "the Savior of the world" (John 4:42).

A review of the content of each gospel should help to convey a picture of the Jesus in whom the Church believed from earliest times. These would have been the colorful Lukan Pentecost of Acts (Acts 2:1-12) or the briefer "Johannine Pentecost" on the evening of the resurrection, with its breathing of Jesus on the disciples and his gift to them of the Holy Spirit (John 20:19-23). Mark has Jesus come to Galilee from his baptism in the South along the Jordan's banks and his testing by Satan in the desert. Back in home territory he begins to proclaim the good tidings of God: what God will do for Israel in the future on condition of its fidelity. But first he must choose companions in the work. Initially they were two pairs of brothers in the fishing trade. An exorcism and a flurry of healings follow. The concentration is Mark's doing, in whatever sequence they actually happened. Is this narrative to be simply a chronicle of the deeds of a wonder-worker? It will be that and more. This thaumaturge is a villager by upbringing who returns to the desert to pray at every turn as he continues to teach. He has a message that is as old as the people Israel but in a sense quite new. "Repent of your sins," Jesus exhorted his listeners, as John the Baptizer was doing concurrently with him. But if John then took his preaching in the direction Jesus did, we do not know that. Mark calls this direction the Gospel, or Good News (*eùangélion*). It was the expectation of the inbreaking of God on Israel's history, liberating it from all oppression in the freedom to live under the kingship of God alone.

Jesus never included himself in his message. It was always centered on the LORD and the reign of the only God over the people of his special care. It was geared to the present in anticipation of the future. The message was very practical: "Love God above all others and above all else. Love other people, whoever they may be. Give them food and drink in their need. Clothe them. Welcome the strangers among them. Care for the sick. Visit prisoners" (Matt 25:31-46).

The Story of Israel Without Which Jesus Cannot Be Understood

The history of the Hebrew immigrants to the land of Canaan from Mesopotamia had been a history of enslavement, first to Egypt and later to the empires of Assyria, Chaldea, Greece, and Rome. Their settlement in parts of Canaan was won by hard-fought displacement of the Semitic tribes of nomads whose pastureland it was. At some point in those centuries they took the name Israel to describe themselves, saying that the LORD had accorded it to their patriarch Jacob. There was a brief interval, say of a century and a half, when the twelve tribes, or bloodlines, into which they had divided themselves emerged as self-governed and in relative freedom. The people's memory was that earlier they had lived under the jurisdiction of itinerant priest-judges, leaders in worship at various shrines and dispensers of justice in litigations over land and property. The best remembered of these and held in veneration was a certain Samuel, an Ephraimite. This means he was sprung from the younger of the two sons of Joseph who was called a "prince among his brothers" (see Gen 41:52; 49:26).

When some leading figures among the twelve tribes (something like today's desert warlords) clamored for a king so they could be like the neighboring peoples, Samuel who had the say resisted bitterly. It was not his own fragile hold on power that deterred him but his insight into what kingship would mean for peoples' lives. His prediction of the form royal rule would take is the classic description of naked power in all the world's literatures. It describes the subjugation of a peasantry, the common folk, to despotic rule (see 1 Sam 8:10-18). But the people insisted they wanted a king and Samuel yielded. He gave them Saul of the small-ish southern tribe of Benjamin. Samuel's prophecy proved tragically true.

Kings and Kingdoms

Saul—tall, handsome of face and figure, successful in battle if not at the last—proved early to be jealous of his throne. He recognized in David whom he had at first favored a usurper. That might have been a simple character flaw in him. There was worse. Saul proved to be psychotic. The biblical narrative of the love-hate relation between the two men is priceless as a piece of writing, although David's respect for the throne rather than the man has to be a case of later editorial embellishment. David got the kingship he craved. He was not only more successful in armed conflict against the neighboring peoples than Saul; he was a con-solidator rather than a divider. Saul was a man of Benjamin, David of Judah. The fact that the two tribes lived close in the South did little or nothing to bring them close against the ten tribes of the North. But, al-though all twelve tribes were of the same ethnic stock, there was nothing like a unified sense of peoplehood among them. David had enough po-litical sense to realize that only the common bond of their religion could achieve it. While at the peak of his power, he succeeded in taking the hill of Ophel from a Canaanite tribe known as the Jebusites. Three places in the Hebrew writings mention "the Jebusite town," adding "(that is, Jerusalem)" in a listing of Benjaminite settlements; or "Jebus which is Jerusalem"; or, again, "David and all Israel went to Jerusalem that is, Jebus" (Josh 18:28; Judg 19:10, 11; 1 Chr 11:4, 5).

It is impossible to tell from these references whether the town had the name Jerusalem among the Jebusites or was given it after the con-quest by David and his men. The third of the citations tells baldly how it was seized from the natives by force. David was attracted to it by its hilly location that made defense easier but also by its presence in the borderland between the southern and northern tribes. Having been king of the two tribes of the South in Hebron for seven years—today the largest town in the West Bank of the Jordan called by its Arab population Al Khalil, "the Friend," meaning Abraham—he then established his reign over all Israel for the next thirty-three years. David is remembered in the Bible chiefly as a victor in battle, at times vindictive over his enemies, at other times clement and forgiving, once lecherously adulterous, twice if his takeover of Nabal's wife Abigail is counted. The Bible does not hesitate to report the darker side of his character.

The second son born to his stolen wife Bathsheba survived as Solomon. He built a magnificent Temple on the site of a threshing floor David had bought from a certain Ornan, a Jebusite, for the purpose. This was possible because of a lull in hostilities from Egypt on one side and Damascus on the other. Solomon engaged tiny Israel in the sea trade for the first time, managing to have cedarwood brought from the forests of Lebanon, bronze from the seaport city of Tyre, and gold from Ophir, which was either in Arabia or on the East African coast. The Temple must have been a magnificent structure and Solomon's palace the same, since it took thirteen years in the building. The king who inhabited it was highly intelligent and knowledgeable, gifts that credited him with being a polymath and the author of 3,000 proverbs and 1,005 songs. Obviously this was the flattering praise accorded a sovereign, whatever the core of truth behind it.

The importance of the David and Solomon stories to Jesus of Nazareth was that by Jesus' day the people had told these tales for nearly a thousand years and looked forward to the time when Israel would again be a conqueror and no longer a conquered people. A hoped-for king would have all the military skill of a David, all the magnificence of a Solomon, and not the Achilles' heel of either. In David's case it was the brutal settling of scores with the leftover army of Saul, in Solomon's the wasteful high living and sexual excesses by which he managed to squander David's patrimony.

After Solomon's death the southern and northern tribes resumed their rivalry, resulting in schism into distinct kingdoms. Conquest of the North by Assyria followed after some centuries, with a resultant population transfer of the best and the brightest to Nineveh. Two hundred years later the same fate overtook the South at the hands of Chaldean forces, with exile to Babylon as its bitter fruit. The latter period of fifty years away from the homeland ended with release by the emerging Persian Empire under Cyrus, whom the book of Isaiah accords the title proper to Judah's kings, *meshiah* (God's anointed). We do not have much information about Israel in the Persian period except that it was a time of relative peace. Alexander's conquest of that empire in the late fourth century was followed by his early death and the transfer of power to two of his generals, one in Syria and the other in Egypt. The dynasty founded by the former assumed the title of king and placed a heavy heel on the neck of Israel. Roman power dislodged the Greek after two hundred years. A brief republic ruled by a triumvirate produced a single ruler who adopted the imperial title Caesar. This signaled the end of anything like democratic government, a development that had marked the Greek city-states. Jesus was born during the long and peaceful reign of one of the three, Octavian, who took the throne name Augustus. He was succeeded by Tiberius as Jesus approached manhood.

The Influence of the Babylonian Exile and Hellenism

Two things of major importance happened during the millennium from David to Jesus. One was the impact of Babylonian culture on the Jewish, which told this people that their God must have a plan for people other than themselves. The other was the cultural and linguistic conquest of the Alexandrian Empire, of greater and more lasting effect than the military on those conquered. Among its outcomes with respect to Israel was a Greek translation of its Scriptures, the Septuagint, used everywhere in the lands to which Jews were scattered. Meanwhile, in Roman Palestine, Aramaic, that is, Syrian, paraphrases to the various books were composed so that the Hebrew, dying as a spoken language, could be understood. These were called Targums ("translations" or "interpretations").

The Roman Empire was very well organized politically, and part of its political wisdom was the toleration of the religions and customs of its various subject peoples, including the Jews. Some of the Roman imperial functionaries were heavy-handed in the manner of Pontius Pilatus, whose prefecture of Judaea replaced the scheme of a Herodian tetrarchy in that province. Elsewhere, however, Jews lived relatively peacefully under Roman rule, Alexandria being the chief exception. The combined cultural and political situation, together with easy if slow travel on the Roman roads and on the Mediterranean, made the expansion of the movement that would bear the name of Christ a distinct possibility.

Jesus, we may assume, was by all means a Jewish patriot, but rousing his Palestinian people to throw off the Roman yoke was no part of his message. Neither had it been that of John the Baptist. The popularity of both preachers of reform with the crowds of Jews in the North and the South, however, made Pilate suspicious that they might be part of a Galilean uprising that he suspected was gaining adherents during his term in office. It is a cruel paradox that two men who preached peace and submission to the will of God should be put to death on charges quite contrary to what they stood for. They were prophets like the prophets of old, to be sure, but while the prophets always had a message touching on political life, they had none such.

Jesus the Quintessential Jew

The history of the Jewish people chronicled in their people's Scriptures is of maximum importance to the Jesus story. Without it, the story cannot be understood. God could certainly have raised up an incarnate Son in any people of God's choice but, if so, that other people would not have known what to make of him. Jesus was intertwined at every point in his life with the people called Israel to which God had been self-revealed over many centuries. Jesus' teaching was identical with that of the prophets in his call for perfect obedience to the God of Israel. This took the form of living a human life as it should be lived, with the constant prayer of praise and thanks and petition included. He summoned the simplest, unlettered people to live lives of highest holiness. Jesus did it by employing the image of God's reign over every aspect of their lives. Samuel had warned the people of the dangers attending human kingship. Complete submission to the will of another human being, even if involuntary, was another form of idolatry. Although the psalms written for the enthronement of a king were filled with high hope, that hope was in almost every case dashed. The LORD alone was worthy of the title and honors due to him, the unrivaled King of Israel. This being so, it is understandable why Jesus should have set himself to proclaim the kingdom, an archaic English word in that context for the reign or kingship, of God. All hopes for a restored royal figure who would set the people free politically were chimeric. Jesus' message, couched in readiness for the day when God's kingship should become a reality, was not chimeric because he taught that only God could bring it about and in God's good time. The human tendency to take the concept "certainly" to mean "soon" led to the understanding that the imminent occurrence of the divine inbreaking on Israel's history was part of Jesus' message, but there is no time frame for God's action. It would happen when it would happen. The sole human response proper to authentic prophetic preaching of God's coming in the future in the person of the Son of God as judge, was to be ready.

The Chronicle Continued: The Markan Story

This widespread expectation among the people of a divine inbreaking accounts for the form Jesus' earliest recorded teaching took. Mark's gospel tells, near the outset, of Jesus' recruiting of disciples for his mission. Then follows a number of his deeds of power that brought instant cure to the ill and to those presumed possessed. After that comes the way the Markan church was, or better, was not, observing the prescribed fast and Sabbath rest. All of this is situated back as if in Jesus' day. The accounts of Jesus driving Satan out of those thought to be infested by evil spirits contain the paradoxical charge that Jesus is in league with Beelzebul, as Satan was contemptuously called (perhaps naming him "Lord (Ba'al) of the House"). Jesus' family members are dismayed by the powers he possesses and try to sequester him from the crowds. It is only after these compressed narratives that we begin to get a taste of Jesus' teaching. It takes the form of four short examples from people's lives about what to expect and not expect in God's future action.

In the first of these examples (Mark 4:3-8), Jesus takes the sowing of seed in the spring, with all the adventures randomly sown seed is bound to have, to make the point that a crop is sure to rise from good soil. No interference provided by rocky ground or a well-trodden footpath or thornbushes rimming the field, or even the birds who see a feast spread out, can keep the earth from producing a yield. And so with God. As with a harvest, God's rule will inevitably come to pass.

In the simile of the clay lamp from the potter's hand with a wick of cloth thrust into its olive oil, the small lamp has only one purpose: to light up the modest house as the farmer's family prepares for bed (Mark 4:21-22). Thwarting the purpose for which it exists makes no sense whatever. Neither is Jesus' message of God's reign meant to be a hole-and-corner affair. It is a matter of tremendous importance. Diffusion is essential.

Again, Jesus' farmer listeners knew how little they had to do after seed was deposited and covered by the soil. It did its thing every spring—slowly, predictably emerging from the earth as green shoots, then stalks, then ears of barley, rye, or wheat. The growth could not be stopped any more than the reign of God as sovereign over the people could be stopped. It was sure to happen.

The progress of the mustard from tiny seed to leafy bush was Jesus' prime example of the progress from the exceedingly small to the flourishing large (Mark 4:31-32). God's way in nature is to bring magnitude out of parvity, the sizeable from the least in size, in a never-ending process. The transcending of nature by the multiplying of pocket breads and fish is not only, or ever primarily, about a miracle. It is acted out, instantaneous growth from little to much, an insufficiency to an abundance. And so with God's reign of the future.

Jesus' hearers knew nothing of cell structure or cell union in human biology. The people of that age thought that the male seed deposited in the female womb did it all. But whether it was agriculture or childbearing, they knew the inevitability of evolving life: great oaks grow from little acorns if allowed their natural progress. So too with the work of God. A gentle reign over God's people was something that, in Jesus' view, was sure to happen—by God's doing, not by human doing. Jesus named the human task as placing no obstacle in the way. Mark tells only one other parable (Mark 12:1-11), this time with a story line like the ones that Matthew and Luke will follow, not simply extended metaphors from tilled fields and peasant dwellings that has been his custom up to this point. The parable is extremely graphic and true to the violence that marked the tenant farming that Jesus' hearers knew all too well.

The landowner has a large vineyard. The grape harvest is good. He sends an agent to collect the quota that has been set months before and that he expects. Instead of the produce that he looks for, rough hands are laid on the agent by the tenant workers. A second emissary is treated worse than the first; the third one is killed. In an excess of violence many more are manhandled or murdered. Brutal times, like the days of the goons trained on California's United Farm Workers. "Ah," says the owner, "I will send my son. Him they will respect." A unique twist among the short stories of God's dealings with Israel is given to this one, told by Jesus to recall the fate of the prophets. Either Mark or the teller from whom he got the story places Jesus in one of his own parables! It is quite unlikely that Jesus would have done this. His business was to proclaim God his Father, not himself or the redemptive act, if indeed he knew anything of it beforehand. It did not matter to Mark that none of the writing prophets is remembered to have been put to death, although Jeremiah, we know, was treated shamefully and exiled to Egypt. The evangelist is a teacher who is aware as were all his hearers of how Jesus ended. It was perfectly in order to identify him as the last in the line of the prophets before new prophets in his name arose in the Church. All were somehow subjected to the violence of rejection. Mark needed to remind his hearers that some would not escape the Master's fate.

The Gospel of which Mark writes (his word for the good tidings concerning Jesus Christ, not this book itself; 1:1) takes the shape of telling of a man with whom God has shared extraordinary powers who will yet come to grief at the hands of others. Mark frequently says he will relate some of Jesus' teaching, but in the event he conveys little of it. The teaching he does report is important: on the folly of substituting human tradition for divinely revealed Torah (7:8-13); on the dangers of accumulated wealth (10:17-22); on the evil of male-initiated dismissal of a wife (10:2-12); on the simplicity of childhood as the condition of entering on God's reign (10:13-16). Jesus was utterly convinced of the importance of his teaching and Mark conveys that conviction. But he multiplies incidents of Jesus deeds of power rather than conveying portions of the many hours of Jesus' teaching. That is because the miraculous signs that attended Jesus' mission were indications for Mark that even superhuman power can be brought low. The relative amount of space he gives to Jesus' sufferings and death makes clear that his whole previous narrative leads in that direction. He provides a clue very early by reporting a plot on Jesus' life, when he has not yet given evidence why anyone should want him dead (3:6). Three times he will give in summary the events of Jesus' last days and hours as if by way of prediction (8:31; 9:31; 10:33). Actually they are meant to prepare the hearer for what will be spelled out in detail, culminating in "and will rise after three days," the outcome of Jesus' life that they already knew.

Mark employs a number of other literary techniques in his narrative preliminary to the climactic crucifixion and empty tomb scenes. One is the story within a story, however brief each may be. They seem to be seven in number and occur at the following places:

3:20-21 [22-30] 31-35,

5:21-24 [25-34] 35-43,

6:7-13 [14-29] 30-32,

11:12-14 [15-19] 20-26,

14:1-2 [3-9] 10-11,

the double inclusion 14:10-11 [12-16] 17-21 [22-25] 26-31,

and 14:54 [55-65] 66-72.

Examination of each discloses that the inner incident somehow sheds light on the one that brackets it, at times with only a verbal clue. Thus, a dead girl of twelve is resuscitated enclosing an account of the cure of a woman suffering for twelve years; the story of Temple cleansing illumines the cryptic parable of the withered fig tree; most important of all, the hearing before the high priest is framed by the denial of Peter by firelight, which has resulted in the literal understanding of a "night trial."

Another device, this one pervasive throughout the gospel, is to have Jesus enjoin silence on the onlookers after he has performed a miracle of healing or an exorcism (literally an adjuring to the demonic powers). The notable exception is the deeply emotionally disturbed man from Gerasa "across the Sea," Lake Kinnereth, or Galilee (Mark 5:1-20; Matt 8:28 has "Gadara"). After driving the unclean spirits into a herd of pigs—in the minds of Jews with their kosher laws small loss for their pagan owner—Jesus by way of exception tells the cured man to announce to his family all that Israel's LORD has done for him. This is one of the hints Mark provides to those new believers in his community who were former pagans: that in Jesus' lifetime God had had as much concern for the gentile world as for the Jewish. The cure of a pagan woman's daughter in Tyre on the Syrophoenician coast where Jesus had gone covertly was another such instance.

But, back to why Jesus should require fellow Jews not to publicize that they had received a marvelous cure at his hands. The answer seems to be that Mark is building up to the ultimate disclosure of Jesus' true identity as the Risen One by a series of nondisclosures of that identity. He has the unclean spirits aware of who Jesus is by virtue of their angelic knowledge, but it is not the knowledge of faith. Jesus' relatives are simply unaware of his true identity, thinking him perhaps mentally unbalanced. The learned from Jerusalem have heard of his powers as an exorcist but attribute them irrationally to collusion with diabolic forces. A human agent of unbelief in who Jesus truly is, the high priest before whom he has been summoned, is made by Mark to get the words right, "Are you the messiah, the son of the Blessed?" But it is not the tune that only faith can supply. Mark has Jesus answer cryptically, "It is you who say so." For centuries this enjoining of *miraculés*, as the French call them, subjects of Jesus' preternatural powers, was thought to be a self-protective device on Jesus' part. He was credited with foreknowing that he would be apprehended and was putting it off until the time his Father had decreed. The explanation is much simpler.

Some one hundred years ago William Wrede, a German scholar of the Bible, concluded that it was not Jesus' unwillingness to have his marvelous deeds widely known but the evangelist Mark's employment of a narrative device. Wrede dubbed it "the messianic secret" but not quite accurately, for it was actually "the Son of God secret." If the high priest's inquiry was correct as to the wording but not based on faith in Jesus, it was at least intended as the second step preliminary to disclosure. That came in a spirit of faith with the centurion's cry elicited by the rending of the Temple curtain: "Truly this man was Son of God." The ultimate disclosure of Jesus' identity is left to the young man in white seated alongside the open tomb where Jesus' body had been laid: "You are looking for Jesus of Nazareth, the one they crucified. He has been raised up. He is not here." The two Marys and Salome had been asking each other who would roll back the stone for them that covered the mouth of the tomb and were utterly amazed to find it rolled back. "It was very large." As they entered the tomb they saw a young man seated on the right side, clothed in a white robe. They were utterly amazed. He told them not to be. "You seek Jesus of Nazareth, the crucified. He has been raised up. He is not here" (Mark 16:6). Their initial amazement was succeeded by bewilderment and trembling. Who would not be awestruck by such a disclosure? But what came next was fear. For when the young man told them to go and tell Jesus' disciples and Peter that Jesus was going before them to Galilee where he would see them as he had told them, they went out and fled the tomb. "They said nothing to anyone, for they were afraid" (Mark 16:8b).

Mark has finally written the gospel he had many times proclaimed orally. It was not only a story that those it was composed for already knew but an extended homily directing them to pass its contents along. Nothing should deter them from doing so. The evangelist concludes by employing the three women for his purpose. They are portrayed as failing to carry out the command to promulgate the mystery of the power of God that "the crucified is the Risen One." Mark's implication is clear: Go, you, and do otherwise! Spread the word, at first to Galilee, where the others who knew Jesus best in life are concentrated. The gospel proves to be all about a man who was raised up from the dead. The only purpose in its writing is to ensure that believers in this mysterious deed of God should spread the word of it far and wide. Knowing something of the man Jesus in his lifetime—his holiness, his deeds, his teaching—proved to be good preparation for accepting in faith the fact that God should have done such a marvel in him. That marvel was not his upraising of the dead, which was but the sacrament or sign of God's deed. The deed was the restoration to God's friendship of an alienated, sinful humanity. Jesus was the agent or instrument God employed to restore to the human race lives of justice, holiness, and goodness. Such was God's original design for human happiness.

Chapter Two

The First We Hear of Jesus in History's Record

The first mention of Jesus in any written source is in a piece of correspondence from a certain Paul, Silvanus, and Timothy addressed to the church of the Thessalonians around the year 51. Thessalonika was the largest city of Macedonia in the northeastern part of what is now Greece. The trio who identify themselves at the head of the letter had evidently brought the good news of Jesus, Christ and Lord and risen from the dead, to this city in the previous year. This would have been twenty years after Jesus was crucified on a false charge and was upraised by the power of God from a rock tomb after three days.

When Jesus is spoken of in this letter it is never by his given name unadorned by a title, *Iēsoûs*, the Greek rendering of *Yeshúa*, "YHWH shall save." It is the same name as that borne by the successor of Moses, Yehoshua, but for one vowel sound, and it was a very common name in the lifetime of Jesus of Nazareth whom this book is about. The onomasticon, or name index, of two works of Flavius Josephus, *Jewish Antiquities* and *Jewish War*, lists twenty men of that name. Josephus writes of the Jesus of our interest: "The tribe of the Christians, so called after him, has still not to this day disappeared" (*Jewish Antiquities*, book XVIII, 63–64; on John the Baptist, 116–19; in Acts below, 17:1-8). He is writing from the court of the emperor of the Flavian house in Rome sometime in the 90s and mentions Jesus only briefly. He reports the death by stoning of James, the brother of Jesus (not one of the two disciples of that name), and others, at slightly greater length. Josephus's account of the imprisonment and execution of John the Baptist is longer still.

Paul was the head of the evangelizing team that brought the message of faith in one God to that large pagan city, a message that its Jewish minority population would not need to hear. The message in its entirety, however, would come as news to those gentiles who were not "Godfearers" of the religion of Israel. These were believers in that religion but whose men did not receive circumcision, hence they were not subject to all the precepts of the Law. The message served as a reminder, as directed to Greek-speaking Jews and gentiles alike, of the word Paul and his team had brought of what God had done a brief twenty years before in the person of the Jew Jesus. The only information we have on how the Gospel (*eùaggélion,* "good tidings") came to Thessalonika is a brief notice in book two of Luke (who also wrote a gospel), the Acts of the Apostles (Acts: 17:1-9). That history of Paul's evangelizing efforts had to have drawn on a defective source, for it speaks of Paul and his chief associate Silas (Silvanus) as having taught there in a stay of only three Sabbaths. They and others were traveling southward from Philippi, the capital of Macedonia. That city had been named by Philip, the father of Alexander the Great, for himself and was the site of Paul's first entry into Europe from his native Asia.

The stop off of the evangelizers in Thessalonika must have been longer, some months at the very least, if they were to convince any sizeable number of its residents of the truth of their message. Acts seems to know, however, of acceptance of it by some gentile Greek men and women only, including a certain Jason, to the intense anger of a segment of the Jewish population. Since the consistent theme of this piece of writing is the favorable hearing non-Jews gave to the Gospel in every city where Paul proclaimed it and the resistance to it by Jews, it is hard to credit the historicity of Luke's account in this instance. What we can be sure of is the substance of the initial proclamation. Luke speaks of the preaching of Paul and company as causing a riot in which Jews drafted some layabouts in the city square to set upon the visitor and the local man Jason in particular. The message that supposedly brought on the violence was that a Jewish religious figure called the Messiah (anointed of God) could be demonstrated from the Scriptures to be one who had to suffer and who would rise from the dead. This figure in the Acts account was Jesus. Luke has Paul employ the familiar rabbinic technique of citing numerous biblical passages that serve to identify a person or occurrence that will supposedly happen in the future but that speaks of a faith in Jesus the readers of Acts already possess.

In addition to the claims made for Jesus, which were assumed without explanation to be inflammatory to his fellow Jews, a part of the incitement to riot was the charge that "these people. . . . All flout the emperor's laws, and assert there is a rival king, Jesus" (Acts 17:7). The book of Acts was written some time well after the adventures of Saul/Paul that it describes, but one thing certain is that Acts echoes the charges found in all the gospels, the one civil and the other religious, on which Jesus was put to death. The proclamation of what God had accomplished in Jesus is accompanied by the claim in Acts and all the New Testament writings that a diligent search of the Jewish Scriptures would disclose Jesus and no other as the one who would be put to death and live again, hence that he was Israel's Messiah. It remains to be seen whether there were any such explicit texts, or whether some were found to be declaring it implicitly after the fact.

The Biblical Title Messiah (Christos), *Anointed One*

The term messiah as an anointed one occurs frequently in the five Mosaic books to describe the descendants of Aaron as priests who were the offerers of public ritual sacrifice. The pouring of olive oil on their heads was the sign of their ordination to office. In the books of Samuel, Kings, and Chronicles, and notably in Psalms, it is the kings of Judah from Saul onward and later of Israel (or Ephraim) who are thus anointed. The interchangeable terms messiah and anointed occur in the Scriptures, therefore, primarily to describe the rite of initiation into kingship. Only once is the word used figuratively to describe a person who is not a Jewish king as an elect of God. The liberator of the Jews from exile in Babylon, Cyrus, is in fact king of the Persians, but he is called "my shepherd" and "the LORD's messiah" in successive verses of the book of the prophet Isaiah (Isa 44:28; 45:1). In the Jewish Scriptures, repeated references to a hoped-for Messiah who would liberate Israel "from sin and sorrow pining," as the Christian Advent liturgy describes centuries of anticipation, are simply not to be found. What you do find in many a scroll of the holy writings is mention of an offspring of David or a Davidic figure who would rule and who would exercise just judgment in time to come.

A passage in Isaiah puts it this way:

> "A throne shall be established in steadfast love / In the tent of David, / And on it shall sit in faithfulness / A ruler who seeks justice / And is zealous for equity" (16:5). Jeremiah expresses the anticipation as follows: "The days are coming, says the LORD, / when I shall make

a righteous Branch spring from David's line, / a king who will rule wisely, maintaining justice and right in the land / . . . This will be the name given to him: The LORD is our Vindicator" (23:5-6). And Amos: "On that day I shall restore David's fallen house . . . I shall restore the fortunes of my people Israel; they will rebuild their devastated cities and live in them, plant vineyards . . . and cultivate gardens." (9:11, 14)

Because David was remembered at his best as a judicious ruler, there was the image of a future king in his mold who would rule justly as few kings of the southern kingdom had done and according to the Bible none of the northern. But David was recalled above all as a soldier victorious in battle who had solidified the tribes of the South and the North by his conquests of the Philistines and other surrounding peoples. Hence, the prevailing image of the messiah or sovereign of Jewish hope was a victor over all of Israel's enemies. As we come to Jesus' day, these enemies would be the oppressive Greek Empire and after that the Romans.

The final chapters of the book of Zechariah appear to have been written later than the first eight, which had as their burden encouragement for the returnees from exile in Babylon. An oracle introduces the concluding chapters in which the Lord, through Israel, is seen as displacing all gentile rule, in Syria to the east and Gaza, Tyre, and Sidon to the west; but then we hear this: "Rejoice with all your heart, daughter of Zion, shout in triumph, daughter of Jerusalem! See, your king is coming to you . . . humble and mounted on an ass, on a colt, the foal of an ass . . . His rule will extend from sea to sea, from the River [Euphrates] to the ends of the earth" (Zech 9:9-10). There is no David-like king in that image. Respectful of Saul's kingship David was; grieving over the death of his rebel son Absalom, to be sure; but never meek. Zechariah then frames the image of David that remained longest and largest in Israelite memory: "On that day the weakest of the inhabitants of Jerusalem will be like David, and the line of David godlike, like the angel of the LORD going before them. On that day I will set about the destruction of every nation that attacks Jerusalem. . . . Then they will look to me, on him whom they have pierced, and will lament over him as an only child, and will grieve for him bitterly as for a firstborn son" (Zech 12:8-10).

Kyrios *as Sovereign Lord or Master*

We cannot know from the letter Paul wrote to the infant church at Thessalonika exactly how he presented Jesus as Messiah of Israel, Christ in Paul's native Greek. Clearly, he most often employs the name Jesus as adorned with one title and sometimes two. He is usually called "the Lord Jesus Christ," "the Lord," "Christ Jesus," "the Lord Jesus," twice "Christ" and once "the Son," but Jesus alone only twice and in the same sentence (1 Thess 4:14). That leads us to conclude that if those are the ways Paul could write about Jesus with customary ease, he must have presented him that way as an object of faith while living in Thessalonika and proclaiming God's deed in Jesus as the Christ and in the Spirit. The honorific "Messiah" would have meant that Paul considered Jesus to be the anointed of God divinely chosen in the mold of King David to lead God's people in the final age of history. "Lord" was *Kyrios* in Greek, *Mar* in Aramaic, and could be the English "Sir" or "Your Honor." The Jewish people already in the days of Jesus and Paul were accustomed to omit pronouncing the sacred name YHWH aloud out of reverence and to speak in its place *Adonai*, "my Lord" or "Master." That word was rendered *Kyrios* in Greek, but to call Jesus Lord was not necessarily to ascribe divinity to him because of its use as a human honorific as well.

To couple the name of Jesus closely, however, accompanied by any of the titles that attribute greatness or importance to a human being with God the Father, again and again as this letter does, is to intimate strongly his participation in the divine life. Jewish practice would never write "the LORD God and Abraham" or "God the Father and Moses," least of all "the LORD and the archangel Michael" as if the two were somehow linked in a way other than as Creator and creature. Saint Paul's usage is totally unusual in this regard. It proves to be unique coming from a Jewish pen when the word about Jesus that Paul had brought the Thessalonians is spoken of as having been received with joy in the holy Spirit, a Spirit of holiness God has given to the members of this church (1 Thess 1:5; 4:8; 5:19). The only conclusion that can be drawn about what Paul thinks of Jesus is that he is a Jew, a human being, who is at the same time a person intimately related to deity as no other had been in the sweep of Israel's history.

The reason Paul alleges for who Jesus is is that he "died and rose"; moreover, that he "died for us" (1 Thess 4:14; 5:10). He could be called Messiah and Lord freely because of the role God had assigned to him. He had been anointed and made sovereign ruler over all humanity because God's Spirit was in him as in no other. Man though he was known to be, he nonetheless partook mysteriously and incomprehensibly of deity.

A second thing we learn about Jesus in this earliest-preserved writing to speak of him is that on the Last Day the just among the dead and those living at the time will be caught up into the heavens, there to meet him and be with him. Paul, like all pious Jews, was convinced that God would be the just judge of the living and the dead at the end of the age. He evidently had taught the Thessalonians, who numbered some Jews among the greater number of gentiles who had "turned away from idols to serve the living and true God," that God had employed the death and resurrection of Jesus as somehow on their behalf. Utter trust in God's deed, which Paul called faith, would achieve a marvelous betterment not only for those who had this faith but for the entire human race. It would not remove the tragic possibility of sin, but it did remove the guilt of all sin going back to Adam. Faith in this deed of God was a remedy for sins committed and a dispeller of the fear of death in the present and the future.

Jesus' Coming (Parousia) at the End in Glory

In this short letter Paul faces a problem that some in the community are having and have proposed to him. Would the Thessalonians' beloved dead be worse off than those living at the time of Jesus' coming in glory, whether in a less-favored condition or, worse still, not raised up at all? Paul's short answer is No. But in developing the answer briefly he reveals how he has presented the mystery of the End, or Last Things, as Jews called it. He must have taught the suddenness of the divine inbreaking as if it could be understood to be imminent or soon, although no time schedule of God's action can be known. Those are the terms, however, on which he bases the scenario of his response. There is every likelihood that Paul would have reviewed his teaching on Jesus' Coming (Parousia, literally, "being present with") at the End, even if the community's difficulty regarding it had not arisen. That is because Paul speaks of it as the final consummation of lives lived in faith in most of his other letters. The teaching quite apart from Paul's response to Thessalonian anxieties was this: those who had responded to God's choice of them with works of faith, hope, and love could, if long dead, expect to be raised up with Christ first and then the living after them to meet the Lord in the air and be with him always. Paul need not have had a special revelation of the future to describe it thus. It was Israelite faith in the last judgment, with a special role expected for Jesus.

All of the above, in sum, is Paul's view of Jesus and what God accomplished through him in the Spirit. The question is, how did he arrive at this lofty concept of a fellow Jew, his contemporary although he had not known him? What could have convinced him that Jesus not only merited the titles Messiah and Lord but that he could be called God's Son in an absolute or unique sense (1 Thess 1:10)? He gives the answer in distressing brevity in another letter, his first to Corinth, by speaking of his direct encounter with the risen Christ (1 Cor 15:8). This would have happened perhaps three years after Jesus' crucifixion and glorification, a date that can be arrived at only by going backwards from the data Paul supplies about his early movements as a believer in the mystery. His letter to the churches in the Asian province of Galatia, which he had founded, is the source. It in turn can be dated with probability four or five years after the first Thessalonian letter. Paul writes there of the Gospel he proclaims as having come to him not through ordinary human channels but "through a revelation of Jesus Christ" (Gal 1:12). There is no preposition "of" in the Greek, but the genitive case of name and title could mean equally "concerning" Jesus or "by" him. A sentence or two later Paul becomes explicit. God by his calling and through God's favor bestowed on him, "was pleased to reveal his Son to me, so that I might proclaim him to the gentiles" (v. 16). We await some words on the circumstances in which the revelation was made and received. No further words are forthcoming. In fact, the claim of this divine self-disclosure occurs only incidentally in a passage in which Paul wishes to make clear that his apostolic calling came directly from God. He says that he did not check it out with the churches in Judaea but launched immediately on a missionary career on his own. He says nothing of the content of his initial Gospel in northern Arabia or Damascus. When he goes to Jerusalem for the first time to confer with Cephas ("Rock," that is, Peter) and James, the brother of the Lord, we have to assume that his teaching about Jesus was identical with theirs or he would have recorded major differences. The same is true of a second visit after fourteen years. Silence on the matter of how God revealed the risen Christ to him!

What did he believe of Jesus in the revelatory experience that sent him on his life's journey? Maddeningly, he does not say. Nor does he say, in a context of self-defense directed to those who are calling his apostleship into question or passing judgment on him: "Am I not free? Am I not an apostle? Have I not seen Jesus our Lord" (1 Cor 9:1). Only that! He goes on to ask rhetorically whether he is not free to eat and drink, to travel with a wife like the other apostles, and to choose to work for a living while teaching, as he and Barnabas do and others presumably do not. We are sure of this much: that the experience of Jesus risen taught him that persecuting believers in that mystery of God was gravely wrong.

Saul/Paul's Faith in Jesus Found in Other Letters

In continuing to track Jesus in Paul's writings we do well to examine the first of two letters he wrote to the church in Corinth. Jesus is accorded the same titles of honor in these letters as we saw above: Lord and Christ. "Jesus," unadorned, appears only in a quoted curse that cannot be uttered under the influence of God's Spirit; similarly, the impulse of the Spirit is required to say that "Jesus is Lord" (1 Cor 12:3), which is sometimes called the oldest and shortest of creeds. Calling Jesus simply Christ, Paul can say that he is within "the law of Christ" to make the point that he is not outside the (Mosaic) Law of God (1 Cor 9:21). And in an expanded figure he says that the rock from which water was struck by a people thirsting in the desert was Christ (Exod 17:1-7). He either knew or made up a midrashic development of the cloud and pillar of fire that guided the people, turning it by verbal alchemy into a traveling rock. Rabbis did things like that all the time. What is important about Paul's use of the image is that he has a preexistent Christ in mind, who centuries before his birth as Jesus is the leader of God's people Israel. He writes quite flatly that man has Christ as his head and God is the head of Christ (1 Cor 11:3). It is a divine-human hierarchy. Where does woman come in? Under the headship of man. Modern women are angered by this concept; but they need to know, although it will give them small comfort, that there is nothing of religious faith about the man-woman relation. It is simply the way family life was conceived in the pagan and Jewish worlds equally. Paul had been expostulating against Corinthian men and women in the weekly assembly in Corinth for not conforming to the Jewish dress code. He is stern about requiring it, but it is fairly certain that he could not enforce it. The headship of men in the family is something he took for granted, as any ancient writer of either sex would.

The mode of dress in the weekly assembly is the first we hear of a cultural custom among pagan new believers that is quite different from that of Jews. It was one that nonetheless continued to prevail in gentile majority churches despite the stern admonition. Paul and all the other apostles to the gentiles must have experienced culture shock in matters like this of covered and uncovered heads in public prayer and more radically different folkways. They had to make distinctions between what was and was not essential for public expression of the new faith by peoples coming from the two major traditions of worship and life, Jewish and gentile. When did Paul conclude that male circumcision and the Mosaic food laws were not essential to pagans practicing the worship of the God of Israel through God's Son, the Jew Jesus in the power of

God's Spirit? There is no reason to think that he came to this conclusion instantaneously upon God's revelatory act. There is so much that we do not know about the roots of Paul's decision on freely eating meats that had been offered in a worship act to pagan gods. It was nearly impossible to avoid them since pagan dedicatory rites, like some kosher and non-kosher decisions, were made right at the public markets (see 1 Cor 8:1-13; 10:14-32).

The discussion of headship, or who is over whom and who is subordinate to whom, leads obliquely but not directly to Paul's view of Jesus as the cosmic Christ whose Church on earth, or any local realization of it, can be thought of figuratively in terms of the human body. For smooth functioning of the body every organ, limb, and body part must fulfill its role and no other. Pagan writers had had such an image of the body politic and the body social. Paul employs the figure of all humanity, whether ecumenical (the Mediterranean "household") or local in a house church, as the one body of Christ (1 Cor 12:12-31; Rom 12:4-8). In that Corinthian letter he speaks of being "in the body of Christ," while in dozens of other places it is simply being "in Christ," "in Christ Jesus," or "belonging to Christ," "being baptized into his death," "dying with him," and above all "rising with him." In general, the Jesus of Paul's letters is not Jee-sús! ("Put your hand in the hand of the man from Galilee") but the Christ now in glory with the Father, with whom every baptized member in all the churches is in an intimate personal relation.

The end of that relationship in life is nowhere in sight. "May the God of peace," Paul prays in one place, "keep you sound in spirit, soul, and body, free of any fault at the coming of our Lord Jesus Christ" (1 Thess 5:23). From Paul's first Thessalonian letter we know what the faith of the early Church in the culmination of all things was: the day of just judgment by the God of Israel with the heavenly Christ given the central role in the power of the Spirit. The much wider and deeper scenario of Israelite imagination had attempted to spell out the successive stages in a cosmic consummation. This picture that Paul must have long entertained is brought onto the screen by Paul's discovery that some to whom he has brought the gift of the Gospel are entertaining doubts that they will be raised up with Christ in the body. We can only speculate as to the roots of their skepticism. They were, after all, men and women of the province of Achaia where the seaport Corinth and Athens, breeding ground of philosophers, were located. Did popular Platonism—with its word of false wisdom, *Sōma sēma*, "The body a tomb"—still hold them in thrall? What, the human soul locked back into the body for an eternity?

Ugh. Or was the gnostic spirit that originated in Persia—with its contempt for matter and its respect reserved for a Gospel that would not be crudely human but a religion of spirit, both in time and after time—already making inroads in Greece?

Philosophical doubt was flourishing among certain intellectuals in the pagan world. Tombstones have been unearthed that read, "He was not. He was. He is not," a succinct statement of disbelief in any life to come. Certainly this total skepticism was not to be found among the members of the new house churches in Corinth. What is much more likely is that the Greek philosophical outlook that some retained left little room for a Semitic religion that looked for a life to come in the body, that death was not the end of bodily existence. That kind of thing, some may have thought, was the view of Egyptians and the Jews but not of believers in the immortality of the soul. In any case, the denial of the possibility led to the apostle's review of the mystery of the resurrection of the body that had the risen and glorified Jesus at its core.

Paul argues in that first letter to Corinth from the resurrection of Christ, which he is confident he can assume, to the resurrection of the just, the matter that some are casting in doubt. The argument is framed in a way that may seem strange to us: "If the dead are not raised, it follows that Christ is not raised, and if Christ is not raised your faith has no substance to it and you are still in your state of sin." In that case, the hypothesis goes on, those who have gone on within the community of Christ are indeed lost. The logic of the steps in this argument may escape us. Paul continues with a summary statement of the wretched condition of those who have no resurrection hope, confident that his argument has established it: "If it is for this life only that Christ has given us hope, we are of all people most to be pitied. But the truth is, Christ *was* raised to life. . . . [Hence] as in Adam all die, so in Christ shall all be brought to life" (1 Cor 15:16-22). Believing this mystery defines what justifies calling oneself a Christian. Adhering to the code of conduct Jesus taught, without this faith, does not do it. It is the litmus test proposed by all who have proclaimed the Semitic apostolic faith in every age and locale.

If what we have seen so far is who Jesus is for Paul and his traveling companions, how can they hold and share this faith regarding him without mention of his public life as a teacher, a worker of miraculous signs, someone who gave multiple evidence in his lifetime of the special relation in which he stood to God his Father? Was not this an essential part of the Gospel proclamation? Our clue to the answer is the fact that no Christian writing in the canon of Scripture, except the four gospels, does this. Only the books called Hebrews and Revelation do a very little more than Paul and the other epistles to elaborate on Jesus' sufferings in his last hours. And none has any reference to his earlier days except to identify some of their teaching as "from the Lord" (e.g., Acts 20:35; 1 Cor 7:10; 11:23) For all of the non-gospel writings, but including the gospels, the Gospel proclaimed was what God had done for the world out of love in and through Jesus as God's Christ and the Holy Spirit. Was it, perhaps, that hearers of one of the canonical gospels—and it would take a century for any local church to hear all four read out publicly—were favored among the early baptized? No, because all four gospels were original compositions in Greek produced outside the land of Israel, whatever the fragmentary Aramaic material was on which they were based that was circulating in Roman Palestine. Could the epistolary silence have been widespread ignorance of the earthly life of Jesus, or even a lack of curiosity regarding it? Both seem totally unlikely. Those events and that teaching would have meant much to the dozens of Palestinian Jews we call the early apostles. They could not not have shared those reminiscences. The same is true of Diaspora Jews like Saul of Tarsus and Barnabas of Cyprus. Simon of Cyrenaica, the cross bearer behind Jesus (Luke 23:26), and his sons Alexander and Rufus (Mark 15:21) who were eyewitnesses of the events, would have spent a lifetime proclaiming them. Could any of those who were not familiar with Jesus in his native Palestine have been totally incurious about his public life and teaching, what manner of man he was that some had thought him intimately related to God and others wanted him dead?

The Silence of Paul's Extant Letters on Jesus' Public Life

Saul stands as representative of many who, having accepted an initial revelation of God concerning Jesus, would have almost certainly learned all they could about him, while knowing that the Gospel they had to proclaim consisted in telling how faith in his death, his upraising from the dead, and his ascent to the glory of the Father made an immense difference to Jew and gentile alike. Paul, Silvanus, Timothy (a half-Jew by birth), and Titus (a gentile by birth) must not be thought of as having brought the Gospel to the gentile world either first or single-handed. We do not know who brought the good news of Christ and the Spirit to Damascus, Alexandria, Edessa, or Rome, except that it was not Paul. Neither should it be thought that the Gospel was brought to the new churches in the exact wording of Paul's collected letters. We can be sure of this much, however: that when Cephas, James, and the other stalwarts (Paul calls them "pillars") of the Jerusalem church first heard the way Paul was proclaiming the Gospel and he heard their way, it had to be substantially the same. Similarly, it was the basic homogeneity of the twenty-seven books that accounted for their finally constituting the canon of New Testament Scripture. Any view of Jesus and his work that departed seriously from the apostolic teaching that came out of Galilee and Jerusalem would not have been accepted. The second- and third-century gnostic gospels that have come to much public notice in the last decade were simply spurned by the main body of Christians. They were not suppressed by the larger body for their important content not found in the canonical four gospels but, rather, because some of what they taught accorded so little with the apostolic teaching. They were works of pure fiction pressing a gnostic line. Orthodox, that is to say, correct Catholic faith about Jesus and the mystery of salvation has many times since had to repudiate a contempt for matter that marks all gnostic systems or influence.

From the sixteenth through the twenty-first century there have been a number of such traditions that purport to teach Christianity as the higher spirituality, a religion of words and concepts and spirit rather than of flesh and blood reality. Christianity is above all not a "head trip," even though like the religion of Israel from which it came it has had to do with the reality of God unseen who is pure Spirit, and good and evil spirits called angels and devils, and the human soul or spirit. It is at the same time a religion of human spirits in the flesh and of a Word or Son of God enfleshed to whom humanity is mysteriously united in a unity it cannot comprehend. From its origins the Church viewed Jesus in that way, as a man of human history born of a woman under Mosaic Law (Paul's wording in Gal 4:4) who preceded history as Son of God with God from the beginning. Christianity like the religion of Israel is an incarnate or enfleshed religion. Some versions of Christianity are embarrassed by its flesh and blood character.

The second letter to the Thessalonian church that Paul may have written (or a later disciple in his spirit more likely) has a view of Jesus identical with that of the first letter. Jesus is very much the Lord who is faithful, who guards and protects the baptized from the evil one, who is himself the Lord of peace (2 Thess 3:3, 16). The members of the church in Thessalonika are presumed to be living their lives in "our Lord Jesus Christ and God our Father" (2 Thess 2:16; see 1:1; 3:5, 16). This epistle presents a different scenario of the "coming" or "manifestation of the coming" of the Lord in glory, describing it as to be much delayed and marked by the apostasy of many believers in the time between the present and the future, but with Jesus as the one who is to come, as in the first epistle.

Saint Luke's book of Acts says that Paul, after an unpleasant experience in Athens, came to Corinth. In that raucous port city, the Big Easy of the ancient world, he met a Jewish couple in the same craft as he, weavers of tent cloth from goat's hair, and stayed there a year and a half (Acts 18:1-11). In the first letter back to this church in Corinth Paul accords Jesus the now familiar titles Lord and Christ, often in tandem. He refers to the future revelation of Christ as "the day of our Lord Jesus," which will be the culmination of a calling to a "share (*koinōnía*) in the life" of him who is God's Son (1 Cor 1:7-9; see vv. 18-31 for what follows). This letter calls Jesus "the power of God and the wisdom of God," the only time that the New Testament accords him that title. He does this to the disappointment of some who wish John had used Wisdom, a feminine noun, in the opening verse of his gospel instead of Word (*Logos*), masculine like the person Jesus. The famed church in Constantinople, *Hagia Sophia*, Holy Wisdom, bears a Christ title.

That wisdom that Jesus is turns out to be his death on a cross, rejected by the world in its wisdom, which in the event proves to be folly: the false concept of salvation without suffering. In a neat twofold paradox Paul has God calling on the fools of this world to confute the wise, the world's weak to overpower the strong, all because a crucified Jesus has proved a fool and weak in letting himself be led to the cross. He did not remain such for long, however, showing himself to be power and wisdom in the flesh when he was raised up by God from the dead. Paul's point in this passage is to bring certain of the Corinthians low in their foolish boasting (1 Cor 1:18-31). They claim to be somebodies by the reckoning of this world. Paul, who knows them very well, writes that until they acknowledge that they are in fact nobodies they do not have a hope of seeing things as they truly are. Once they grant that Jesus was the world's great Nobody and become like him in that—accepting the cross in their lives as the one sure sign of God's wisdom and power—they cannot be reckoned somebodies in the image of him who indeed *was* Somebody.

Jesus in Paul's Corinthian Correspondence

Christianity has often been accused of finding human suffering to be a good in itself. Friedrich Nietzsche, born into a Protestant family, declared in mature adulthood that Christianity was a religion for weaklings. It sapped the human will to overcome all obstacles, thus to prevail as the Super Human. He was certainly influenced in his thinking by a prevalent position of his boyhood that saw Jesus' humiliation at the hands of bullies as his finest hour. A healthy theology of human salvation does not teach this. Neither did Paul or the four evangelists on whose writings such an erroneous construct is based. Jesus' coming forth from the tomb glorious and immortal was his finest hour.

Christian faith in what God accomplished through Jesus for the human race holds him to be a human being in every respect, sin alone excepted. It was concluded of him at an early date that this "descendant of David was established as Son of God in power by his upraising from the dead." That is a snatch of a creedal statement that Paul incorporated at the head of the latest written of his letters that we possess, the one he sent on ahead of him to Rome, where he hoped to stop off on his way to Spain. All other proclaimers of the Gospel had come to the same conclusion as Paul from the fact of Jesus' resurrection. No other view of this man who died as a criminal emerged from the earliest communities of believers in God's deed done in him. That faith took the following form: if this teacher who reflected in his person the holiness of the All Holy God, who performed many miracles of healing and of control of the forces of nature, and who had more than once escaped being apprehended by inimical forces, could let himself be captured and led to his death, he must have had all the limits of human nature, including mortality. That is why the central prayer of the eucharistic rite in all languages says after the word death, "a death he freely accepted." This means that a man who could have avoided it went to his death. It does not mean that Jesus reveled in suffering or invited his captors to finish him off. It means that God had raised up one man totally obedient to the divine will, that is, without sin, who though innocent of any crime had been executed in a cruel manner. Simply that.

Jesus' death on the cross was God's answer to the anguished cry of Job and to the multiplied plea of the psalmists, "Why do these terrible things happen to me?" "Why do you let your enemies, O God, prevail over Israel, sack your holy city Jerusalem, kill those who serve you faithfully?" Jesus' death was a powerful lesson, divinely taught, that God lets the good and the wicked suffer terrible injustices at the hands of other humans without interfering in the evil exercise of their freedom. The unique character of Jesus' case was that God vindicated him, set right the imbalances of the scales of justice, by raising him up from death to new life after three days. In all other cases, God will do perfect justice to the good and the bad alike on the Last Day when the Son Jesus comes in the Father's glory.

In the mean time, the time between, the whole Church along with Paul has called the cross the wisdom of God and the power of God because this death was the means God chose to inaugurate a new life for all humanity (1 Cor 1:18-24). The question so often asked, "Where was God when . . .?" is not the right question. It supposes God should time after time have interfered with the evil in the human heart or, in other catastrophes, with the course of nature. Christianity does not believe in such a God. The God of its awestruck faith respects human freedom even when exercised at its worst and knows the complexity and terrible fragility of the created cosmos, not stepping in to halt the laws of destructive nature.

When Paul later in this letter scolds some in Corinth for living lives unfaithful to their calling he uses language that modern Westerners find hard to comprehend. This is especially true in light of the Church's centuries-long resistance to a false interpretation of the Gospel as directed to the human spirit only. Paul at some point has chosen a vocabulary of "flesh" and "spirit" as plainly contrary to each other. How can this be? Careful inspection of his use of these terms reveals that he does not mean by them the body with its passions and the soul with its intellect and will in a struggle to do the right thing. He does portray the interior struggle between flesh and spirit in that sense in a later letter (Rom 7:4-25). In his first letter to Corinth, however, he uses the two nouns in a different way. Having spoken of the Spirit of God as the only agent of divine self-knowledge, he says that the human spirit similarly scrutinizes human things. But the human talent is confined to ordinary happenings and things of this world. To understand the things freely given us by God and the words addressed to us by God a further gift is required, because "no one knows what pertains to God except the Spirit of God" (1 Cor 2:11; see 2:10–3:3). This sets the stage for a spirit-flesh discussion of the two as polar opposites, in no way able to act in harmony. He calls the human open to the guidance of God's Spirit "spirit" (*pneûma*) and as resisting that guidance or direction as "flesh" (*sarx*). In other words, the two words describe human nature at its best and at its worst.

If the two nouns used in this way are puzzling to us moderns, the two adjectives are even more so. Seventeenth-century Bible translations, Catholic and Protestant alike, spoke of the natural man, or the carnal or sensual man, versus the spiritual man. "Carnal" correctly translates the adjective made from *sarx*, the Greek word for human nature or flesh, as in man and other animals, but the modern translation "fleshly" is no better. For centuries Bible readers in English took carnal to connote the sex passion, which if misused is one way of living in the fashion of "this world." In fact, the example Paul provides for non-spiritual living or infancy in the Christ life is rivalries in the community, bickering over self-importance. Any other thwarting of maturity in Christ is done by resisting God's grace, which is the gift of the Spirit (1 Cor 3:10; see vv. 1-21 for the full discussion). From the apostolic age onward, living a spiritual life has meant one thing only for the Christian: the openness of the human spirit to the prompting of the Spirit of God. Much contemporary "spirituality" is something else, namely, cultivating the human spirit, the better self, without any reference to eternal God. Practices like meditation, interior reflection, and yoga are by all means a good thing so long as they are not confused with religion. Religious reflection begins with one's self, one's spirit to be sure, but it turns shortly to the praise, the thanks, and the petition directed to Another. Christianity sees much modern spirituality as natural, not spiritual, in the Pauline sense.

This letter of Paul devotes space to exhortations to harmony in the community. All human beings have an ego problem. It is impossible not to have one. Corinth seems to have been gifted with an extraordinary number of inflated egos, taking the familiar form of "anything you can do I can do better." Paul's main concern in correcting the behavior of some is their outlook on Jesus' body, the Church. Saint Augustine would later put it as, "You who eat the body of Christ *are* the body of Christ." The thought is Pauline and probably older, since all life in common with others is corporate. The *corpus* in this case is the body of the Lord. If a human body were to be made up of all eyes or all ears, all feet or all hands it would be a monster. Similarly, a local church that was all apostles or prophets or teachers would be a monstrosity. Yet some in Corinth seemed to wish to have it that way. Name your role. Speaking in tongues? "I can do that." Interpreting the incomprehensible gibberish of a tongue speaker? "I can do that too." Healing, deeds of miraculous power, assisting others, administering community affairs? "I'm your one. Step aside, please." The human tendency to put oneself forward is not, however, the matter Paul is chiefly concerned with. It is the local community of faith, the baptized, as being nothing less than the Body of Christ on earth. Every local church is the one Church in the little. Christ is in the members of his body and they are in him. The heavenly Christ has mystically incorporated men and women into his body, his very self.

But "the body of Christ" meant for Paul more than Jesus' glorified body or corporate life in him. It was the same for all the far-flung apostles. They remembered that on the night before Jesus died he had taken bread in his hands and after he had given thanks to God, broke it, and said: "This is my body, which is for you; do this as my memorial." In the same way he took the cup after supper and said: "This cup is the renewed covenant sealed in my blood. Whenever you drink it, do this in memory of me." "For every time you drink this bread and drink this cup," Paul added, "you proclaim the death of the Lord until he come" (1 Cor 11:23-26; see vv. 26-29 for what follows). The apostle and his team must have participated in this ritual many times in the year and a half they stayed in Corinth. They almost certainly knew these words of Jesus by heart. Paul must have felt, however, that he had to rehearse them for emphasis; for in the class conflict attending the rite that had been reported to him, he feared that the Corinthian church had lost not only the solemnity but even more the unity of mind and heart that the consecrated bread and wine symbolized. In brief, all the grains of wheat that make up the large loaf of pocket bread and all the drops of fermented juice of the grape in the large vessel are the one bread and the one cup that show forth the one body of the Lord that the church at Corinth both eats and drinks and is (10:16-17).[1] As disunited, as individuals going their own way in the assembly, they are no longer symbolized in sacrament by the one loaf and one cup.

The bond that held the LORD, the God of Israel, and this people together was called a covenant (*b'rith*), a unilateral agreement first offered to Abraham, then to his issue Isaac and Jacob, afterward renewed through Moses on Mount Sinai, and again with the whole people upon their return from exile. In every case it was the one covenant renewed. But there is no word "renew" in Hebrew or in the Greek translation of the Hebrew Scriptures. There is no problem of God's doing something new for his people. In fact, the book of Jeremiah has the LORD say in words of promise: "I shall establish a new covenant with the people of Israel and Judah . . . not like the covenant I made . . . when I took them out of Egypt . . . a covenant they broke" (Jer 31:31-34). But the prophet then says that the covenant the LORD will give will be written on the peoples' hearts and will say, "I shall be their God, and they will be my people." Those terms are not new. It is only the mode of reception by the people that is

---

[1] *The Teaching [Didachē] of the Twelve Apostles* of the early second century has a eucharistic prayer that features the many fragments of the one loaf, 9.3-4.

new. Similarly, Jesus' words at the Last Supper had to have referred to the Abrahamic covenant once more renewed, since there can be no change of the divine mind and starting over.

What was its newness? Again, the character of the recipients who were welcoming the gift of the covenant held out. Since the liturgical formula of Jesus' words was the one in place in a mixed congregation of Jews and gentiles in Corinth—and presumably the same combination marked the churches of Matthew, Mark, and Luke that had substantially the same words—the newness consisted of a covenant accepted by Jews and non-Jews and not the people of Israel alone. This was indeed an absolute *novum* in all religious history. From a very early date, perhaps as soon as the Gospel was brought outside Roman Palestine to the near Diaspora and former pagans were incorporated into the life of the Church, the one covenant was renewed for an entirely new population.

The Hebrew word translated "covenant" can be rendered into English as "compact," "contract," or simply "agreement," for that is what it is. The terms of a covenant, if it is to be validated, must be accepted by those to whom it is offered. In the first instance and throughout Israel's history the sole terms were fidelity to the God of Israel, not only by reposing total trust in the LORD's providential care but by living lives of the kind expected by this All Just, All Holy God. Unlike the deities of the pagans who had no such concern, the one God expected ethically upright lives in his human creatures, the only kind of life that befitted their human nature. A lofty ethos characterizes the perfection of the human being. Evil choices mark its imperfection. Paul has been charging this infant church with disorderly conduct, even raucous behavior arising from factionalism, at the weekly assembly. He would have the Lord's Supper, as he calls this ritual meal, celebrated quite separately from a meal of choicest foods and too much wine brought from home by the upper class—and not shared with the great unwashed in the same congregation. Only then would the bread and wine, now become the body and blood of the Lord, serve its symbolic purpose, namely, stand for a unified community by bringing about that unity.

After quoting the words of Jesus over bread and wine at his last meal with his friends, Paul follows with a warning about eating and drinking unworthily. Each person must do an interior search to see whether there is some sin unrepented that will bring God's judgment. Paul calls such an unresolved state of conscience failure to "discern the body." At first it seems that he means a self-examination to see if the one who eats and drinks believes that it really is the Lord's body and blood. A closer look at the context of the warning shows that faith in the mystery is not in question. That seems to be assumed. But if the *discerned* body and blood means the community—the whole Christ that needs to be discerned which may have been sinned against by some—then the unworthiness of proceeding to eat and drink becomes clear. All consciences must be free of sin for the "Supper of the Lord" to be a true sign of unity, not a false or lying sign.

The Jesus of the Epistolary Corpus

To review, we need to ask who Jesus is in the faith of Paul's churches and all the churches in the mid-first century. He is the risen Christ and Lord, now at the right hand of the Father, who will come in glory at the End to summon the living and raise up the dead to be with him always. He is, at the same time, not only with God but also in and with those who believe in him, both individually and corporately. He is, lastly, present to the Church as the literal food and drink that nourishes the bodies and souls of those who have been baptized into his death. This is the one, undivided Jesus whose multiple presence is possible because he is the Son of God as well as the son of a Jewish mother through whom the Spirit of God is active in this world and throughout the cosmos. "All things were created through him," as we shall see in later written New Testament books (Heb 1:2; John 1:2).

Paul named Sosthenes, the man whom Acts identifies as a synagogue official in Corinth, as the co-sender with him of the first letter to that church. The second letter to the Corinthians, which may be an edited joining of several pieces of correspondence, is sent by Paul and Timothy. Jesus is not spoken of in any way different in the second letter than in the first, but the apostle does employ some fresh figures to describe who Jesus is in Paul's and the people's lives. Thus, we hear, "God leads us as in a triumphal procession in Christ" and those who believe in him become "an aroma of Christ for God" on their way to salvation; if to perdition, then as a foul odor (2 Cor 2:14-17). Continuing the metaphor, the letter speaks of the sweet odor of life and the stench of death. Paul is aware in all his letters of those who do not give the Gospel a hearing and, even more, those who at first profess belief in it but then desert that path.

He frequently warns against judging others and, like Jesus, counsels leaving that to God. At the same time Paul often sounds like the psalmist who is quite sure of the harsh judgment some will receive at God's hands. He entertains no doubts that there are "those who are perishing." He goes on to name the reason for his travels as "the gospel of Christ" and says he needs no introduction to or from this community: "You are all the letter I need, a letter written on our heart" (2 Cor 3:1-3). It is not a letter written in ink on papyrus or vellum, least of all on stone-hard clay tablets. The people are a letter that has come from Christ, given to the apostles to deliver.

The distinction between two kinds of letters, one inscribed with a pen or stylus and the other enfleshed in the hearts of sender and receivers, leads Paul to create another contrast, still in figurative language. This one has in Christian memory been misunderstood almost as much as it has been understood. The faithful Jew Saul, ever ready to proclaim that God has done something new for Jews but also for gentiles, wishes to set two epochs one against the other: one of death, the other of life, one of a covenant renewed by the tablets of Torah, the other of a covenant further renewed of justice leading to glory. Knowing well the Sinai story of Exodus that is retold in Deuteronomy, Paul puts it to use for his purpose but changes it in light of the point he is making. The resistance to the Gospel he encounters from fellow Jews is almost certainly based on the belief of most Jews who are contemporaneous with Paul that the deliverance of the Law on Mount Sinai was God's last word. How *could* there be anything new, they wondered? Hence their resistance to God's deed in Christ as a new revelation, updating the renewal of the Abrahamic covenant through the Lawgiver.

To controvert this position that is in opposition to the Gospel, Paul tells of Moses coming down the mountain with face resplendent, reflecting the glory of God. That is part of the story in the Scripture, as is Moses having to veil his countenance while speaking to the people. Paul adds a detail that the scroll of neither Exodus nor Deuteronomy contains. He alters the Exodus account to say that he does this "to keep the Israelites from seeing the end of what was fading away" (2 Cor 3:13; see Exod 34:29-35; Deut 9:12, 15). This was Paul's way of saying that conformity to all the ritual precepts of the Law was not God's final revelatory word. He says this in anger at the fellow Jews of his day who will not accept the possibility of a newer revelation. In making this case he distinguishes between the "old covenant . . . [inscribed] in letters on stone-hard tablets" and "an epistle of Christ administered by us written . . . by the Spirit of the living God." The Greek word for covenant in this passage (v. 6) became *testamentum* in the Vulgate translation, hence "Old and New Testaments" in Christian speech. Further, the words *gramma* and *pneûma*, "letter" and "spirit," became a proverb about the letter and the spirit of Mosaic Law. The tragic Christian misunderstanding that came of this passage, because there is no word for "renew" in Greek, is that there was a new covenant in Christ offered by God to replace the old covenant renewed on Sinai on tablets of baked clay. This erroneously conceived replacement of the one by the other is called supersessionism. Paul teaches no such thing nor does any proclamation of the Gospel in the apostolic age, although Hebrews comes perilously close.[2] Unfortunately, the nonbinding of new believers from paganism to Jewish ritual customs, and these rites being rendered a matter of free choice for ethnic Jews, has for centuries been taken by gentile Christians to mean that one revelatory act of God has been replaced by another.

The fact that the Church from its origins accepted the Old Testament as its Scriptures, however, means that being a Christian involves believing in the religion of Israel. That it has been updated by God's revelation in Jesus, Christ and Lord, has done nothing to abrogate it. Such belief in Jesus makes proclaimers of the Gospel like Paul and his team, as Paul says, slaves of those to whom it has been delivered for Jesus' sake. "The light shining out in darkness" dispelling pagan gloom meant for Isaiah the religion of Israel practiced in northern Assyrian-dominated Palestine (Isa 9:1; see 8:23). Paul sees in that text a light that has "shone in our hearts to bring to light the knowledge of the glory of God on the face of Christ" (2 Cor 4:6). Such is Jesus consistently for Paul: the glory of God on the face of Christ.

Paul prefers leaving the body and going home to the Lord, that is, Jesus, to living on in the body, knowing that like everyone else he must appear before the judgment seat of this same Lord (2 Cor 5:10). He once knew Christ according to worldly standards (literally, "the flesh," 2 Cor 5:16-17). Now, that is no longer the case. To be "united to Christ" is to be part of a new creation. He is the one through whom God has reconciled the world to himself. All this is so because Jesus died and was raised to life: "He died for all so that those who live might no longer live for themselves but for him." This phrase that sums up life in, through, and with Christ Jesus is incorporated into one of the eucharistic canons (2 Cor 5:15). What follows in this passage is the place the glorified Jesus has in what will later be called the economy, or plan, of salvation. God's design is to reconcile the world alienated by sin to God's own self through Jesus: "Christ was innocent of sin, yet for our sake God made him one with

---

[2] Heb 7:18, *anōphelés*, "useless" or "inoperative" but often rendered "abrogated"; a variety of ritual precepts is meant, certainly not the whole Mosaic corpus.

human sinfulness so that in him we might be made one with the justness of God" (2 Cor 5:21). Such is the mystery of human redemption. To believe in it as a member of the Church is not simply to love Jesus intensely, which some contemporary evangelical preachers make the sole condition for being "saved," but to understand however basically the way God employs the human Jesus as humanity's redeemer.

What can Paul possibly mean when he says that Christ cannot be in accord with Beliar (other, later manuscripts read "Belial"; 2 Cor 6:15)? He is making a list of opposites that cannot coexist, among them light and darkness, belief and unbelief. Beliar ("worthlessness," although literally "lord of dung" or "of the flies") was a popular contemptuous dismissal of the devil or Satan by Jews. Paul is warning against too close association with a pagan or pagans lest it imperil the new faith of believers. Although this is less likely, it could be the taunt of some, recorded in the gospels, accusing Jesus of being in league with demons as the source of his powers. The greater likelihood is that Paul employs a word out of his Jewish vocabulary to describe the pagan religions he normally refers to as the worship of idols.

Paul returns to Jesus in the first of his two letters of appeal for famine-stricken Jerusalem by calling Jesus rich by nature but having adopted the Corinthians' poverty so as to enrich them (2 Cor 8:9). They, in turn, must contribute to the Judaeans in their need should it occur. Continued faithful confession of the Gospel is termed obedience to Christ (2 Cor 9:13; 10:5). Departure from a sincere commitment to Christ will result if the people attend to the preaching of "another Jesus" than the one Paul preached (11:4). This can only mean the presentation of an erroneous or adulterated version of the way God employs Jesus to enrich believers in him. We know from several of Paul's letters, but this one and the one to the Galatian churches especially, that Paul fears the influence of persuasive proclaimers of the Gospel who have not got it right. The apostle is convinced that all the persecutions and hardships he has endured in spreading the Gospel validate the authenticity of his version of it. If that were not sufficient proof there is the snatching up of one, described obliquely, to the third heaven—Jewish cosmology conceived of three heavens while Greek thought has seven spheres within spheres—described by the Persian word Paradise (2 Cor 11:23–12:10). Surely Paul is reporting a mystical experience in which he heard words in a secret language that human lips could not repeat. After all his strictures regarding boasting, he feels he must not describe the vision in the first person. He casts it rather in terms of his weakness and vulnerability, speaking of a thorn in the flesh or an angel of Satan sent to buffet him. What can that be? Kidney stones, the impaired vision he hints at in the Colossian letter, the illness that he says brought him to the Galatians, his stammer that renders him near speechless when he gets excited? There is no way to know.

Signs of Jesus' Jewishness Wrongly Imposed on Gentiles

With his strong pen Paul can say by letter exactly what he wishes to say. He knows that he is strong in this medium, whereas his oral presentation is rightly accounted weak and his physical appearance perhaps repulsive. Paul's epistle to the Galatian churches is triggered by his anger on learning that some among his new believers have been taken into camp by false brothers, "pseudo-apostles." These may be ethnic Jews or, with an equal probability, Godfearers or proselytes, pagans who have adopted Jewish customs in part or whole (acceptance of circumcision made the difference) upon adopting the religion of Israel. Paul argues in Galatians that gentiles need not live as Jews in matters such as circumcision, abstaining from nonkosher foods, and perhaps fasting practices and Sabbath rest. The reason that some thought that gentiles had to adopt all the observances required of Jews in the Scriptures was that these books were now *their* history. There was the additional fact that Jesus, whom some pagans now believed in as the world's redeemer, was a Jew. Saint Paul, in the letter he wrote to the church at Rome before he arrived there, engages in a defense of his teaching, going so far as to say that faith in what God has done for all humanity in Christ and the Spirit has rendered the distinctive signs of Jewishness neutral even for Jews. In other words, ritual practices proper to Israel now contribute nothing essential to faith in God's redemptive act. Demanding that the observances continue among Christian Jews as well as being freshly adopted by gentiles is identified by Paul as a false reading of the one Gospel. He can even speak of "the circumcised" or "those from James" as being brought in "to spy on our freedom" after he has made a second visit to Jerusalem with the uncircumcised Titus and others (Gal 2:3-5). The infant Church did not adopt this position because Paul promulgated it. He promulgated it because it was the Church's position (see Gal 2:11-14).

At times, some post-Holocaust Christians, anxious for good relations with Jews, will make a point of the Jewishness of Jesus, expecting that that might establish a bond and pave the way for dialogue. Unfortunately, it does little or nothing to achieve that end. Jews can only remember the persecution of their people by Christians. It blocks out every other consideration including the historical. Moreover, recalling Christian origins is of little help, since Jews who know their history know that early believers in the crucified Jesus risen from the dead were admitting gentiles into the religion of Israel wholesale, without attending to it as exclusively the religion of a people. Rather, they attended to the biblical prophecy that at the end of the age all peoples would worship the one God by maintaining that God had revealed the final age as having begun. Christians sometimes say in their naïveté, "Remember, Jesus was a faithful Jew true to the Torah." Of course he was, but that tells us little of the observances he engaged in. We simply do not know what that meant in his day, if anything beyond circumcision, the food laws, abstention from work on Saturday, and going to the Temple on the three pilgrimage feasts if the opportunity afforded. Christians need to recall, as Jews very well do, that the schism or split between Jews of the synagogue and Jews of the Church came very early and was over peoplehood: "Who is a Jew?" The legions of ethnic non-Jews who later in the first century declared themselves to be Jews in religion if not in ethnicity was the straw that broke the camel's back. Christians need to remember that the religion of Israel proclaimed as the religion proper to the entire human race is the reason why many Jews could not accept the idea, while some did. It was not the proclamation of Jesus as fully divine as well as fully human—which Christians and Jews alike assign as the teaching that Jews generally could not accept. We have no idea that they could not accept this as a revelation of God. We do know that they were not ready for a dilution of their peoplehood in the revelation they had long ago received, that the God of Israel was their God only. They could not imagine becoming one among the peoples of the earth, and one in the midst of idol worshiping, morally debased peoples at that, which was their view of every ethnic stock other than their own.

One happy outcome of the struggle over whether Jews and gentiles could be of the same religious *faith*, hence of the one *Church* on totally equal terms, was the exposition of the mystery of Christ Jesus that Paul engaged in as part of that argument in the letters to Galatia and Rome. He does the same more briefly in other epistles. The anonymous authors of the pastoral letters to Timothy and Titus, the catholic letters attributed to Peter, James, and Jude, plus the John epistles, Hebrews, and Revelation all allude to God's revealed work in Jesus in the same way as Paul, if usually very succinctly. Only Hebrews explores at any length who Jesus is as well as the work God raised him up to do. There has not been any attention paid to the tension between Jews and gentiles in the Church since the year 200 or so, by which time Christian Jews had become relatively few. The Reformers of the sixteenth century resurrected the debate on quite erroneous terms by identifying the Catholics they had been as no better than Jews in relying on their works of piety—pilgrimages to holy places, the veneration of saints and their relics, and ultimately all sacramental prayer as achieving self-salvation by dint of human effort. Paul's writings had nothing to do with that case, least of all did he declare Mosaic Law null in its entirety because replaced by grace, as some in that era maintained. He did teach clearly that God was the redeemer of the entire human race through Jesus Christ and the Holy Spirit, no longer of Israel only through the ritual practices prescribed in the Law. The entire apostolic Church was teaching, as was Paul, that by God's gift humanity had achieved reconciliation with God, justification (a legal figure) and sanctification, with salvation or rescue from reprobation in prospect at the end of days. It was all couched in language like that of the psalms and hymns of the Old Testament, since the earliest proclaimers of the Gospel were Jews who found in Jesus the fulfillment of all biblical prophecy. Saint Paul writes in Romans that Christ is the end of the Law, meaning the goal toward which all that is written there tends (10:6). That the Law is finished, over, done with—and, hence, that the vocation of the Jewish people is finished as well—is an absurdity that some Christians have entertained even to today.

How, then, does the Galatian letter view Jesus and his role in Jewish and world history? The answer is through faith, by which Paul always means complete trust in what God has done in Christ, not belief in God or religious faith generally but in God of whom he could write, "you are all children of God through faith in Christ Jesus" (Gal 3:26). The "all" are the gentiles to whom this letter is primarily addressed but also the relatively few Jews of the Galatian province who have the same new faith. "For all of you who were baptized into Christ have clothed yourselves with Christ" (3:27). This figurative language may suggest being wrapped in a white garment after being immersed in water or having it poured on those liberally who stood in a pool or stream. In any case, the "clothing" stands for the mystical union of the new believer with the person of Jesus, God's Christ and Lord of the Church since his ascent to the Father. Since Paul is arguing the relation of observance of the ritual precepts of the Law to faith in what God has done in Jesus he devises another figure that onlookers of the wealthy would recognize immediately. He speaks of the Mosaic Law as a pedagogue leading to Christ (Gal 3:24-25). That noun in English has come to mean a teacher but its original meaning was a person charged with the safe conduct of another, specifically a slave who saw that a child went unharmed to school and back. "Disciplinarian" is the rendering of that word in several modern Bible translations but it has too harsh a ring. Paul uses it to convey the Law's function during the 430 years between Moses and Christ. It was the way the Jewish people knew what was right and what was wrong in human behavior. "Transgression" is the usual biblical word for sin, namely, of the Law's boundaries. The purpose of the Law for Paul was to lead to Christ. In the apostolic preaching, Christ's role and function is to lead to God.

This Jesus is, in the Pauline term, a mediator between God and a covenanted people who exercises a function that not even the Law could serve. That is because the covenant made by God with Abraham included the promise that in Abraham all the nations of the earth would be blessed. Even though the Jewish people thought that the presence of any of them in the midst of a pagan horde was a blessing to those people because of the Jewish faith in the one creator God and Israel's lofty morality, very few pagan peoples thought the Jewish presence to be a blessing. Paul, like all the apostolic preachers, was convinced that the promise was fulfilled by the holding out of a blessed condition to all the world's gentiles through the glorified human being Jesus, who was constituted by God the middleman between God and humanity (see Gal 3:15-20). In this extension of the divine blessing, namely, sonship and daughterhood of God in a fuller sense than that of creaturehood, which is already a blessed condition, the Law does not contradict the promises. It could not since God cannot be self-contradictory. Faithful observance of the Law by Jew and gentile proselyte alike brought justness under the Law, but it could not bring the greater good that Paul terms "life" (Gal 4:1-5). Some centuries later a creed for public recitation would call the Spirit of God "the Lord and giver of life," but this gift is none other than that bestowed through Christ the mediator. It is the one gift to all humanity from the one, indivisible triune God: new life in Christ Jesus.

The Galatian letter is a spirited, angry denial that the ritual observances of the Law can in any sense profit the newly baptized gentiles. The apostle argues the case with the aid of several other images besides that of a will whose original bequest goes unchanged by the later addition of codicils (viz., the promise to Abraham followed by the Law given through Moses; Gal 4:21-31). Among these is an heir of minor age whose condition of ownership is no different from that of a slave while trustees act as guardians until he comes of age (Gal 4:1-5), and the biblical tale of Hagar the Egyptian slave whose offspring are born into slavery while the freeborn Sarah's issue is the freeman Isaac (Gal 4:8-10). Paul makes this story an example of two covenants, the one promulgated on Mount

Sinai and held binding in contemporary Jerusalem, while the other the renewed covenant of the heavenly Jerusalem, a figure of the Church.

The apostle Paul is a Diaspora Jew who does not hold the holy city in complete respect because he attributes to its church the continuing demand that new gentile believers in the Gospel adopt Jewish folkways. There are two aspects of his argument that need to be emphasized. When Paul speaks pejoratively or even dismissively of the Law he has in mind only the ritual precepts that are the special signs of Jewishness, not the whole body of laws that are exclusively ethical, including those culturally modified by the years of desert wandering and the conquest of the tribes of the new land. Second, the Galatian letter discusses the adoption of precepts of the Law proper to Jews by gentiles newly baptized, even when a phrase speaks of falling back into enslavement. Paul knows that there was no such observance when he brought the Gospel to the gentiles or when he left them. Some other evangelizers, either local men or men coming from outside, have deceived people whom Paul knows well into thinking that Paul did not promote some essential religious behavior, notably, circumcision, while with them (Gal 5:1-12). We know that Paul's target recipients of this angry letter are former pagans, as is seen in phrases like "God has now acknowledged you" and "How can you turn back to those feeble and elemental spirits?" the supposed deities guiding the movements of the heavenly bodies, entering once again into their service by "keeping special days and months and seasons and years" (Gal 4:8-10).

To conclude: although the adoption by gentiles of the "special laws" of Torah (as Philo, a Jew of Alexandria, termed them) has not been a problem in the Church since the earliest centuries—not even in the Reformation period when Paul's argument in Galatians was erroneously applied—it had the virtue of bringing into full light the gift of God of new life to the whole human race. With God's choice of Jesus as intermediary in the renewal of the covenant first given through Abraham, the promise that all the peoples of the earth would be blessed in his descendants was fulfilled.

Jesus in the Last Written Extant Letter of Saul/Paul

All the evidence from within Paul's epistle to the church at Rome indicates that he felt it necessary to get in the record before visiting the imperial capital exactly what his teaching in all the churches has been.

It seems to be not so much a correction of what is found in Galatians as a careful spelling out of the presentation he has made everywhere regarding the relation of Jews and gentiles in Christ. There evidently was strong anti-Paul sentiment abroad due to his perceived favoritism of gentiles over ethnic Jews and, far worse, an apparent misprizing of the Law that contained the terms of God's covenant with the people Israel. The major omission of Paul's discussion of that question in the Galatian epistle was where the newly baptized Jews stood in the matter of the special laws of Torah that were the signs of Jewishness. The Roman church, a mixture of ethnic Jews and gentiles, was undoubtedly curious to know the position of this influential apostle, who had brought the Gospel to so many other churches. It is almost certain that the church in Rome numbered some and perhaps many, Palestinian Jews. The short answer to the question, which is not the major question relative to the role of Jesus in God's redemptive design, is that Law observance by Jews may be expected to continue provided it is not considered essential to faith in God's deed in Christ. Those special signs of belief in God's self-disclosure to Israel have been rendered neutral by God's recent revelation in the Son and the Spirit. Although Paul never says it explicitly, Jews can continue to practice these signs out of centuries-long familiar habit so long as they are not thought a necessary complement to faith. "The promise [of God to Abraham] was made on the ground of faith in order that it might be a matter of sheer grace and that it might be valid for all Abraham's descendants, not only for those who hold by the Law, but also for those who have Abraham's faith. For he is the father of all, as Scripture says: 'I have appointed you to be the father of many nations'" (Rom 4:16-17a).

Knowing that Aquila [Onkelos] and many other members of the Roman church were circumcised Jews, Paul deems it important to discuss whether this places them in a superior position to others in the community, as they may be claiming over gentiles. He writes that circumcision has great value in every way because it always testifies publicly to God who is faithful, however unfaithful individual circumcised Jews may be. In fact, however, circumcision is a matter of the heart, not a scar on the body. A real Jew is one inwardly, not outwardly. An uncircumcised pagan who keeps the precepts of the Law will be counted as circumcised, while a circumcised Jew may be a transgressor of the Law. Paul's crowning argument is that Abraham was as yet uncircumcised when he received the promise of fatherhood of many nations. Now, the promise has been fulfilled in the many uncircumcised peoples.

But all this argumentation in the primitive Church could divert us from our main purpose, which is to see who Jesus is in the faith of all who accepted the Gospel. He is no different in the epistle to the Romans than in any previously written Pauline letter. At no point is he the Jesus of his earthly days until "he died at the appointed time for those who knew not God" (except in Gal 4:4; see Rom 5:6). Jesus in this letter is consistently the glorified Christ in whom God's justice is now made manifest. God's grace is freely given through redemption in him. "God designed him to be the means of expiating sin by his death, effective through faith" (Rom 3:25). Elsewhere Paul couples Jesus' upraising from the dead to his death as achieving life in the present for believers and the hope of resurrection in the body and salvation in the future (Rom 6:3-11).

A Pauline Letter That Paul Did Not Write

The letter called Ephesians is a marvelous catechetical summary of Paul's teaching designed for circulation in the province of Asia. Understandably, the role of Jesus in God's redemptive design is identical with that in the writings of Paul and others of the apostolic age. More briefly than in the long passage cited below,[3] the author says of Jesus in an address to gentiles:

> Once you were far off, but now in union with Christ Jesus you have been brought near through the shedding of Christ's blood. For he is himself our peace. Gentiles and Jews, he has made the two to be one and in his own body of flesh and blood has broken down the barrier of enmity that separated them; for he annulled the Law with its rules and regulations so as to create out of the two a single humanity in himself, thereby making peace. (Eph 2:13-15)

These three verses are in a sense the saddest in the New Testament for they unknowingly testify to the brief period when the enmity between Jew and gentile was put to death and the two were reconciled in a single body through the cross. The harmony between the two ethnicities in the churches of Asia Minor was short-lived. Before long the gentiles gained the ascendancy in numbers and influence and began to accuse the Jewish

---

[3] See Eph 1:3-22, where the mystery of redemption in Christ is spelled out in the author's majestic style.

populations of the area with refusing to accept the mystery of God's act that the cross represented.

Jesus in Hebrews and Revelation

Another first-century writing in Greek that is impossible to date, although Alexandria seems to be its provenance, is one that concentrates on Jesus in his dying and rising. This book was erroneously called Hebrews at an early date because it was thought to be an appeal to Jews to believe in what God had achieved through the crucified Jesus in his role as high priest. The treatise acknowledges that Jesus was a Jewish layman and not a hereditary priest. It casts him in the role of priest, however, by identifying him as mediator of a new and better covenant "established on better promises" (Heb 8:6, 13). Mediation between God and the people was a priest's sole office through his offering of Temple worship. Hebrews says that we have in Jesus a more excellent priest because he does not have any sins of his own for which to make sacrificial satisfaction. More than that, while all high priests are fated to live and die, Jesus' priesthood in the sanctuary beyond the veil of the heavens is unending.

It was pointed out at the beginning of this chapter that Jesus was termed Israel's Christ and Lord from the first proclamation of him as upraised from the dead. The deliverer of Israel who was hoped for had to be an anointed king in David's mold. But priests were also anointed and prophets too, figuratively, in virtue of their calling (Exod 29:29; Lev 6:22; Isa 61:1). It is no surprise that the one human being whom God restored to life after death and burial should immediately be viewed as the LORD's anointed: king and priest but also prophet, that is, spokesman for God. Hebrews makes the most of the risen Jesus not as priest only but as high priest. The Scriptures designate one priestly functionary as high priest (Num 35:25; 2 Kgs 22:4) and have him in Aaron's mold sprinkling the blood of a bullock and a goat on the cover of beaten gold over the ark "in atonement for the sins of himself and his household and the whole Israelite community" (Lev 16:15-17). Even while the Temple stood in the forty years between Jesus' heavenly glorification and its destruction by the Romans, believers in his resurrection tended to see Jesus as priest and victim in the shedding of his blood in atonement for the sins of the world. Such voluntary victimhood on behalf of the human race is testified to in fragments in various New Testament writings, but it is given full treatment in Hebrews.

That book spells out the role of Jesus as high priest, a man called by God as Aaron and Melchizedek were but, unlike them, was God's Son:

> In the course of his earthly life, he offered up prayers and petitions, with loud cries and tears, to God who was able to deliver him from death. Because of his devotion his prayer was heard: son though he was, he learned obedience through his sufferings and, once perfected, he became the source of eternal salvation for all who obey him, and by God he was designated high priest in the order of Melchizedek. (Heb 5:7-10; see Ps 110:4, which the passage quotes)

That king of Salem in Genesis, a priest of God Most High, was designated of another order by the psalmist, one in which some newly inaugurated king of Judah was being enrolled, than the corrupt hereditary priesthood. In Hebrews' four short verses, there are combined the anguished outcry of the dying Jesus mentioned in the gospels and his perfect human obedience which God made the source or origin of the deliverance of all humanity from sin and the fear of death and judgment. They contain the elements of what a later theology would call the mystery of redemption: God who alone can forgive the sins of all humanity, which are at base acts of disobedience of the divine will for human happiness, accepting one totally obedient man (viz., "without sin") to represent the human race as mediator with God in the process of reconciliation. God alone is the "savior" of humanity, meaning its rescuer from ignorance, sin, and death as the psalms so often say, but the new situation is that God's elect in reconciling an alienated human race is not any prophet, king, or priest but a human priest who is uniquely God's Son. We do not know the steps by which the infant company of those who reflected on Jesus' resurrection and ascension, all of them Palestinian Jews, came to conclude from his glorification what God had meant to do by his life and death. We only know what they concluded.

Temple worship, carried on every morning and evening but more elaborately on the three pilgrimage feasts, one each in spring, early summer, and autumn, was the public prayer of the whole people. The lyrics of the Psalms were the playbook of that ongoing liturgical drama. The people knew the symbolism of the blood of beasts and birds they had bought with Temple coinage, slaughtered by butchers but then smeared on an altar of stone by priests. It stood for *their* blood, their lifeblood, meaning their obedient lives. The Psalter spoke in words what the priests offering blood sacrifice spoke in act: glory to Israel's God, the LORD;

praise for his great goodness; thanks expressed wholeheartedly; but, above all, the awareness that the fashioner of earth and sea and sky and all that is in them had a special concern for them, the people Israel. The common folk knew that the Temple priests in their day were a venal lot, toadies of the empire more than obedient servants of God. The hundreds of men of Aaronide stock and their wives who lived among them, the priests of the twenty-four courses who might never be drawn by lot for Temple service, were no such sort. The compromised character of the Temple priesthood by contrast, however, proved no deterrent to the people's commitment to the sacredness of their function. Whatever their ethical lives, the Temple priests were universally acknowledged as the officers of liturgical intercessory prayer through blood sacrifice.

To repeat, we do not know the steps by which the earliest Jerusalem and Galilean churches went from experiencing the risen Christ to concluding that the lifeblood of this perfectly obedient man was accepted by God as shed in perfect sacrifice for the lives of the many. Saint Luke in the early chapters of Acts has Peter presenting to Jerusalem crowds within days a full-blown theory of how God employed Jesus' death and resurrection to achieve the restoration of a fallen world to God's friendship. But these snatches of proclamation and apologia come from the Lukan church of the late first century. It is only from the correspondence of the non-Palestinian Jew Saul/Paul in the 50s that key words like "death," "blood," "resurrection," and "life" provide hints that even the churches that did not originate from Palestinian Jewry were seeing in the events of three days in Jesus' life the accomplishment in one stroke of what Temple worship achieved from one year to the next in the lives of Jews at prayer. Whoever held the office of high priest and whatever his character, his work was intercessory prayer in act on behalf of the whole people. When the priest offered symbolic sacrifice, the victims were always subhuman creatures. Israel repudiated human sacrifice totally. That is what the tale of the binding of Isaac in Genesis is about. The question remains, was Jesus' voluntary self-sacrifice an act of suicide thinly veiled?

When Christian liturgies describe Jesus' death as "a death freely accepted" they mean precisely that. Jesus surely could have avoided it, on the evidence of the three persons the gospels say he resuscitated from death. Nor did Jesus obediently fulfill a decree of the Father that he should proceed to an ignominious death. That decree is the fiction of a theological speculation and a bad one at that. God is hardly to be thought of as passing a sentence of condemnation to death on the innocent, for whatever good might come of it. The God of Christian belief, like the belief of Jews before them and ever since, does not operate humans robotically to achieve the divine purpose. The interaction between human freedom and providential design is a mystery that eludes us. It is enough to say that Jesus' enemies in life thought they had reason to silence him with finality and so brought about his condemnation and execution. He for his part acted freely, it would seem, to let the process go forward. The only intervention by God into human nature and history was to upraise him from the dead. The only reason to believe that it happened as reported is to accept the testimony of witnesses to him who had experienced him as thoroughly lifeless, dead, as restored to life. And if he were believed to have ascended to the Father as the culmination of the redemptive mystery, would it not make sense to interpret his death and resurrection as modeled on the high priest's role of "offering gifts and sacrifices for sins" by offering the gift of his life? Since he made that offering once for all and not repeatedly as the high priests did, his priestly intercession in the heavenly court had to be conceived as the one timeless act. Its effect was achieved on the earth over time, however, through the sacramental sacrifice in bread and wine that was his body and blood eaten and drunk.

There is another New Testament writing that, like Hebrews, is a treatise, not a letter (although some earnest scribe at a later date appended four verses to Hebrews to make it seem like a letter from Paul). That other writing takes its name from its first word "Revelation," in Greek, *Apokálypsis*, "unveiling." What is disclosed is what the author says must come to light very soon, the punishments that a just God will have to visit on an empire whose emperor and magistrates are frenetic over the refusal of some in the province of Asia to participate in the worship of the gods of Rome, including the emperor as a god. Jerusalem's Temple may well not be standing as the treatise is written, but the demand by local functionaries is firmly in place to put a pinch of incense on a burning coal before an image of a deity or, as it may be, the Emperor Domitian. The writer finds himself "on the island of Patmos, because I proclaimed God's word and gave testimony to Jesus." He seems to know of numerous "slaughtered saints" although he names only one, the martyred Antipas of Pergamum (see Rev 1:9; 2:13; 6:9). Listed in the book are a variety of bizarre tortures and punishments that the empire, bloated with riches, can expect to receive at the hand of a just God. These are often taken to be the subject of the revelation (hence the title "Revelations" accorded it by people who have not read the book). But what is primarily revealed is not the way the persecutors will themselves be persecuted but a person, the Lamb, who was slain and who lives again (Rev 5:6, 12; 7:14, 17; 13:8; 14:1, 4, 10; 19:7; 21:9). The author calls his book a prophecy. Jesus in glory who will achieve justice for his beleaguered friends is the fulfillment of that prophecy.

At times Revelation calls Jesus the Christ or Anointed but not often, only at the beginning and end of the book (Rev 1:1, 2, 5; 20:4, 6). Jesus the Lamb is the most usual designation. He has a bride or spouse (Rev 19:7-8; 21:2, 9; 22:17). This wife of his proves to be the Church who, in another figure, is the holy city Jerusalem come down out of heaven from God (Rev 21:2, 4, 10).

The husband is first described as "a figure like a man who is standing among seven lampstands of gold in a robe that came to his feet with a golden sash encircling his breast. His hair was like snow-white wool, his eyes flamed like fire, and his feet were like burnished bronze refined in a furnace" (Rev 1:13-15). He holds seven stars in his right hand; a sharp, two-edged sword emerges from his mouth. Clearly we are in the realm of vision and figure. It is no surprise that his voice "was like the sound of a mighty torrent" or that "his face shone like the sun at full strength." He speaks: "Do not be afraid. I am the first and the last, and am the living One; I was dead and now I am alive forevermore, and I hold the keys of death and Hades." By this time the visionary reports that he has fallen at the feet of this glorified human figure as if dead, but he is told to get up and write down what he has seen, "both the now and what is to take place hereafter." When the one like a son of man, a human one, proceeds to inspire seven letters to churches on the Asia Minor mainland they are instructive and corrective more than terrifying. The writer may have been ignominiously deposited in the penal colony on Patmos, but he has lost none of the authority he knows he possesses. Six of the letters are largely censorious in tone. Only one praises a church for its fidelity. All are in the stern tone of one who speaks for another. That other is the Christ of so many apsidal mosaics, with his coal-black eyes, hair like tar, and a nose like an eagle's beak. Faithfulness to the Gospel once delivered is the subject of all seven letters.

There is an eagle screeching in the sky and a destructive thurible of burning incense poured out on the earth and seals of wax broken and unbroken, but images of a plague and ruin are not the prophet's main concern. He is concentrated on ultimate victory not on defeat, whether in the short term or the long. He knows of resisters to the imperial decree and these he portrays, all dressed in white bearing branches of palm on their shoulders, the ancient sign of victory. The predators, the men of death, appear to be the winners, but the author of the drama knows them to be the ultimate losers. Like any persuasive writer of argument the Seer depicts the opposition in its strengths, not her weaknesses. The obscene amount of wealth amassed by the commercial whore in her sea trade could not be better conveyed in words. It is cast in the form of a prayer:

> Pay her back as she has paid others.
>> Pay her back double for her deeds . . .
> for she said to herself,
>> "I sit enthroned as a queen;
>> I am no widow,
>> and I will never know grief" . . . [Yet],
> Nations, populations, races, and languages . . .
> will strip her naked and leave her destitute . . .
> Plagues shall strike her in a single day,
> pestilence, bereavement, and famine, and she
> shall perish in flames; for mighty is the LORD God
> who has pronounced her doom. (Rev 18:6-8)

How or when all this will come to pass the Apocalyptist does not know, only that the smoke of the pyre of the great city will one day rise to the skies. The LORD will accomplish it. Of that much the writer is sure. Israel's God will achieve it through an agent, concerning whom the empire, collapsing into ruin, cannot have a clue. Creatures called angels of whom pagan Rome knows nothing speak in a voice of authority: "Fallen, fallen is Babylon the great . . . the kings of the earth have committed fornication with her, and merchants the world over have grown rich on her wealth and luxury. . . . Alas, for you, great city, mighty city of Babylon! In a moment your doom has come upon you" (Rev 18:2-3, 10).

What sounded like a vast throng in heaven is heard shouting: "Halleluiah! Victory and glory and power belong to our God. . . . He has condemned the great whore who corrupted the earth with her fornication; he has taken vengeance on her for the blood of his servants" (Rev 19:1-2). And again, a vast throng cries out in what sounds like a mighty torrent or great peals of thunder: "Halleluiah! The LORD our God, sovereign over all, has entered on his reign. Let us rejoice and shout for joy and pay homage to him, for the wedding day of the Lamb has come! His bride has made herself ready, and she has been given fine linen, shining and clean, to wear" (Rev 19:6-7; note the resemblance in figure to Eph 5:25-27).

This is not a call to the Asian church for readiness for further martyrdom but a rallying cry of victory over the enemies of the bride by the power of the One who sits on the throne. Where is the Lamb in the impending wedding banquet, to which an invitation has been sent out "in the very words of God," transmitted by an angel? That messenger says he is not to be worshiped, in what has to be a warning against incipient angelology in the infant Church (Rev 19:10). He, like his fellow servants, is but bearing witness to Jesus in the worship of God, who alone is to be worshiped.

Up to this point in Revelation (*Apokálypsis*) the Lamb has been depicted with the marks of sacrifice on him, standing between the throne in heaven—on which sits One whose appearance is like jasper and cornelian and behind which is a halo of emerald—and the twenty-four elders in the court (Rev 4:2-4). This Jesus has been called "the Lion from the tribe of Judah, the shoot growing from David's stock" (Rev 5:5). Clearly he is a human being, a Jew, but so intimately united to the One on the throne that they receive blessing and honor, glory and might together and act as one against the enemies of God and God's servants. There has been previous brief mention of an unnamed rider on a white horse among three other varicolored horses, their riders all bent on death and destruction (Rev 6:1-6). Not so this one who reappears, late in the book. Heaven is opened to reveal the white horse "whose rider's name is Faithful and True, for he is just in judgment and just in war . . . Written on him was a name known but to himself; he was robed in a garment dyed in blood, and he was called the Word of God." An English poet of the turn of the twentieth century rendered the scene faithfully, calling the crucified Jesus now in glory *The Veteran of Heaven*:

> 'Twas on a day of rout they girded me about,
>> They wounded all My brow, and they smote Me through the side:
>> My hand held no sword when I met their armèd horde,
>>> And the conqueror fell down, and the Conquered bruised his pride.'
>
> What is this unheard before, that the Unarmed makes war,
>> And the Slain hath the gain, and the Victor hath the rout?
> What wars, then, are these, and what the enemies,
>> Strange Chief, with the scars of Thy conquest trenched about? . . .
>
> What is *Thy* Name? Oh, show!—'My Name ye may not know;
>> 'Tis a going forth with banners and a baring of much swords;
> But My titles that are high, are they not upon My thigh?
>> "King of Kings!" are the words; "Lord of Lords";
>> It is written "King of Kings, Lord of Lords."   (Rev 19:16)
>>>>>>> Francis Thompson

Revelation has the armies of heaven following the rider "whose eyes flamed like fire, and on whose head were many diadems," all of them "riding on white horses and clothed in fine linen, white and clean" (Rev 19:14). The writer then deserts metaphor, but not entirely, as he dips into the history of his times, well known to the first hearers of his poetry in prose if not to us. The beast of his early narrative and a false prophet— obviously a baptized person who worked closely with imperial author- ity—are taken prisoner and, here we are back again in imagery, are thrown alive into a lake of sulfurous fire (Rev 19:20).

The book has achieved its purpose. God the just judge ultimately punishes the wicked, when and in what ways known to God alone. The LORD of Israel, the only God, has a human ally in the work of ultimate justice. It is Jesus, Yeshúa, "the LORD saves," a man so close to eternal God that God can be spoken of in his work of rescue or salvation as working in tandem with him.

Do the New Testament portions composed before the four gospels, which was the case of Paul's authentic epistles, or after them, as in the other books commented on above, refer to or describe Jesus' place in the proclaimed Gospel differently than in the places just explored? Hebrews certainly does in its introductory portion before getting to its main busi- ness, which is to establish that the glorified Jesus is now interceding with his Father for those who call him "brother," in his office of high priest in the heavenly sanctuary. He is qualified for this office because he is God's Son whom "God has appointed heir of all things and through whom God created the universe" (Heb 1:2). This is a thumbnail christol- ogy if not yet a soteriology. "He is the radiance of God's glory, the stamp of God's very being, and he sustains the universe by his word of power" (Heb 1:3). The only one who can be described in these terms is someone who possesses deity in its fullness. As a man, though, with human limi- tations, he can make progress. He has done so by bringing about "puri- fication from sins." In that short phrase Hebrews sums up the work of the sinless on behalf of sinners: his obedient death, his vindication as totally innocent by being raised up from the dead and enabled, by that act of God, to clear the slate of human sin of all the ages.

The paean of praise to this Son takes the form of proclaiming his superiority to the whole company of angels—an embodied creature high above pure spirits—who will survive even the dissolution of the cosmos. To no angel was the phrase in the psalm ever spoken: "Sit at my right hand until I make your enemies your footstool" (Heb 1:13). The only role of angels remotely comparable to his is in the service of humans destined for salvation. God will not subject the world to come to them but to Jesus. The argument of the anonymous author goes this way: The psalmist says in praise of man that all things are subject to human dominion, but look around you, obviously it is not true. Some persons, some things escape it. There is one situation, however, open to the eye of faith in which all things can be seen as "subject to him." "We do see Jesus, who for a short while was made subject to the angels, 'crowned now with glory and honor' because he suffered death, so that by God's gracious will, he should experience death for everyone" (Heb 2:9).

How early was this theory of human salvation through the death and glorification of Jesus arrived at? We have no way of knowing. A number of recent books have espoused the theory that it must have taken some decades for a Mediterranean peasant, a Jew at the margins of society, to have gone from his status of itinerant teacher in a far-off corner of the empire to a figure now in the heavens worthy of divine honors. In brief, how Jesus became Christ is confidently explained. These theories are theological fiction of the crassest sort. For Jews to have venerated, even adored a human being, not in his humanness but in what was divine in him—and a company of Jews were the first to have this conviction—would not have taken years of reflection on the holiness of Jesus' life. What it would have required and did in fact receive was the personal encounter of some hundreds of these Jews with a man they respected and loved in life, whom they had seen bludgeoned and beaten to death, deposited in a tomb like any corpse, and experienced again alive in a matter of days. That would have been enough to send the learned among them scurrying through the Scriptures that recounted the long history of a people to discover what God meant by this marvel: one man, one Jew, anticipating the bodily resurrection of all the just on the last day, chosen by God to act somehow on behalf of a whole believing people. That this is the conclusion they came to the record shows. The conviction would not have taken them long to arrive at. Experiencing a dead man alive again changed the thinking of a company of Galilean Jews on every matter in heaven and on earth. This should not surprise us. What came of it was the religion of Israel in a new phase, called very early in the second century, *Christianismós*, to distinguish it from a contemporary development, *Ioudaïsmós*. These are the two traditions in which the religion of Israel continues to be known, through the Mishnah and Talmuds in one case and the New Testament in the other.

Chapter Three

Knowing Jesus from What He Taught

The Gospel according to Mark gives us quite a lot of information about Jesus, both what he did and what he said in his short public life and what was believed about him after his resurrection from the dead. These data come to us in edited versions of collections of Jesus' deeds and teachings that we do not possess in the original. Although some of Mark's sources may have been quasi-biographical in character, Mark did not set himself to write a biography of Jesus in his public career, despite what seems to be one. He composed, rather, a lengthy homily that has as its rhetorical purpose confirming hearers in a faith they already possess. They are to pattern their lives, in the measure that this is possible, on the way Jesus lived his life. He was a man empowered by God throughout his days as they are now empowered, although differently from him. He challenged the power of evil as they must, even showing contempt for it. Despite his life of justice and innocence before God, there was no protection for him against suffering and death from evil forces. Similarly, a life of moral uprightness such as he taught was no guarantee of a life of invulnerability. Mark makes clear that suffering and death lay ahead for Jesus as for the whole human race. But in reminding his hearers that God crowned this life of endurance of cruel torment and death with new life in another sphere, Mark makes the point above all that living a life of discipleship must entail accepting mental and physical pain as Jesus did. Mark does not get into belief in the resurrection of the body with Christ on the last day, which, like all in the apostolic age, he believed. He satisfies himself with the graphic reminder that the endurance of whatever suffering a disciple has in store—and its acceptance in a spirit of perfect trust in God—is the condition of a life with him "who is not here; who has been raised up" (Mark 16:6).

From Matthew and Luke there is much more to be known about Jesus by what he taught than from Mark. Each of the two gospel writers gives ample evidence of possessing a copy of Mark. Matthew employs almost the entire content of Mark and its sequence of events as well, at times repeating portions verbatim. He tightens Mark's prose, however, and will situate passages in different settings. Both he and Luke have access to some dozens of Jesus' sayings that they will employ in nearly identical wording. They also have a few incidents, like the scenario of his temptation by the devil, before he launches on a career of public teaching (see Luke 4:1-13; Matt 4:1-11). If the content of any of the duplicated passages labeled Q[1] by modern scholarship is the same as or close to Mark's, their wording of it will never be like his. Besides this reliance on Mark as their chief source, both have sources independent of him and of each other.

All three of these gospel writers were distinct literary geniuses, not apart from but in concert with the coauthorship of their writing with the Holy Spirit. The Church has believed from an early date in the inspired character of these writings by viewing them as on a par with the Jewish Scriptures on which they were based. Although all three wrote in Greek as their native tongue (and John the same), they betray their Semitic origins by employing at times figures of speech proper to Jewish culture rather than that of the Graeco-Roman world. These turns of phrase and rich metaphor, while proper to the biblical writing that preceded them, are not to be found in the pagan writings of Europe or North Africa. A consequence is that the generations of gentile believers that came after them often took the figurative in the gospels for the literal, thereby misunderstanding them. The story of the cursing of the fig tree in Mark is such an example, the destruction of the Gerasene swine by Jesus another (see Mark 11:12-14, 20-25 and Matt 21:18-22; Mark 5:1, 11-20 and Matt 8:28-34). Matthew will correct the latter to Gadarene, knowing that Gadara is much closer to the Sea of Galilee than the far distant Gerasa. That tale pays its respects to the occupying Roman army by having the man's infesting demons say, "My name is Legion, for we are many," at the same time showing contempt for the pagan pig farmer who would presume to multiply nonkosher food rather than good Jewish lamb.

---

[1] Q is the designation devised by nineteenth-century scholars for the approximately 235 verses common to Matthew and Luke in Jesus' identical or near-identical wording. They are some fifty-three of his sayings and two dozen more in which the phrasing is similar but not exactly the same.

Jesus' Many Teachings in Matthew

Matthew provides five collections of Jesus' teachings, each of them preceded by a narrative section and a sixth that is not. All were undoubtedly delivered on a variety of occasions. The gathering into a single discourse is Matthew's doing. They are:

chapters 5–7, remembered as the Sermon on the Mount because the introduction has Jesus going up onto a mountainside;

chapter 10, with Jesus' instructions sending his disciples on mission;

chapter 13, with six parables, to which allegorical interpretations have been added to two by an early editor or Matthew himself;

chapter 18, which contains instructions on how disciples should relate to each other and is illustrated by two parables;

chapters 24 and 25, a slightly edited version of Mark 13, which tells of how things will be when the Son of Man comes in glory;

finally, we find in chapter 23 a harsh denunciation of the scribes and Pharisees preceded by no narrative setting other than questions of interpretation of the Law put to him by Pharisees and Sadducees.

Matthew's gospel overall can be described as a handbook of polemic, or How to Counter Pharisee Demands of Torah Observance with Jesus' Demands. The accusations of Pharisee behavior come from Matthew's day. How close they are to the heated exchanges of Jesus with other teachers can be arrived at only in a general way by eliminating phrases that seem to describe life in Matthew's church rather than in Jesus' lifetime. While negative teaching against opponents in debate is characteristic of this gospel, there is a far greater amount of Jesus' positive teaching. This means that Matthew is a rich resource for what Jesus was like: how he thought deduced from what he taught. Matthew never has Jesus claim that the interpretations of difficult passages in Torah are his own. He says more than once that the opinions he puts forward are not his but, rather, what the Father means by what is said in the Scriptures.

Jesus was remembered as a very wise man from his early youth. One can be immature at fifty, a perfect fool, and a reflective, judicious person at twelve. It was recalled when he first came on the public scene that he had not trained under a rabbi (see John 7:15). That was the only way in the culture of the time that one could gain wisdom from Torah. But not quite. The other way was to be attentive to every bit of Scripture read out in Hebrew and expounded in Aramaic by Nazareth's most learned teacher, whoever that was, and pondered deeply from boyhood until you were thirty. Jesus must have gone that route. Medieval theologians would speculate that if you were a divine-human individual, as Catholic faith from the beginning was convinced Jesus was, surely deity would so illumine humanity that he would have had limitless knowledge and insight. That is not very good thinking about the incarnation. If Christians believe Jesus to be fully human they cannot eliminate human limitation as thoroughly inoperative in his case. It would take the edge off all his mental and emotional joys, sufferings, and ordinary human responses to life. It is thoroughly human to take delight in family celebrations and in the achievements of younger members, just as it is grim to be betrayed by friends into a situation of excruciating pain. In this false hypothesis, Jesus might have thought: "I am surely going to die on this cross. But in the Father's plan, which I can clearly foresee, I should be delivered from all this in a few days." That is theological nonsense.

On the other hand, endowment with a keen intelligence coupled with a young manhood of constant prayer must have helped Jesus conclude as a young workman that he had a great work to do under God. If, later, the learned rabbi Akiba could become convinced that Bar Kosiba, who took the name Bar Kokhba, "Son of the Star," was the messiah of Israel fated to throw off the Roman yoke, why could Jesus not have had a similar conviction about his calling under God? Such would have been his vocation to the work of proclaiming the future reign of God over Israel on far better terms than the military and political. Whatever Jesus' thoughts might have been, we know what he did about them. Having served briefly as a devotee of the fiery preacher John the Baptizer, he is known to have set out on his own public teaching career that incorporated repentance for sin and a realistic hope of liberation at God's hands, liberation not of the political kind. Jesus never presumed to set a date for this, as visionaries before and after him had done. He set himself to preach the conditions of readiness for that liberating rule of God. That could only mean utter fidelity to Torah by a whole people to whom God had given guidance through Moses and the prophets who came after him.

The Beatitudes and the Woes

The Sermon on the Mount is Matthew's account of Jesus' early start on the project. His gospel assembles the teaching of Jesus from several

sources, beginning with a set of eight conditions of happiness or blessedness (Matt 5:3-9). In form they are like the opening phrase of the book
of Psalms, which tells the way of the just but immediately contrasts it
with the way of the wicked. Luke does this in his version of those who
are happy by adding four woes or miseries (see Luke 6:24-26). Matthew
does not. Omitting the wretchedness that follows from evil behavior,
Matthew's eight states of blessedness imitate the Psalter's beginnings.
Luke, having given four of Matthew's expectations of living joyously in
the final days, immediately adds four states or conditions that will result
from sinful living. All eight of Matthew's beatitudes are promises of how
it shall be under the future reign of God. The clear implication is that the
mourners of the present time should take comfort from the fact that at
the end of days they will rejoin those they have lost in death. The peasantry will in the future possess the land they worked so hard for others.
Those who hunger and thirst for justice will in the final days receive
justice in full measure. The ones who practice merciful deeds will know
the mercy that was not held out to them by their debtors. The non-
duplicitous, the persons who struggle to make the peace, and the persecuted will all experience a reversal of their situations.

Jesus was a Jew of his time. This means that he looked forward to
salvation, a word for deliverance from God's just punishments for all
except the non-repentant, on the Last Day. Unlike many teachers of his
time Jesus did not predict liberation from the yoke of political oppression. All the failed messiahs of whose careers he would have heard are
scarcely remembered as they lie on the scrapheap of Jewish history. Jesus
wisely situated the ultimate outcome of his people's present condition
in the distant future, God's future. In doing this he has been remembered
as the proclaimer of God comforting the meek and consoling the sor-
rowing, the perfect executor of justice for those who in life experience
little justice. "Clean" or "pure" of heart does not connote chaste living
but describes persons of integrity whose actions correspond not only to
their words but also to their intentions. Jesus was interested in future
happiness for all those suffering now who could be sure of a present
measure of happiness by a clear conscience and would be rewarded on
the Last Day. Under eight headings he knew that his Father in heaven
would keep every promise ever made to Israel. Some disciple or perhaps
Matthew himself added a ninth beatitude. The insulted and the persecuted for adherence to the name of Jesus could expect a present reward
for their perseverance in loyalty to him and by all means a fitting future
reward.

Jesus, like any teacher, featured the benefits of fidelity to his teaching. There was quite enough opprobrium to go around for those who heeded his teaching, but discipleship was not a matter of public repudiation in the form of persecution only. Certain satisfactions were in store for those who knew that the mode of fidelity to the Law he taught was the right one—enough to constitute his followers salt on the earth and light in the world, a city gleaming white on the top of a hill as the rooftops of Sefad in Galilee did in his day. Matthew's theme throughout, like that of Luke especially, was that the teaching of Jesus, if followed faithfully, could reverse all human fortunes, turn the topsy into turvy, literally stand the world on its head.

Many of the psalms, and Mary's *Magnificat* and Zechariah's *Benedictus* composed in their spirit, predicted an immediate, impending future in which God would fill the hungry with good things and the rich would be sent empty away (Luke 1:46-55; 68-79). The LORD would bring redemption to his people and a knowledge of salvation through forgiveness of their sins—but not in the form they expected. When Jesus began to teach publicly, his message was one of preparation now for living as subjected willingly to God's kingship over them later. The way to ensure it was fidelity to the precepts of Torah in a spirit other than that of certain Pharisee and scribal teachers. Their mode was a literal and minimal observance of all the written commandments and prohibitions found in the Mosaic books and those deduced from them by teachers of the "Oral Law." Jesus' mode of observance was figurative and maximal. He taught, in a word, "Do more."

Matthew proposes six specific ways in which Jesus taught that injunctions in the Mosaic books were to be obeyed, with Jesus quoting each injunction as "ancestral," that is, traditional, teaching. Jesus cited the Sinai precepts on murder, adultery, divorce, and swearing on one's oath, then, in addition, the law on retaliation or paying back in kind and of hatred of God's enemies. Following the enunciation of each from the ancient biblical code as found in Exodus and Deuteronomy, Matthew has Jesus say, "But I say to you" (Matt 5:21-48). That is the literal Greek phrase, but while adversative in form it is not adversative in meaning. A better rendering would be: "This, I propose, is what the commandment implies."

The six pairings have been called antitheses but they are not that; rather, they are theses in the spirit of the divine Lawgiver, Israel's LORD. Regarding the prohibition of taking a life, it includes uncontrolled anger and the hate speech that can end in killing. All such sins are just as subject to God's judgment as killing itself. The evangelist Matthew adds as a coda to that interpretation three remembered sayings of Jesus: settle arguments with others before you engage in any act of religion, do it quickly on the way to a rabbinical court, and if the judge's decree is prison find a way to pay to ensure release. Jesus was totally realistic in his teaching, never theoretical as if operating on another plane. He made people face their actual ethical dilemmas and proposed the solutions that Torah held out.

"Do not adulterate the marriage bed, either yours or another's." The precept is brief in its biblical phrasing: *Lo tinoph*. Jesus taught that the intention stood for the deed, the lustful gaze that said inwardly: "I would bed that man's wife if I could." The very desire is sin as Judaism teaches in its stress on *kavvanah*, intent. Again, Matthew adds apothegms to this prohibition from Jesus' remembered teaching: "Gouge out your eye. Cut off your hand. Better to go maimed in your lifetime than be thrown whole into the fires of Hinnom," Jerusalem's ever-burning garbage dump. The figure of speech is Semitic hyperbole, of course, but one of which Jesus' hearers could not miss the meaning. A third Scripture citation on marriage in Deuteronomy, written much later than the first four Mosaic books, allowed an exception that Jesus did not allow (24:1-4). A technique of interpretation in rabbinic argument in his day, and indeed ever since, is to find a compromise position to resolve a contradiction between two passages. The hypothetical case in the deuteronomic writing was of a husband's discovery of "something unclean" in his wife, a blanket term the meaning of which Jesus' recent contemporaries had been debating hotly. Shammai, a hardliner, took the adjective "unclean" to mean her unfaithful conduct, that and nothing else, while Hillel, normally more understanding, was in this case more understanding of the man's desires than the woman's rights. He took the term to mean her unsuitability on any ground, even to the consistent overcooking of her husband's food. Jesus would have none of this. With other teachers of his day he took the two precepts, "The two shall become one flesh" in Genesis and the man's permission to send his wife packing for unspecified cause in Deuteronomy, to be irreconcilable. Such divorce by male fiat would mean, Jesus taught, that the next union of either would be adulterous of its nature. He did not elaborate on his view in this instance but in another place he called it simply male arrogance that created the exception, the *machismo* of later Spanish speech.

To complete the six commandments and their "fulfillment," in Jesus' term, there is first the nonnecessity of swearing to the truth of a trivial matter on one's oath. An Aye or a Nay should suffice. In the English phrase, one's word should be one's bond. There evidently were a number of bogus oaths abroad in Jesus' day. Matthew names four of them. Modern Italians say, *Per Bacco!*, the British, *By Jove*, but neither the god of wine nor Jupiter is being called on seriously to attest the truth of a statement. Swearing by the heavens or by the earth, by Jerusalem or by one's own head, must have been real in Jesus' day, harmless in wording but with intent to deceive or withhold the truth. In Jesus' graphic phrase, "They are from the evil one." "An eye for an eye and a tooth for a tooth" is a truncated version of a longer series that begins, "If injury ensues you must set the penalty at life for life," and rolls on sonorously, "hand for hand, foot for foot, burn for burn, wound for wound, stripe for stripe" (Exod 21:23-25). Again, figurative language is at work, limiting compensation for an injury to the extent of the injury, certainly not proposing killing, maiming, or wounding as the correct response to any such offense.

The previous verse gives the clue to what this language of violence is getting at when it mentions payment in the presence of a judge. The phrase that has been quoted for centuries as if it meant a positive sanction on vengeful behavior in fact meant a just limit on claims of indemnity, no more than the loss or damage incurred. "Grave bodily harm," in return, in the phrase of modern law, was figurative Semitic speech. So it was understood in Jesus' day, when a payment in money was the usual means of settlement.

This was the hypothetical case that immediately preceded in Exodus at 21:22, of a woman who has miscarried when caught in a melee among men. Jesus knew the tit-for-tat mentality that went back to early desert days and says it must be replaced. He proposes responding to a blow on the cheek by asking the assailant for another, a bizarre suggestion if taken literally. Again, we are faced with Semitic metaphor. Do not become anyone's punching bag, is the intention of the phrase, but do retaliate evil with good. Achieve a mastery of peaceful resistance in action. Sued for your inner garment, offer the outer one as well. Walk a second mile when asked for accompaniment on a thief-infested road of one mile. If asked by a beggar for a handout, shell out, do not falter. When you lend be prepared for the borrower to default (Matt 5:38-42).

Jesus in all these examples interprets the basic deuteronomic command, "You must love your neighbor as yourself." The popular understanding of God's hatred of Israel's enemies, so pervasive in the psalms, was that hating your enemies was permitted, even encouraged. However erroneous the supposition, Jesus countered it with a demand to love your enemies and pray for your persecutors. Here we have no metaphor, no figurative speech but a stern injunction of Jesus to those who wished to be his followers: "If you love only those who love you, what reward can you expect? Even the tax-gatherers [known for their dishonest ways] do as much." "Pagans greet fellow pagans on the street" (Matt 5:46-48). All this is natural, normal. Jesus proposes a totally abnormal way of life. He calls love of enemy perfection: humanity made perfect by doing the opposite of what comes naturally.

The Our Father

It would have been helpful for the ages if Matthew had provided the many other virtues and vices encompassed by the major commandments besides the six from Jesus' teaching that he chose. The evangelist went about conveying that teaching in another way. He warned against giving alms to the poor just for show, against praying ostentatiously to be admired, against multiplying words of incantation like the pagans who hoped their deities could make sense of their babble. But Jesus was not basically Mr. No. He was Mr. Yes, and as such he taught: "This is how you are to pray." His prayer to God as universal Father followed. The Matthew version found in 6:9-13 (cf. Luke 11:2-4) caught on in Christian liturgies and private recitation rather than the shorter version in Luke. Just as was the case with the beatitudes, each petition after the opening words of address is oriented toward the end time. The LORD, the God of Israel, is spoken to as "Our Father," as had long been customary in Israel. The people were calling on God as "my Father," at least back to Jeremiah's time and more recently in Malachi, the anonymous self-designated "my messenger" (Jer 3:4, 19; 31:9; Mal 1:6; 2:10). Luke omits the "Our" and begins abruptly, "Father." Matthew locates the unseen God in the heavens, as did all Hebrew cosmology. He has Jesus demand that the Name of God that stands for God's person be held sacred, as it is to this day. *Baruch ha Shem* ("Blessed the NAME") can punctuate any modern Jewish conversation after "God" or "Adonai" has been spoken. Jesus' prayer then expresses the hope that God's reign may come—swiftly rather than soon—and that in the meantime his will be accomplished by people here as it is by the angelic hosts in the heavens. The word in Matthew's Greek and in Luke's for "daily" bread, which seems to ask for sustenance on each successive day in life, may not be that. It is hard to know because the word (Englished literally as "over other substance" by the fourteenth-century priest of the Diocese of Lincoln John Wycliffe and as "supersubstantial" in the Reims version of two centuries later) does not occur in any other writing in Greek. If the evangelists or their source coined it they may have wished to record Jesus' Aramaic word cognate with the

Hebrew of Proverbs 30:8 and properly rendered "daily bread." The other possibility is "bread for the morrow," meaning in the age to come. That would have been patterned on Moses' censure of those who kept some manna over for the next day instead of trusting that more would be available on the morrow (Exod 16:19-20). In any case, once end-time thought grew dim in Christian memory the phrase came to be taken as a plea for sustenance on each and every day rather than for life at the end of the age.

As to the prayer for forgiveness on condition that we forgive, Matthew has the Greek words for debts and debtors at 6:12, while Luke in the parallel place (11:4) speaks of "our sins" and says "we also forgive every one that is indebted to us." Where, then, do the words translated by the noun and verb "trespass" in Catholic and other versions of the prayer, which is basically Matthean, come from? The answer is, from the King James rendering (1611) of Matthew 6:15, which has the words as Jesus continues to speak. The Reims Version (1582) has "forgive you your offences" in that place while it, like KJV, has "dettes" and "deters" three verses earlier.

Now to the prayer as recited differently by Catholics and many Protestants. Up to about 1500 or so, *Pater*, *Ave*, and *Creed* were normally memorized and recited in Latin, even by the illiterate. Among the earliest manuscripts of a book called *The Prymer* of prayers in the vernacular from about 1400, this one is perhaps the best:

> Fader oure that art in hevene halwed be thi name, thi Kyngdom come to, thi wille be doon in erthe as in heven, oure eche daies bred gif us to day, and forgive us our dettes, as we forgive to our detoures and lede us nought into temptacion bote delivere us from yvel. Amen.[2]

A printed book of a century later gives, "and forgyve us our synnes as we forgyve other," while shortly after that under date of 1506, we read: "and forgyve us our dets as we forgyve our dettis [dettoris?]."[3] To complete the early sixteenth-century confusion, another much printed

---

[2] MS. G. 24 in H. Littlehales, *The Prymer* (London: St. John's College, 1891), 20 as cited in Herbert Thurston, S.J., *Familiar Prayers: Their Origin and History* (Westminster, Maryland: The Newman Press, 1953), 24. *The Kalender of Shepherdes* (London: R. Pynson), 1506. Ibid., page 25.

[3] *The Myrrour of the Chyrche* (London: Wynkyn de Worde, 1521). In the translation that was executed for the Bridgettine nuns of Sion, near London, of the *Mirroure of Oure Ladye*. Ibid.

book provides: "and forgive us our trespasses as we forgive our trespassors." William Caxton (d. 1491) was a printer, editor, and enthusiast for standardizing the English language who expressed unhappiness at praying the Psalter and other prayers in the vernacular. He allowed the practice to some if it stirred them to more devotion and to the love of God, "But utterly to use them in English and leve the Latin I hold it not commendable."[4]

In *The Manuell of Prayers or the Prymer in Englysh* prepared by a certain Bishop Hilsey at Thomas Cromwell's instance in 1539, the following version, declared official in a preface, occurs. Note that St. Matthew's debts and debtors have yielded to Luke's trespass as noun and verb.

> Our Father whiche arte in heven, hallowed be thy name. Thy kingdom come. Thy will be done in earth as it is in heven. Gyve us this day our dayly bread and forgyve us our trespasses as we forgyve them that trespass against us. And let us not be led into temptacyon. But delyver us from evyll. Amen.

Thus did Catholics receive their familiar wording, paradoxically by the "Commandment" of King Henry VIII who broke communion with that Church. The "whiche" yielded to "who" and "in" to "on" among Catholics in the late seventeenth century but was retained by Anglicans. Protestant usage meanwhile retained the "debts" and "debtors" of Matthew in the Authorized or King James Version. The doxology at the conclusion of the "Our Father" in Matthew, "For thine is the kingdom and the power and the glory, for ever. Amen" (6:13b; 1 Chr 29:11), occurs in the King James Version because those learned translators worked from later Greek manuscripts than the earliest ones of the fourth century not yet available to them. The concluding doxology was eliminated from Protestant Bibles around 1885 on a critical-text principle but is retained in all public recitation of the prayer among Protestants and in the eucharistic liturgy of Greek Orthodoxy. This venerable prayer was made a prayer of the people as an embolism or insertion after the phrase "but deliver us from evil" in the restored Roman Rite after Vatican II.

The Devil in the Desert

If the beatitudes and Jesus' Prayer to the Father are the best remembered of his prayers, his threefold response to the devil as tempter in the

---

[4] *Chastysing of Goddes Children*, cited by Thurston, *Familiar Prayers*, 26.

scenario envisioned in Matthew 4:1-11 and Luke 4:1-13 is surely next in order of memorability. The proverb, "The devil can quote Scripture to his own ends," comes from here, as does the improbable leading of Jesus about by Satan, first upon his return from forty days of fasting in the desert and then to the pinnacle of the Temple and onto a high mountain. The latter two scenes are in reverse order in the two gospels. Whatever the words of Jesus were in dismissive contempt of diabolic power, this drama of challenge and response is what came of them. The devil is made out to be testing Jesus in the three areas where Israel was most sorely tested in its forty years of desert wandering: hunger, security, and power, or rather the total lack of the latter two. Jesus is portrayed as he must have been after his preparation in solitude for his mission: craving food, vulnerable to the wild beasts, and utterly powerless. Israel's hoped-for deliverer would be in no such condition. Would Jesus have bread to eat of the desert's stones, trust himself to angels to raise up his battered body, accept dominion from the ruler of this world (see John 12:31; 14:30; 16:11)? Jesus answers out of the same Scriptures from which the devil makes his fraudulent case: "Not by bread alone does man live, but by every word that comes from the mouth of the LORD your God" (Deut 8:3); "You shall not put the LORD your God to the test" (6:16); "The LORD your God, shall you fear and him only shall you serve" (6:13). Thus was the devil worsted in a contest of biblical texts.

It was not to the prince of fallen angels Jesus gave the curt command, "Be gone!" but to another tempter, Simon Peter, who in this case was no Rock. He acted as an evil counselor, rebuking Jesus for predicting his need to suffer. "Out of my sight, Satan! You think as men think, not as God thinks" (Mark 8:33). This command, like that to the devil in the desert, is not a prayer to God but an exorcism, a driving out of diabolic power. Jesus was well remembered in his public teaching for having declared more than once that his people's fear of the devils of hell was ill-placed. A thoroughgoing trust in the power of God could and must bring an end to it. Whatever the source of apprehension of baleful forces, real or imagined, Jesus taught that people had to be rid of the incubus. An invocation of the All Holy could alone accomplish it.

Recorded Prayers from Jesus' Lips

Three other prayers of Jesus come to mind. One would have been voiceless if the evangelist Luke had not given it tongue. Jesus, kneeling, prayed: "Father, if it is your will take this cup away from me; still, not my will but yours be done" (22:42). Another prayer, not nearly so well remembered, perhaps because delivered in complete confidence and not in anguish, is found in nearly identical wording in Matthew and Luke (11:25-27; 10:21-22, respectively). It deserves to be set apart from words about his life of prayer. Luke has Jesus rejoicing in the Holy Spirit as he prays:

> I give you praise, Father, LORD of heaven and earth, for although you have hidden these things from the wise and the learned you have revealed them to the childlike. Yes, Father, such has been your gracious will. All things have been handed over to me by my Father. No one knows who the Son is except the Father and who the Father is except the Son and anyone to whom the Son wishes to reveal him.

The Lengthy Prayer Spoken at the Last Supper

The extended prayer of Jesus to his Father at the Passover Meal in John's gospel—roughly chapter 14, with an extended development of its content in the next two chapters and a distinct prayer, chapter 17, in which Jesus prays for all who will come to believe in him—could not have been framed by that evangelist had he not received the earliest tradition that Jesus Christ Risen stood in a unique relation of Sonship to God and therefore must have done so all along. This is a reminder that what we know of Jesus' life and teaching we know in retrospect from faith in his having been upraised from the dead and ascended to his Father in a glorified body. The four evangelists tried to convey his brief public career in outline but they were able to do so only through the lens of his glorification and hoped-for return. This was inescapably the starting point of all the use they made of the collections of his sayings as a teacher, his short stories, his interaction with the crowds and with his closest friends. An awareness of his glorified state and expected return necessarily colored the accounts of his arguments with other teachers about how to live out Torah faithfully, his rebuffs at the hands of antagonists, and his arrest and execution.

All this is to say that the gospels were an existential literature of the writers in their place and time. Their intention was to help the members of their respective communities live their lives "in Christ," to use St. Paul's phrase from an earlier date. They were not concerned primarily with writing lives of Jesus but with showing how the hearers of their writings in a basically oral culture could pattern their lives on his. Jesus was a man whose deed of God in him they already believed in. The gospels were intended as a confirmation of that faith.

Jesus' Descent from a Long Line of Storytellers

Because Jesus' ancestry was known in a culture that was alerted to these matters, Matthew and Luke provide family names of the man Jesus of the tribe of Judah and the house of David. The ancestors went back as far as Abraham in one case and to Adam in the other. Both lists culminated in an immediate forebear of Joseph, from whom land and property, if any, would pass to Jesus. The people's Scriptures would have been the source, needless to say, although where the two quite different lists of names after the return from exile come from we have no way of knowing. Jesus' Davidic ancestry is certainly at the root of his birth in Bethlehem, David's city. Luke and Matthew possess in common eleven details about his birth to Mary, without Joseph or any man as his father. The tradition of his virginal birth must have been fixed well before either gospel was written. Luke has an account of Jesus coming to Jerusalem on one of the pilgrimage feasts from Nazareth with his parents. Matthew has told a similar tale of his parents' flight to Egypt to escape the wrath of the dying tyrant Herod. These are stories so palpably based on what was known to lie ahead for him that their historicity cannot be established. In any case, a precise history, modern style, was not the major concern of either evangelist.

If the gospels are a tissue of stories quite like the *aggadic*, or narrative, element of the Jewish Scriptures, it comes as no surprise to learn that Jesus was a master storyteller. His dozens of recorded parables—a Greek word for parallels—were not told to illustrate his teaching. They *were* his teaching. Without telling these brief made-up tales Jesus did not teach. Some of them, like his proverbs, may have had a history going back centuries, like the axioms of Ben Franklin's *Poor Richard*. For those that Jesus told he provided a new context while composing parables of his own. He was a sharp observer of life around him and fashioned his tales on the lives of his people. He never told a fable, that is, a story in which members of the animal kingdom spoke in human language. The Old Testament has only two such fabled characters, the talking snake of Genesis and the ass in Numbers who chided Balaam for having beaten her in anger three times.

There is one other fable in Scripture that features, not animals with human characteristics as in Aesop, but talking trees. It is a story told in the book of Judges to make the point that the *vox populi* can make some tragically wrong choices. Gideon had a son named Abimelech in the time of the judges when the people had reverted to the worship of false gods known generically as the Baals. Abimelech challenged his mother's extensive kinsfolk in Shechem, modern Nablus: "Which is better, that the seventy sons of Jerubbaal rule over you or one man?" Not surprisingly, the speaker is that man. The people opt for a local person who by this time has gathered the worst types of thugs around him as a private army. He has them dispatch the seventy Jerubbaalites who are his kinsmen, making the people begin to realize what kind of man they have elected to power.

One son of Jerubbaal, Jotham, escapes the slaughter. He climbs Mount Gerizim in Shechem and tells a story: "Once the trees went to anoint a king over themselves." They said first to the olive tree, then to the fig tree, then to the grape vine, "Reign over us." Each in turn refused the honor. The first was too busy producing the rich olive oil that serves to honor men and gods, the fig tree would not yield up "its sweetness and good fruit to wave over the trees," while the humble grapevine was equally disinclined to give up its wine that cheers gods and men and go to wave over the trees (Judg 9:7-20, 52-53). Saint Thomas More once said to Henry his king, "I would not be as a mathematical point, having position without magnitude." The buckthorn was ready to take on the rule even though its piercing spines, like the horns of a young buck, were well known. Jotham, a son of Jerubbaal, who alone had survived the slaughter of his seventy kinsmen, rose to remind the people of the bad bargain they had made in appointing Abimelech king: "I give you the joy of him and may he have his joy in you. But if not, let fire come forth from him to devour the people of Shechem."

And so it happened. It was a clear case of the anarchy that follows when good men do nothing. Abimelech the buckthorn ruled only three years before the people came to realize what a good king the olive tree, the fig tree, or the grapevine would have made, and they revolted. Abimelech and his men put down the rebellion bloodily, killing at least a thousand. But then an enterprising woman took half a millstone and dropped it on his head from a tower, crushing his skull. The world's buckthorns always get theirs, however long it takes. Jesus said once: "He who lives by the sword will die by the sword." In the vernacular, time wounds all heels.

Jesus' parables are normally not so bloody, but when Matthew edits a few he will have them end in the cruel reprisals that marked the tribal warfare of Israel's history (see Matt 13:41-42, 49-50; 18:34; 21:35-39). Luke is by all odds a gentle storyteller and will not have Jesus' tales end in carnage. Matthew carries on a fiercer verbal polemic against certain public figures than anything found in Luke. He castigates some for practicing piety in order to be seen, accusing them of the blast of a trumpet as they drop alms into a public chest (Matt 6:2-4). "Hypocrites" is Matthew's charge, a word that literally meant actors in a play and would have had double force since Israel had no drama (7:5; see 23:1-36). Hoarding money was the great sin for Jesus, almsgiving the great virtue. He is reported in Matthew and Luke in nearly identical wording as saying that God and money cannot be served with equal devotion: "It must be the one or the other" (Matt 6:24; 6:25–7:29). A high priority on food, drink, and clothing is something the birds and the field flowers are not anxious about, but they are the things some people make their primary concern. Even Jesus' peasant listeners, some mired in poverty? Evidently yes, for he never spoke to no purpose. "You will be judged at the Great Assize in the measure you judge," he said. "Take that wooden beam out of your eye. That might help you to find the speck in your own." "Ask and it will be given to you, knock and the door will be opened." The asker receives, the seeker finds. But watch out for a smooth stone in place of a pocket bread or a snake when you expect a fish. In sum, "Do to others what you would have them do to you." "The gate that leads to destruction is wide and the way is easy." Not so the narrow gate and the hard road that leads to life. False forth-tellers are all around you, frauds who do not have a clue regarding the future. They are wolves clothed in wool. Be on guard. Watch out!

Proverbs, maxims, words of wisdom. Jesus, tell us a story.

Do grapes grow on a thornbush, figs on a thistle-rich tree? Good fruit grows on healthy trees, bad fruit on dry branches. More wise sayings! Give us a story.

Once upon a time a man built a house on a rocky promontory overseeing the sea. The rain fell, the floods came, the winds blew. They beat upon that house. It stood standing. It was built on rock. A neighbor named Habens, Minus Habens in fact, who had a few tiles missing from his roof bought a plot of sandy land because the price was right. Same storm, same wind, same flooding rain, and down came that house in a mighty roar (Matt 7:24-27). Folly exacts a high price.

Much too simple a story. Did Jesus tell any tales with a complex plot? It does not have to be a long story. Well, there was the one recalled from David's time, calculated to deflect the Pharisee charge against Jesus and his friends of unlawful Sabbath activity. The disciples were hungry, like poor scholars everywhere. Heads of grain were in the fields for the picking (Matt 12:1-8; 1 Sam 21:2-7). Rub a few vigorously between two palms, blow the husks away, and you have a snack of barley flour, or it may be wheat. The challenge the men encounter surprises us. How could it have been unlawful activity on the Sabbath as charged? It seems a stretch to us, but the accusation was of taking in a harvest, a specification of the oral law that prohibited work on the day of rest. Jesus knew his people's Scriptures well and assumed his challengers did the same. He reminded them of the story of David who, in full flight from Saul and desperately hungry, approached a sacred shrine alone, his companions encamped at a distance, and begged some bread from the priest in attendance. Offered some loaves of the holy bread displayed ceremonially at the shrine and replaced daily, David accepts them with gratitude.

Jesus' argument directed at the Pharisees went this way: if sacred food reserved for the priests could be given to David, the man who would be king, why not to Jesus and his famished men? The argument is actually the evangelist's, based on an incident lodged in community memory. Mark, from whom Matthew takes the story, observes that the priests alone were privileged to eat the bread, Sabbath or no. Matthew knows that Jesus was a Jewish layman, not a priest. But in reporting the exchange over Sabbath observance he places on Jesus' own lips: "I tell you, something greater than the temple is here" (Matt 12:6). It is, of course, the evangelist's conviction.

The gospel writers possessed a variety of remembrances of Jesus' words and deeds. Often they repeated them as they had been preserved in group memory, that is, as the knowledge that the sayings and deeds they recounted were those of a man whom God had raised up from the dead, a man now in heavenly glory. Their narratives are inevitably edited without any attempt to suppress that knowledge but, rather, be colored by it. Thus, while Mark's enunciated axiom, "The Sabbath was made for man, not man for the Sabbath," is a clear echo of the place in the Greek Bible that says this of the sacred shrine or sanctuary, it is all of a piece with Jesus' teaching that a concern for people's needs outruns all religious observance (see 2 Macc 5:19). When Matthew comes upon it while copying out Mark faithfully, and Luke the same, he omits it in favor of quoting Mark's watchword on the sovereign rule Jesus now possesses in the eyes of the Church: "For the Son of Man is lord even of the Sabbath" (Mark 2:28). Jesus out-Davids David and any holy shrine on every count: "I tell you, something greater than the temple is here" (Matt 12:6).

Matthew's first collection of parables is derived from Mark's, with the exception of the latter's image of the seed that grows both silently and inevitably without the farmer's attending it. He adds one of his own, the tale of a man whose enemy at night over-sowed his wheat field with *zizania*, a weed that resembles wheat. The owner's slaves reported the dastardly trick when wheat and weeds grew high enough to be distinguished. They proposed plucking up the troublesome weeds. It was patently impossible to uproot the one without the other, so the landowner ordered: "Let both grow together until the harvest. Then you can separate the two, burning the one and storing the other." This has to be a tale of how it will be on the last day: an illustration of the way the LORD lets the wicked live alongside the good without interference. Only at the point of judgment will perfect justice be done to both.

Matthew and Luke adopt Mark's thoroughly puzzling explanation of why Jesus has taught in parables. To employ metaphors or images in illustration of a point is the oldest teaching technique. Expanding them to story length may include some cryptic elements not readily grasped on a hearing. But every teacher teaches to be understood, certainly not with a view to not being understood. Why, then, is this put forward as Jesus' intent and coupled with a quotation from Isaiah that any schoolboy of the time could have taken for heavy irony, as in: "All right! All right! Don't listen. You might learn something." Notice that Mark distinguishes in his opening phrase between "you who have been given the secret of the reign of God" and "those outside" (v. 11). Matthew corrects the latter phrase to an indefinite "them," Luke to "others." All three append a saying rich in paradox to the effect that the gift of the original revelation will be added to, while the little the have-nots already possess will be taken from them. The evident conclusion to be drawn is that believers in the Gospel have been enriched while others, for whatever reason, have not. Then comes the mind-numbing part. Jesus has taught in parables the clear meaning of Isaiah's verse but now taken literally—precisely so that on hearing them some will not comprehend them. This is a clear case of an effect explained as if it were a cause. "I am; therefore I think." Descartes before the horse. The evangelists who interpret or apply ancient texts with Semitic logic take literally a prophetic utterance they know to be Jewish irony. To what purpose? To account for a fact of their experience. They have been quoting Jesus' parables as part of their proclamation of the Gospel. Some hearers have accepted it. Others have not. Attributing a divine intent to all that is written in the holy books and to their evangelizing activities as well, they find the form of Jesus' teaching off-putting to some *by God's design*!

More of Jesus' Teaching in Matthew

If Matthew employs and adds to Mark's parables, which others are unique to Matthew? First, a succession of short ones illustrative of a life lived in response to the gift of the Gospel proclaimed. A treasure buried in a field turned up by happy accident is then buried while the finder sells all he has to buy the field. The same story is told of a dealer in pearls who has been examining a lot not likely to bring a great price when he comes on one that surely will. He too sells all his possessions to buy it. A seine is cast into the sea by commercial fisherman and is drawn up when it is full for the normal sorting-out process. The Mosaic kosher laws at Leviticus 11:9 and Deuteronomy 14:9 say a sea creature must have fins and scales to be edible, so the rest are thrown away. In Jesus' telling, angels will sort out the wicked from the good at the end of the age, but in Matthew's retelling the unjust will be tossed into a furnace of fire as they weep and gnash their teeth. One can deduce this, Matthew supposes, from the bad end to which those hearers of Jesus will come who do not repent in response to his teaching and lead upright lives.

Matthew has a parable in act that is unique to him. It is told to illustrate the superior position of the disciples of Jesus in their own minds to other Jews as a result of their faith in what God has done in him. A precept of the Law levied an annual tax on all Jews for the upkeep of the Temple, a matter of two drachmas in Greek coinage, or a half shekel per person (Exod 30:13). Matthew's parable makes the fulfillment of a religious obligation stand for the favored condition of Jesus' followers by virtue of their anticipation in faith of God's reign. They are Jews and so the answer is "Yes" to the question to Peter, "Does your teacher pay the Temple tax?" (Matt 17:24-27). But afterward in the house Jesus quizzes Peter on a basic point: "Do the powerful exact tribute from their own or from others?" From others is the obvious answer. Whether the people in power are the imperial house or Jewish petty kings, their sons do not pay. Their subjects do, is Peter's answer. Israel was a subject people so Peter's response came immediately. The parallel situation with a hint of "so much the more" is placed on Jesus' lips: "Then the sons are exempt." With respect to Temple upkeep the followers of Jesus are the new royalty, sons of God's household and therefore not obliged to payment. But as Jews they were thought to have the obligation and so Jesus instructed them to pay to avoid giving scandal. Matthew continues his story by telling of the catch of a fish with a stater in its mouth. The coin was worth a shekel and paid the tax for two. The early Church in Roman Palestine was evidently paying the tax but knew it did not have to. As Matthew writes, the people's worship of Israel's God was no longer in the Temple but somehow in its ruins. Believers in Jesus' body raised up as the new Temple were worshiping God through this priestly advocate, the heavenly Christ. The gospel writers felt free to compose parables of their own like this one because they had such a harvest of the Teacher's parables to draw on and to modify for their teaching purposes.

A second parabolic action follows immediately (Matt 18:1-5). It derives from Mark but is equally about the condition of the disciples as the coin-in-the-fish's-mouth story. This time the parallel is made with the child whom Jesus calls over and places in their midst. A child by definition is open to instruction. Learners from the Master teacher Jesus need to become like children—the phrase is, literally, "come close to the ground"—if they would enter upon God's rule over them. That an openness to his teaching is the meaning of this act in metaphor is signaled by his description of them as "little ones" (Matt 18:6). This can of course mean children, but elsewhere in the gospels the word is rendered "least" as in "the least of my brothers." There, it is not children referred to but, rather, the lowliest in society, the marginalized. Such seems to be the meaning here. It is not the rich and powerful but the peasantry who will hear Jesus' teaching and act on it.

A succession of metaphoric acts follows, which describe how to deal with those who put a stumbling block in the way of the faith of simple folk: "Better a great millstone be hung about the neck of such a one and he be drowned in the depths of the sea" (Matt 18:6). It is figurative speech to be sure, but then Jesus is a Jew and his Aramaic tongue was a treasure house of images. Woe to those who lead others down the path of an evil life. It is "you, you, your" in the singular whose hand or foot is better cut off, whose eye is better plucked out than that one lead another into sin. We have already seen this wording in Mark's Jesus. Better eternal life populated by the maimed and blind than by the comfortable rich who are whole and sound.

Did Jesus have a miserable end in view for the rich? Did he declare them no candidates for a life under God's rule in the future? It seems so. His word to the earnest young man who had kept the commandments from his youth was to sell it all and give the proceeds to the poor (Matt 19:16-30). Old Christian catechisms—of not so long ago, in fact—used to call voluntary poverty "a counsel of perfection," meaning a laudable thing to do. But the poverty of the world's poor has always been involuntary. And it has always been the direct result of the conduct of the rich, a result that occurs even today in this and other rich countries of the world. Jesus' teaching was a command not a counsel, and he acted authentically in delivering it. For the only biographical note we have on him was that he sold his trade as a craftsman and went on the road, "living rough" as the British say. There was a distant memory of it as the evangelists wrote, "The birds nest at night, foxes retreat to their burrows, but the Son of man has nowhere to lay his head" (Matt 8:20; Luke 9:58). Again, Semitic hyperbole, but it sounds like living the command himself that he laid on others. Nowadays we call it the equitable distribution of the world's resources. Christian peoples have never practiced it, not even halfheartedly. They have contented themselves with thinking Jesus must have meant something else, like becoming a missionary sister or friar or a wealthy philanthropist like Bill Gates. He meant simple living for any who would be his followers.

Some Further Matthew Parables Explored

Matthew's parable of the day laborers in the vineyard—stoop workers, because one can pluck only some of the grapes and none of the peas or bush beans while standing—is his alone (Matt 20:1-16). The opening line says that Jesus' intent is to parallel the vineyard owner with the reign of God. This does not make him a figure for God, as Isaiah does in the song of the vineyard in his fifth chapter. It is all about labor relations in the ancient agricultural Middle East. The center of gravity of the story is the payment practice of that distant age, much like that of today's world in many quarters of the globe. A verbal contract is struck in the cool hours after dawn, "a day's pay for a quart of flour, a day's pay for three quarts of barley-meal" (Rev 6:6). Thus does another New Testament writing record the purchasing power of the age. A second crew in the market square at nine in the morning is hired and sent out with the promise of the same rate of a day's pay; so too with others at noon and three, even at five in the afternoon. How will the owner work things out at payment time at the end of the day?

At this point there is a bit of fuzziness of detail in the story but never mind. The latest hired with their full day's pay will probably have fled the scene, so too the other latecomers, either chortling at the size of their coins or else failing to reveal the amount to others, lest violent hands be laid on them by the dawn-to-dusk laborers. For purposes of the story, however, all must stand around knowing what each received. Otherwise, the declaration of the landowner would not have been heard by all to the effect that his openhandedness with some should not be resented by others. They have no reason to complain. He has kept to the terms of the contract entered into with all.

As with Jesus' teaching generally, it is impossible to know the wording in which he delivered it. There is every evidence of editing by either the evangelists or their sources for homiletic purposes as they address specific congregations. We cannot know whether Matthew had in mind repentant sinners as the latecomers equally rewarded, or the gentiles with their millennia of not having known the true God vis-à-vis Israel with its centuries of fidelity to Mosaic Law, or some third situation from that age. It does not matter because the parable conveys Jesus' teaching, which had also been that of his religion of Israel, that God is infinitely just but also boundlessly generous and merciful. "My thoughts are not your thoughts nor are your ways my ways, says the Lord" (Isa 55:7-8). A review of the way human justice is exercised and the way human generosity beyond justice is so little exercised shows Isaiah for the prophet that he was.

Matthew at this point has Jesus enter Jerusalem for the last time, so all his later public teaching is delivered there. A short parable found in his and no other gospel is forceful in its brevity. Just as with the day laborers, here it is not clear who the two sons are meant to be (Matt 21:28-32). Matthew has made it applicable to those who considered themselves just under Mosaic Law but did not heed John's preaching of the Law's demands, and the prostitutes and tax gatherers who did. Families that include among their siblings one ant and one grasshopper or a cheerful brother and a surly brother are familiar enough for Jesus' hearers to have given him an immediate hearing. But his story was over almost as soon as it began. One son is the big talker with no action—no remembered promises ever kept. The other is sullen and silent but then has a change of heart. Whether streetwalkers and tax skimmers are meant to be represented by brother number two as Jesus told it is an indifferent matter. As it comes to us, the difference between action and inaction could not better be portrayed in as few words, nor could change of heart when people of any sort, sons or daughters, come to their senses. The father had a right to filial obedience. And so with all humanity's obedience to God, whether it be given early or late.

The personality of Jesus, as we call it nowadays, comes through in his stories even more than in his proverbial utterances. He wishes above all that his hearers be faithful to the terms of the Abrahamic covenant renewed through Moses on Mount Sinai. He knows that such obedience for fellow Jews and gentile fellow travelers is the key to happiness. Yet he does not chant "the Lord, the Lord, the Lord" as a first-century mantra (see Dan 9:19; Matt 7:21-22). He looks for totally upright ethical behavior, but he is no tedious moralist. Boring as a teacher Jesus was not. He caught his hearers' interest with his first sentence and stopped at the moment he might be losing it.

The remaining parables that Matthew provides from the tradition are spoken as if delivered after Jesus' entry into Jerusalem for the last time, as was the parable of the two sons (Matt 20:18; 21:1, 10). A longer one features another vineyard owner, this time with thugs in his employ who bully, beat, and finally murder the slaves he sends to collect the season's yield (Matt 21:33-41). Matthew copies this parable out quite faithfully from Mark, as does Luke, but at its end he has the owner not lease but, rather, give the vineyard to others. This certainly does not mean to gentiles but to Jews and any others who would make up the Church.

A later brief narrative comes from Mark and is similarly agricultural. This one is little more than a parallel between the course of nature of a fig tree in spring and the day and hour of the LORD's expected inbreaking on Israel (Matt 24:32-33). A warning for watchfulness is contained in the story of a wealthy man who departs on a journey, leaving his slaves in charge and directing them to oversee the investment of his money. This detail occurs in Matthew and Luke but not in Mark, who contents himself with the master's instruction to the doorkeeper to stay awake, watching for his return (Matt 25:16-17; Luke 19:13, 16-19; Mark 13:34). Different sums of money are left for investment in Matthew and Luke, but the difference is of no consequence. Luke uses the term "deposited in a bank," while Matthew employs the more delicate phrase "worked up" the various sums of *talenta* to double the amount in three cases. The story in all three versions is about what should have been done, whether by way of investment or trading, with specific amounts of capital. However Jesus told the tale, the evangelists seem to have made *him* the man on a journey between his ascent to his Father and his return, who expects the multiplication of deeds of justice and charity in his absence. But that is not what rich men who lend money expect.

The interesting question is whether Jesus told a fictitious tale that included the taking of interest on invested money. Matthew's word *tókos* meant precisely that in the ancient world. Torah sternly forbade interest taking from a fellow countryman, something Jesus and Matthew after him would have known well (Exod 22:24; Lev 25:35-37). Both places in the Scriptures that do not permit it to the Israelite specify a poor neighbor as one from whom interest may not be taken. Were the rich disregarding the prohibition in Jesus' day and did they have a lively trade in money going, possibly with gentiles like Syrians or Egyptians, with whom some kind of banking business was being carried on? Whatever the case, the parable reflects life either in Jesus' day or in the gospel writers' later day in the Diaspora. Commercial life was very hard on the poor in any case, but Jesus did not tell his parables to deplore that fact. He chose realities out of people's lives to make another point. If such and so is the way of the world, consider what must be the case between the God who is LORD and the people of his concern. Matthew's nonprofiting slave has been cast out into outer darkness in his parables, while Luke's highborn lender to his slaves is hated by them and goes abroad to seek governance or rule of some sort. He has an enemies list, and when the profitless slave has had his one *mina* taken from him and given to another, the returning despot has those who had resisted his gaining more power summoned to be slain before his eyes (Luke 19:27). This grossly unhappy ending seems to be a coded account of the well-known journey of Archelaus, a son of Herod the Great, who went to Rome petitioning kingship in his father's place, to be given only tetrarchy under an imperial official of senatorial rank. A delegation from Judaea followed him to Augustus Caesar's court and may have contributed to the thwarting of his hopes. He was remembered for his cruelty by Luke who is the only evangelist to trace the Herodian house in any detail (see Matt 2:22; Luke 3:1; 23:12).

Of the three Matthean parables not yet reported on, two are drawn from a source he has in common with Luke. A third is exclusively his own. In the first of these Luke tells of a man who once gave a banquet to which he invited many (22:1-13). Matthew does not miss the opportunity to make it a king who gave a marriage feast for his son (14:16-24). The symbolism is obvious. The invited guests made excuses not to attend: a farm and a business operation in Matthew's case; the better-remembered purchase of a field, the testing of five yoke of oxen, and a recent marriage in Luke's. The recounting by the first evangelist is characteristically gory: the slaves who tendered the king's invitation were killed and his anger at the refuseniks took the form of equally bloody reprisals. Did Matthew draw on some known *casus belli* in the Herodian or imperial household? Or was the high sensitivity of the powerful to perceived insult simply presumed to be the way petty sovereigns would react?

The two narratives have in common the great unwashed as those successfully drafted to come, "as many as were found" (in Matthew), "from the streets and hedgerows of the town" (in Luke). Matthew makes them the bad and the good, Luke the maimed, the blind, and the lame, which is the description of the animals not fit to be offered in temple sacrifice (Lev 22:22). Matthew's detail of the king's anger when some appeared without a wedding garment may have been part of a separate parable, but it seems an irrational demand in any context. Were suitable garments made available to the guests in that era, like jackets to men and shoulder scarves to women in today's upscale restaurants? Or was it that, since we know of the trinitarian baptismal rite from Matthew, either a literal baptismal garment was meant or the upright life that should have characterized some of the baptized but did not? Our unfamiliarity with Semitic symbol in word and act makes this hard to answer.

There are several parabolic fragments that Matthew has in common with Luke but which neither develops: the chaos attending the coming parousia of the Son of Man in which one would be taken and one would be left (Matt 24:40-42; Luke 17:34-35). Since no one knew the day or the hour, all must be ready so as to avoid the same plight of the unwary in Noah's day (Matt 24:36-39; Luke 17:26-28, followed by Lot's escape from Sodom fire and sulfur). "They married and gave in marriage," in Hilaire Belloc's verse, "And danced at the county ball/And some had a horse and carriage/And the flood destroyed them all." There is the briefly developed account of the slave put in charge in his owner's absence who in a drunken orgy beats his fellow slaves and faces severe punishment upon the owner's return, surprisingly among Matthew's favorite target the hypocrites, the hyper-observants of the Law (Matt 24:45-51; Luke 12:41-46). The last parable in his arsenal is the much-misunderstood tale of the sleeping wise and foolish virgins, five of whom upon coming awake at the groom's approach had remembered to bring oil for their small clay lamps while five had not (Matt 25:1-13). It is a story of the provident and the improvident. The foolish virgins are the scatterbrained young whose folly had nothing to do with their virginity. When the door is shut on them against entry to the marriage feast, the reality of a wedding party yields to parousial prophecy.

What is to be said of Jesus as he is portrayed in Matthew's parables overall? This much at least: that he is made stern and severe to the point of punishing those who do not accept his teaching. That teaching had as its centerpiece the reign or rule of God. But it is Matthew who, in conveying that teaching to his contemporaries, made the risen Christ a character in Jesus' parables in ways he doubtfully spoke of himself. The one whom the early Church called "the Lord" had beyond question taught his hearers to live in a manner befitting the LORD God's future inbreaking on Israel. This evangelist and the two who like him had access to the sources containing parable material left the Church the legacy of Jesus' genius as a teacher. Matthew's polemic stance against his religious adversaries resulted in his "editing in" some aspects of Jesus' character that need to be edited out for clearer hindsight into the manner of man he was.

Luke's Teachings of Jesus Special to Him

The parables of Jesus proper to Luke are more helpful to discover the skill of the Master as teacher than would be the small ways in which he edited the material he got from Mark or had in common with Matthew. The major concern underlying each distinct literary product provides the key. Mark proposes Jesus as a man gifted with divine power to bring order to a disordered world but who must suffer and die if his tomb is to be found empty after three days by the Spirit's exercise of that power. Matthew presses the ways in which the Risen One had taught that the Law should be lived contrary to the way other teachers taught it, who themselves failed to live it. Luke's conviction that Jesus died and was raised up to achieve the remission of sins contributed to his portrayal of Jesus as a man of great compassion for weak humanity in its sinfulness. All three wrote from the vantage point of believers that the sufferings of the innocent Jesus were not to no purpose but had been endured for the sake of all, and that his coming at the end of the age would mean a resurrected life in the body for all.

Luke has incorporated some brief parable material into his gospel, like the sower and the seed and the lamp whose light cannot be hidden, before he turns to the first full-length story that Jesus told. If Jesus was a superb storyteller Luke was not far behind. The way he clothed his narratives in detail has resulted in their being remembered and repeated for centuries. His excoriation of the lakeshore towns of Chorazin and Bethsaida is no fit example of his literary style, for he and Matthew have it in almost identical wording from their source. Surely it is a reproach of the church of Palestine to these places for having rejected some early proclamation of the Gospel. This is not to say that Jesus did not wish his teaching to be received but that it was not so revolutionary as to be rebuffed upon a hearing. The presentation of his death and resurrection, faith in which could make a difference to all humanity and not Israel only, could easily have caused incredulity at such a wild tale and cosmic claim. Some of Jesus' parables as he presented them could also have had an adverse effect. They were all of a piece with the narrative of Jesus' townsfolk stopping up their ears in his home synagogue in Luke's fourth chapter, as it came to be numbered. On that occasion it was not only that this well-known local figure was claiming to wear the mantle of Isaiah but that God should be thought to have an equal concern for the pagan Sidonians and the once conquering Syrians as for Israel. Xenophobia, fear of the foreign or the different, is arguably the oldest and deepest flaw in the human character.

Jesus' first recorded story from Luke's pen shows him challenging that deep-seated tendency (Luke 10:29-37). A roadside mugging in Jesus' day was a common occurrence. The sympathy of his audience for the victim would have been aroused immediately as he began to describe such a case. The Jericho road had no human habitation on either side and was a prime target of brigands. Priests and Levites coming from Jerusalem could be presumed to be in full Temple service. They were targets of another sort, the people's scorn. For although that magnificent structure was the pride of common folk and its ritual praise, thanksgiving, and repentance, something they participated in willingly, the conduct of its custodians did not share in the admiration. The reason was money. The temple priests not only lived well but were charged with acting as agents of the empire in collecting taxes from the people. Needless to say they were suspected of withholding too much for their services, besides having the choicest of meats held back from sacrifice for their table as specified by Torah.

Jesus' story opens predictably and continues until he comes to the traveler moved with compassion at the victim's plight. When Jesus identifies him as a Samaritan his hearers might have immediately wished he were the victim and not the hero of the tale. The antipathy between Jews and Samaritans, even though the latter were ethnically Jewish, was intense. It went back many centuries to the days of their return to the Northern Kingdom from exile in Assyria, at which time they were falsely accused of going over to false gods (see 2 Kgs 17:30-31; the five deities listed became the "five husbands" of John 4:18). Their real fault was having resumed Israelite practice on Mount Gerizim in Samaria, not Mount Zion in Jerusalem. Worse still, at a much later date they had accepted funds from Alexander's Greek Empire for the building of a temple on Mount Gerizim. What Jesus' Galilean audience knew about Samaritans better than any history from the past was that, as pilgrims to and from Jerusalem on any of the three annual feasts, Galileans had to travel on the east side of the Jordan through pagan territory to avoid being pelted with stones. Despite the satisfaction Jesus' listeners might have taken from the heartlessness of the priest and Levite, the notion of the Samaritan as "good" was a full-frontal attack on their sensibilities. The tender care of the man's wounds would only have wounded the Galilean psyche, compounded by his being transported on the Samaritan's beast to a caravansery for further care. Two hundred years later in the collection of rabbinic decisions called the Mishnah ("Oral Instruction") the Samaritans are consistently spoken of as another people and coupled with the gentiles. Hence a Jewish Good Samaritan Hospital is an oxymoron one will never hear of.

This first Lukan parable was spoken by Jesus in response to an earnest inquiry by a scholar of the Law as to who, exactly, was meant by one's neighbor in Leviticus 19:18. There the word *re‘a* is placed in apposition to "one of one's people," a fellow countryman or Israelite. The scholar's question as to the meaning of neighbor could only have been a Lukan cue to bring on Jesus' response. In the parable, not only every fellow human, but even one's enemy was the Levitical meaning of neighbor for Jesus.

That powerful short story places in parallel the action of one person with what Jesus expects the actions of all in his hearing to be. The evangelist has situated it within the narrative of Jesus' journey to Jerusalem that runs from chapters 9 to 19. All the memorable parables recounted by Luke occur in this setting. The fierce denunciation of Pharisee conduct that he has in common with Matthew is found there, but then comes a story that underscores the folly of piled-up wealth. It comes in the form of a harvest so bountiful that a farmer has to tear down his barns and build new ones to accommodate it. The description may be exaggerated to ridicule the rich landowners for whom the tenant farmers, who are the bulk of Jesus' hearers, slave in the fields. It could also have been a recent case both Jesus and his outdoor audience knew of. The sudden and unexpected deaths of the prosperous were a matter of the experience of the poor. God speaks: "You fool, this very night you must surrender your life; and the money your have made, who will get it now?" (Luke 12:20; see Eccl 2:18-21; 6:1-2). What use is it to be Mr. Moneybags, Jesus asks, if one is a pauper in God's sight?

A short parable on the virtue of humility is found in Luke's gospel only. True humility is a fitting self-image. Its opposite is the illusion of self-importance. This parable places Jesus in the improbable situation of chiding fellow guests whom he observes jostling for places of honor at a dinner in the house of a leading Pharisee (Luke 14:7-14; cf. 1:52; 18:14b; Matt 23:12; Ezek 17:24; 21:26c [NAB 31d]). The improbability consists in the brief scenario Jesus conjures up. The host approaches a person who has seated himself in a place reserved for a more eminent guest and says, "You are in this man's seat." Abashed, the man who has put himself forward retreats to the lowest place. Had he taken it initially he might expect to be told, "Come up higher, my friend," and then his fellow guests would see the respect in which he was held. Luke likes to end a parable with a remembered watchword of Jesus. Here he adds one that occurs more than once: "For everyone who exalts himself will be humbled; and whoever humbles himself will be exalted." To this there is appended the suggestion by way of commentary that when you play the host you should have the maimed, the lame, and the blind as your guests. The reason is that they cannot repay you. Be assured that, in the resurrection of the just, you will be repaid (Luke 14:12-14).

There is a fine sense of paradox in Jesus' parables, however brief some of them may be. When he is recalling a fact that is not a fiction, the slaughter of some Galileans by the brutal Roman prefect Pilate, he makes their presumed innocence the occasion for repentance by the guilty (Luke 13:1-5). He cites the deaths of eighteen other men in an industrial accident, the collapse of a tower in Jerusalem. They had done no wrong whatever. But those who most certainly have done wrong need to repent. Failure to do so could lead to a similar tragic end.

A cryptic brief parable that is likewise about repenting while there is time follows. Olive oil was a cash crop for the Jews of Roman Palestine, besides their putting it to many uses domestically. Figs and grapes were other objects for export as well as at the family table. This meant that one dying fig tree could represent economic loss. Jesus told the following parable. A man had a fig tree in his orchard which, upon inspection at the proper season, had no figs among its leaves. Impatient, he ordered it cut down, for it was only taking up the ground. His overseer intervened and asked for one more year's attention via soil enrichment in the earth around it. "It may bear fruit in the future," the orchard tender said. "If not, you can cut it down" (Luke 13:6-9). End of story. Jesus' parables were like that. No need to say more if the point has been made.

A parable unique to Luke is a warning by Jesus of the cost of becoming his follower. Since it has the phrase "must carry his cross" and speaks of breaking all human ties, including ties with the family, it was either edited or composed after his death in that cruel fashion. Briefly, the builder of a tower must calculate the cost beforehand; similarly, a warlord should figure both his and his enemy's troop strength before risking attack (14:26-32). In the same way, potential disciples must sell all they have before joining Jesus on his teaching mission.

What is perhaps the best-loved of all Jesus' Lukan parables is really two that have been joined together, one about a wastrel son, the other about a forgiving father. First, however, this gospel will deal with two less emotion-laden images. The one it has in common with Matthew tells of a shepherd who will leave a flock of ninety-nine nibbling at desert grasses while he goes in search of one that has wandered off (Luke 15:1-7).

Setting it happily on his shoulders once he finds it is hardly a show of affection as with a pet. The recovery means overcoming potential economic loss, just as with the fig tree. Jesus was always alerted to the lives of marginal income his peasant hearers lived. In telling stories illustrative of life under Israel's God and with their neighbors—the latter often rivals rather than partners in eking out a livelihood—he knew that even while listening they were worried about the next shekel, the next food on the table. That is why a housewife's loss of one coin meant domestic tragedy (Luke 15:8-10). If it were sizeable, say worth one hundred of today's dollars and one of the ten coins her father had saved up as her dowry at marriage, it would have been a hedge against either widowhood or her husband's incapacity to work through illness or accident. No wonder she threw a neighborhood block party at the find—without cagily disclosing the size of the coin to her friends like any mother of a family living at the edge.

Prodigality Can Mean Generous Giving but Not Here

Now the story of the father and the son (Luke 15:11-32). The young man asked and received the share of his father's inheritance that would come to him at the father's death. Being the younger son he knew that his older brother would inherit any property the father possessed. Off he went along the primrose path of pleasure, squandering the sum— whatever that was—on the equivalent in Jesus' day of fast women and slow horses. At rock bottom and in a famine-stricken land far from Israel, he got work in a pig farm. He was perfectly free to eat the animals' fodder. When even that was gone he came to his senses and began to journey home on foot repentant, ready to ask his father's forgiveness and for a job along with the hired men if the father would have it. End of story number one.

Number two begins with the young fool of a prodigal, wasteful, that is, in his giving and spending, walking slowly, painfully toward the house he grew up in. His father spied his trudging figure in the distance and, pitying the beaten young man, did what no prosperous farmer who owned a few slaves would do. He ran, ran like a young lad to meet and greet his son. This he did with an embrace and a kiss in the oriental manner, cheek to one cheek and then to the other. He called out over his shoulder "Quick! Fetch a robe, the best we have, and put it on him; put a ring on his finger and sandals on his feet. Kill the fattest calf in the stalls. We're having a coming home party." All was done as directed.

At that point the older son who had not figured in either story heard the sounds of music and dancing and asked what was going on. When he was told he refused to join the dance. He went instead to his father and angrily challenged him for making all this fuss over his no-good brother. "What's going on here? I've stayed home and worked this property day after day the way a good son should and what did I get for it? Not so much as a young goat for a meal of celebration with my friends." He shouted this at his father, refusing to go in to the house. "Relax, son," the older man said, "Calm down. You are here with me always, in and out of season. Everything I have is yours. So come and do some celebrating." He is your brother, after all. He lived *la dolce vita* and it turned out to be bitter, not sweet. We have him with us now. "We *have* to celebrate and rejoice. He was dead and has come back to life. He was lost and has been found."

Whom did Jesus have in mind as father and son? He does not say. He does not make application at the end of his stories, like a pathetic humorist who explains his jokes. The evangelists sometimes append allegorical applications to one or other parable, such as the sower and the seed or the wheat and the weeds. That is a help to know that Jesus must have meant more and other than the explanation they attempt. Mercifully, Luke has left it to his hearers to work out these images of tension and division in a family. Is that alone what Jesus meant to convey? It would be quite enough: youth and age, folly and wisdom, the absolute need to forgive ungrateful behavior. Or are grave sin and repentance primarily to the fore here? The setting in Luke's gospel after the tales of rejoicing over the recovered lost sheep and lost coin incline us to think so.

What of the older son as Israel that had borne the heat of the day's labor in dogged faithfulness to Israel's God and the younger son as the gentile world that in the Jewish mind was given to every sort of immorality and idolatry, now side by side with Israel in worshiping communities everywhere in the Diaspora? Jesus does not say. He lets people puzzle out his meaning in freedom to find there every meaning they can discern. His parables always end in the unspoken word: if the shoe fits, wear it.

Even more challenging is the parable of the crooked farm manager, as Luke proves by applying five proverbial sayings of Jesus at the end in the hope that one may provide the key to Jesus' meaning (Luke 16:1-13). The brief narrative is fairly straightforward, requiring in the original hearers a knowledge of an extortion technique they already possessed. The owner of a landed estate has evidently agreed with his manager on the quotas of olive oil, wheat, and the rest that the latter will be able to deliver at harvest time. Suspected of sharp practice by his boss, he sets about cooking the books. He directs the men in charge of the olive orchards and the wheat fields to write down commitments of fifty and eighty percent of his earlier estimates, hoping to take the loss but still pocket the difference that remained. When the owner learns of the scam he commends the perpetrator for acting astutely. Again, end of story.

But how can the owner respond that way, centuries of Christian congregations have asked? The short answer is that he would not be the victim of the failed scheme. The manager once discovered gets none of his expected cut and probably loses his job besides. The owner is certainly deep in the business of defrauding the working poor and so he simply recognizes a good "con" when he sees one. It meant no loss to him. He would see to it that the original amounts of produce were delivered to him as promised. The first explanation of the sense Jesus' parable would have made to his hearers might well have been his signature statement: "Take a leaf from the book of the worldly wise. See that you scheme to perform acts of justice as carefully as they do acts of injustice." The evangelist may think he has shed light on the parable by appending the four money sayings that Jesus spoke on other occasions, but strung together this way they lose their force. Only one seems apposite: "No servant can serve two masters. . . . You cannot serve God and money" (v. 13).

Jesus taught powerful tales to bring sin in the economic order to light: the judge who dispensed little justice to the widowed poor (Luke 18:1-8); the repentant public official for whom theft was a way of life (vv. 10-14); a beggar's sores licked by dogs at the gate of the rich man at whose flesh flames were licking in *sheol* (Luke 16:19-31). In one real life story Jesus' treed quarry Zachaeus was given a second chance (19:1-10).

What do we learn about Jesus from his teaching in aphorism, parable, and lengthier discourse? Despite the fact that this material in the gospels has been edited by the various evangelists and probably by their sources before them, the following things about his message and his method come through as very clear:

- He was a superb teacher in the open air in the manner of teachers of his time.

- He was considered by the crowds to be a better teacher of the Law than his learned contemporaries, although without having been schooled in it by any teacher.

- He was a master of his culture and of the day-to-day lives his audiences lived by dint of his native intelligence and his keen powers of observation.

- He could count on the knowledge many of his hearers would have of the people's Scriptures read out in Aramaic paraphrase and expounded in the Sabbath synagogue assembly.

- He knew that the hardscrabble existence most of them were living was uppermost in their minds, surely occupying more of their thoughts than religious reflection or prayer.

- He had a great conception of the Lord who was God and the relation in which people stood to the majesty of deity unseen whose voice they never heard.

- He thought, along with the prophets and the sages, that the God of Israel had a special care for the people Israel but, unlike most other teachers, a concern for gentile peoples as well.

- He spent much time alone absorbed in prayer and, when speaking of God, was remembered by his followers to have claimed an intimacy that took the form of calling the Lord God "my Father."

- He had a great love for people, sinners as well as saints and all between.

- He wished for his hearers lives of love of God and love of every fellow human being in which alone was their peace.

- He was stern and serious in manner, not a scold, but at the same time a person compassionate for people in their weakness and in the circumstances of their lives they could not control.

- He relieved what suffering he could, often by miraculous means.

- He was remembered above all as one whom God had restored to life three days after his death by crucifixion. This fact, unique in human history, was affirmed by many witnesses. It is the climax of each gospel narrative. Without it they would have had no reason to commemorate Jesus as Lord and Christ as they did. He might have been remembered for fifty or one hundred years as one more powerful preacher eliminated, like John, son of Zechariah and Elizabeth. But the known fact that he had been resurrected by the Spirit's power colored everything the evangelists wrote about him, including his teaching as recollected and recorded by a chain of witnesses.

Jesus taught not only verbally and by the example of his life but by signs and wonders. The miraculous deeds reported of Jesus are so many and so varied that it cannot be that none of them occurred, as rationalists love to maintain, although the details in some may well have been elaborated in the telling. They are chiefly of instantaneous cures and healings, which is a requirement for the claim of an authentic miracle. A listing of these occurrences as the four gospels record them would show that some are described as happening in two different sets of circumstances. This would be the work of the gospel writers or the sources on which they drew. The placement would be their doing for narrative purposes.

Jesus as Exorcist and Wonderworker

The first miracle in Mark's account is the cure in a synagogue of a convulsed man thought to be possessed by an "unclean spirit" (1:21-28). Whether it was a true inhabiting by a diabolic presence or was a case of schizophrenia or epilepsy cannot be determined. The symptoms that are described make the cure miraculous, as will be the case with the numerous other exorcisms performed by Jesus with a spoken word or a verbal exchange with the victim.

The next healing is of the mother of Simon's wife in the house where he and his brother Andrew grew up (1:29-31). She was ill with a fever that sure wouldn't leave her, like Dublin's Miss Molly Malone. Jesus assists her to her feet, "and she resumed serving the men" (1:31; see also 2:5; 5:43). That phrase has nothing to do with female servitude or even the role of housewives. It is a verbal cachet to indicate the conclusion of the brief narrative. Similar phrases are found in the other healing accounts, the most common of which is, "Your sins are forgiven," or, "Go and sin no more" (2:5; see John 5:14; 8:11). In one resuscitation of a child from death the incident's end is marked by, "He told them to give her something to eat" (Mark 5:43).

Mark next mentions a whole clutch of instant restorations to health in which he is careful to distinguish between demonic possession and some physical or emotional malady. In quick succession this gospel reports on the healing of a victim of *lepra*, any of a variety of contagious skin diseases but not Hansen's; of a man long paralyzed lying on a pallet and another with a withered arm; of still another victim of violent seizures, this time apparently a pagan from one of the ten cities east of Lake Kinnereth and the Jordan. A nature miracle has intervened, the calming of the inland sea in a heavy squall. Mark describes these acts contrary to nature as "deeds of power" (*dynameîs*). Jesus' sole resuscitation of the dead in Mark (Luke and John will each have one) is a girl of twelve and is bracketed between the cure of a woman sufferer from (probably) menstrual hemorrhaging over a twelve-year period. The multiplication of bread and fish to feed a crowd of thousands with some left over is reported twice in this gospel (Mark 6:34-44; 8:1-10). The number of wicker baskets to contain the uneaten loaves is given as twelve and seven, two important numbers for Jews. This and the repetition of the miracle patterned on the manna event followed up with a quiz on the significance of the event, discloses Mark as the catechist that he is.

Jesus' walking on the sea follows the first narrative and contains the detail that "he was about to pass by them" (6:48), a thoroughly puzzling phrase to later gentile readers until they realize that "he treads on the crest of the sea" (Job 9:8) lies behind the account. So do several places in the Scriptures where the verb "to pass before" is a technical term for the presence of Israel's LORD to Moses and Elijah (Exod 33:19; 34:6; 1 Kgs 19:11). Similarly, after Jesus climbed into the boat with the disciples, how was their utter astonishment at what they had witnessed related to their incomprehension of the incident of the loaves, "because their minds were closed" (6:51-52)? Was it meant to be a prelude to the second narrative of multiplied loaves, after which they forgot—incredibly—to bring bread along, for which Jesus chided them harshly: "Do you still not understand? Are your minds closed? Have you forgotten?" There follows what can only be called a catechetical review (8:19-21). The evangelist may be describing the slow comprehension of the Master's closest friends as to who he is. It is likely that Mark is deploring the closed-mindedness of some in his day to the proclamation of the one through whom God had worked such marvels. As to the disciples having forgotten to bring bread after its recent proliferation, the "one loaf" with them in the boat has to be Jesus himself. Surely this is Semitic language in symbol that the evangelists, like their biblical forebears, use throughout.

A final indication of metaphoric use in Mark is his miracle of restoration of sight to two blind men who came to "see," one of them in stages, who Jesus is (Mark 8:22-26; 10:46-52). The first is an anonymous villager of Bethsaida in Galilee and the second, the son of Timaeus, a resident of Jericho in the South. The miracles serve as brackets enclosing the three predictions of Jesus' sufferings, death, and uprising, each of them a summary of the climactic events of the gospel up to which all else leads.

The most important thing about these signs of God's power shown in the man Jesus is the compassion he displays in each case, a sufferer with fellow sufferers in their suffering. When Jesus says to Bartimaeus as he sends him on his way, "Your faith has healed you," we know what Mark means to make of these two stories. The newly sighted pair have trusted in God to do this thing through Jesus, but their faith has a wider compass: the faith of the Markan church in God's deed in Christ's sufferings, death, and resurrection, spoken of three times within the bracketed restoration to the sight of faith.

One often reads or hears the Fourth Gospel, John, characterized as theological, while the first three are called historical. The distinction is quite wrong. Jesus' setting in John is in fact more historical as to place, time, and religious culture than the other three, while they in turn are equally concerned with the theology of who Jesus is and specifically with soteriology, that is, his role as divinely designated savior. The Gospels according to Matthew, Mark, and Luke are often called synoptic, meaning "at a single glance." If the bulk of their content is placed in parallel columns, or even if one goes back and forth from one to another in a specific saying or story, their similarities and dissimilarities in wording can be seen immediately. All three are interested in presenting Jesus as a teacher and a person endowed with miraculous powers but as much more than that. In two places Mark will indicate who Jesus is in the faith of the Church through what God has accomplished in him. Matthew simply copies him out in the first of these: "For the Son of Man did not come to be served but to serve, and to give his life as a ransom for the many" (Mark 10:45; Matt 20:28).

A Brief Foretelling of Jesus' Life, Death, and Resurrection as Bringing Redemption

Ransom and redemption are the same figure of speech, descriptive of buying back captives in war. As used in the New Testament in other places than the gospels, it means being brought from a condition of captivity or enslavement to a condition of freedom (see 1 Cor 6:20; 7:23; 1 Pet 1:19, "set free by his blood"). The whole human race, in other words, is in a vastly improved situation by virtue of God's deed in Christ and the Spirit. The rescue is not from danger, bodily infirmity, or mortality but from the power of evil, in a word, sin and its effects.

In a second place, following Mark's gospel, Jesus will say while holding bread in his hands, "This is my body"; and after he will say: "This is my blood, the blood of the renewed covenant, shed for the many"

(Mark 14:24; Matt 26:28, who adds "for the forgiveness of sins"). The covenant was first made with Abraham and renewed through Moses, with a further renewal prophesied by Jeremiah. These are but two of the many places that depict Jesus as having had the role of reconciler of a humanity alienated from God. All of them were arrived at by profound reflection in the primitive Church on the meaning of a life that seemingly ended in a cruel death but that was revealed, in a reversal of death, as an initiation into a new and glorious life. Luke chooses to express the Church's faith in Jesus and his work early in his gospel when he has Gabriel tell Mary not to fear because God has been gracious to her:

> You will conceive and give birth to a son, and you are to give him the name Jesus. He will be great, and will be called Son of the Most High. The LORD God will give him the throne of his ancestor David, and he will be king over Israel forever; his reign shall never end. . . . The Holy Spirit will come upon you, and the power of the Most High will overshadow you; for that reason the holy child to be born will be called Son of God. (Luke 1:31-33, 35)

That is a Synoptic Gospel expressing faith in Jesus as both human and divine—as the other two do and not John only—but, more than that, in a kingly or royal role. David, in spite of his major flaws of character, had other outstanding virtues, like his forgiveness of his son Absalom who mounted a revolt against him. David went on to rule his people in perfect justice as no Israelite sovereign had done before him or since. Jesus' greatness outstripped that of David by an infinity. He was the very Son of God who as an Israelite achieved for his people, indeed for all the peoples of the world, the peace of assurance that their sins are forgiven and they need no longer live in fear of death, for it is not the end but a beginning.

Chapter Four

What John Does with the Figure of Jesus

John is often called the Fourth Gospel because of its position in all the earliest manuscripts. This does not mean that it was the last to be written. That is something we cannot know, only that like Matthew and Luke it was written after Mark. John goes about telling the Jesus story in a series of vignettes, actually one-act plays with dialogue and characters assigned. Some characters are unnamed, like a man paralyzed for thirty-eight years, the unnamed mother of Jesus, and those never called by name like "the sons of Zebedee" and "the disciple whom Jesus loved." Others are designated by name: Nathanael, Nicodemus, Andrew, Philip, Thomas, the Bethany family of three adult siblings, Simon Peter, his father John or Jona, and Mary Magdalene. Like Mark, John has no account of Jesus' conception and birth, preferring to begin his account with Jesus' coming on the scene in tandem with John, the son of Zechariah (whom he never calls the Baptist or Baptizer). This introduction of Jesus is done through the alternation of a prose poem about a Word who was with God "in the beginning" and who was born a man of flesh, with a prose narrative about John's testimony to that individual. He is described as the true light that sheds light on everyone and who was even then coming into the world. It is not possible to be sure which writing was interspersed with portions of the other. Often the poem that states in its opening phrase, "and what God was the Word was" is voted in first place with a narrative insertion, both because the gospel opens with it and because timeless existence is infinitely superior to time-bound humanity. On the other hand, "A man named John was sent from God" is the obvious introductory phrase to all that is narrated in the gospel. Whichever the case, the double orientation, both to eternity symbolized by the Word who was with God in the beginning and to the thirty-five or so years of Jesus' lifetime, will persist throughout the gospel.

A second important characteristic of John's Jesus is that he speaks of himself in the way that all in the primitive Church believed in him, if not in precisely Johannine terms. Jesus, in other words, is made the exponent of the early community's christological faith from which the Church never afterward departed. This is not done throughout with the aid of Greek poetry with an Aramaic substrate, as in the early paragraphs referred to above. The technique, rather, is a historical act of Jesus that is followed by an extended discourse. Thus, when John's disciples report to him that Jesus is baptizing and drawing great crowds, John responds at length that he is best man to the groom, Jesus, in a figurative marriage rite, concluding: "He must increase; I must decrease" (3:30). Then follows a long paragraph of disquisition on the relation between Jesus and God that ends: "The Father loves the Son and has given everything over to him. Whoever believes in the Son has eternal life [i.e., the Life of the Final Eon], but whoever disobeys the Son will not see life: God's wrath rests on him" (John 3:35-36; cf. Matt 11:27; Luke 10:22). John, like Matthew, is quite secure in bringing divine censure on the heads of those who are not accepting the Gospel.

More often it is Jesus himself who is made to respond to a crowd of Jerusalem "Jews," probably a self-denomination of those committed to the Oral as well as the Written Law who were convinced that they alone were *the* Jews. They have challenged Jesus on a Sabbath healing that they take to be work and thus prohibited. Here John the evangelist inserts a threat on Jesus' life. Why was he threatened? "By calling God his own Father he was claiming equality with God" (John 5:18b). Any such phrase as "my Father" intermingled with "our Father" could hardly have merited a death threat, whereas the kind of teaching that immediately follows the heated exchange could well have led to violence in John's all-Jewish community:

> Jesus answered . . . the Son does . . . only what he sees the Father doing; whatever the Father does the Son does. For the Father loves the Son and shows him all that he himself is doing. . . . As the Father raises the dead and gives them life, so the Son gives life as he chooses. . . . The Father has given full jurisdiction to the Son; it is his will that all should give the same honour to the Son as to the Father. (John 5:19, 21, 23)

That is by all means a claim of equality with God and could have sounded, in the ears of Greek-speaking Jews in John's Diaspora city, to be a denial that God was both one and unique. At this point in the justification for his action, Jesus continues at twice the length to maintain that the Father not only empowers him, places all judgment in his hands, and testifies to him, but the works the Father has sent him to accomplish also testify to him, and the Scriptures do as well. They will reveal it if they are diligently searched. All give witness on his behalf.

If fully half of this gospel is devoted to Jesus as expositor of the Father-Son relation, the narrative portions that provide the occasion are as interesting as any in the other gospels.

A Pharisee named Nicodemus who has a position of some authority, perhaps on the Great Council, comes to Jesus by night for enlightenment. The visit results almost immediately, without being triggered by anything Jesus says, in a discourse on the necessity of birth from above in water and the Spirit for all who would enter upon the reign of God. When the brief exposition of the importance of baptism seems to have ended, it is followed by another, likewise delivered as if at night, on the irreconcilability of light and darkness. Greek-speaking Christians ever since have used the word *phōtismós*, enlightenment, for baptism (see 2 Cor 4:6). It is unlikely St. Paul ever heard of Gautama, the Enlightened, when he spoke of the light cast on the face of Jesus. "For God so loved the world," John wrote, "that he gave his only Son, so that everyone who believes in him might not perish but have eternal life" (John 3:16; through him will come not a judgment of condemnation at the Last Day but rescue [salvation] from it [v. 17]). This teaching of Christian faith is often quoted in isolation but, as with anything in John, context is all. One is not free to accept the declaration of divine love and its major consequence, a new kind of life, without believing all that is written in this book and in the canonical Scriptures in which it is set. "This saying is hard; who can accept it?" (John 6:60) some asked who had been exposed to the totality of teaching contained in this gospel. The saying they had just heard was, "Whoever eats my flesh and drinks my blood dwells in me and I in him." John had placed his church's teaching about the inaugural ritual act, namely, baptism, in a conversation with an inquirer whose opening line was an acknowledgment that Jesus is a teacher sent from God. This gospel will teach the essential character of a second rite, "eating the real food and drinking the real drink" that is the flesh and blood of the One sent by the living Father (John 6:53-58). The other gospels also teach the necessity of a bath in water as the symbol of new life in Christ and a meal of bread and wine as the symbol that does not merely stand for but is this Christ. John teaches both in his way, which is never quite the same as the other three.

John's Technique of Having Jesus Mystify, Then Explain

John employs another one-act play to teach the healing of an old schism in the family of ethnic Jews. A woman has come alone to a well at high noon to draw water. A man who at the moment is alone approaches her. The conversation of strangers of the two sexes does not strike modern Westerners as particularly odd. This encounter is unusual not only because it contravenes cultural mores but for a much more important reason. Only people at enmity with a neighboring people for centuries can take in the full force of the encounter. For, "Jews do not share drinking vessels with Samaritans" (John 4:11). Half a world away on two continents: "For colored only." In much tribal life, mere treading on another's land can mean death. In a Johannine conversation the opening gambit is often so naïve as to be opaque: "Sir, you have no water and the well is deep, so where can you get 'living water'?" Before it had been: "But how can someone be born again when he is old? Can he enter his mother's womb a second time and be born?" (John 3:4). Later still: "Sir," they said to him, "give us this bread that comes down from heaven now and always" . . . (John 6:34, 41-42). "I am the bread that came down from heaven" . . . "Surely this is Jesus, Joseph's son. We know his father and mother. How can he say, 'I have come down from heaven'?" In all these cases total mystification is expressed, leading to Jesus' exposition of a quite different matter, religious mystery. He brings an end to ignorance with knowledge, to darkness with light. Time and again Jesus is the teacher in John, always anachronistically relative to his earthly life, teaching the Church's faith in him as the Son of the Father. The wider Church adopted John's Word-made-flesh christology, but it did not need that image for its faith. It had in Jesus a person anointed by God (*meshiaḥ*) whose humanity was seen indwelled by divine Sonship on every page of this gospel.

Several times more John will resort to the narrative technique of initial incomprehension by onlookers or Jesus' own disciples to provide an opportunity for Jesus to teach so as to be understood. Some Pharisees object, for example, that Jesus is testifying to himself, a thing totally disallowed in any court of law. He responds by calling on the Father as a fellow witness, citing Torah—which says that a minimum of two is necessary—as he does so (John 8:17-18; see Deut 17:6; 19:5). A group of fellow Jews who have believed in him bristle at being told that standing by his teaching would make them truly his disciples and thereby free. They say that as sons of Abraham they have God alone as their Father and have always been free. "If God were your Father you would love me," says Jesus, "for God is the source of my being and from him I come. . . . But because I speak the truth you do not believe me. . . . The one who has God for his Father listens to the words of God. You are not God's children, and that is why you do not listen" (John 8:42-47). In just such a heated dialogue as this John reports on the resistance he meets daily to the truth of God about Jesus, a truth that liberates from ignorance and sin.

A man born blind receives his sight from Jesus who has called himself the light of the world. The man Jesus is a stranger to him. Quizzed by some Pharisees as to who might have done this "work" on the Sabbath, the man says he does not know. His parents seem to know but will not tell. The badgerers say they are disciples of Moses, not of this Lawbreaker, which is the key to the whole exchange. The newly seeing man makes a spirited defense of Jesus, saying in tones of heavy irony that it is an even greater marvel that God should use a sinner as the instrument to achieve the restoration of sight than the miracle itself. Jesus then speaks in response to the feigned incredulity of his adversaries that such as he should have done this thing: "It is for judgment that I have come into this world—to give sight to the sightless and to blind those who see. . . . If you were blind you would not be guilty, but because you claim to see your guilt remains" (John 9:39, 41). Once more we are let in on the heated argumentation that proclaimers of the Gospel in one Diaspora city were party to. It is important for gentile Christians of a later day to know the abuse their Jewish forebears in faith were subjected to and the kinds of arguments they employed in response. It is equally important to know that the terms of that early polemic cannot be easily understood and should not, in any case, be replicated in modern attempts at evangelizing. It is Semitic argumentation of a kind many other peoples on the globe are unfamiliar with.

One of Jesus' two disciples named Judas asks a question about the seeming waste of money for a liter of costly perfumed oil for anointing Jesus' feet. The gospel writer calls this man surnamed the Iscariot a thief, hence his supposed interest in wasteful expenditure. Jesus responds that the generous woman, Mary of Bethany, who applied the oil to Jesus' feet and dried them with her hair, should keep the aromatic ointment for his burial (John 12:4-7).

Again, two disciples with Greek names from a Galilean lakeshore town, one of them Simon Peter's brother, are deputed by gentile proselytes on their way to Passover worship in the Temple to gain an audience for them with Jesus. The request brings on a lengthy discourse by Jesus about his death and the glorification that lay ahead:

> Unless a grain of wheat fall to the ground and die, it remains that and nothing more; but if it die it bears a rich harvest. . . . Now my soul is in turmoil and what am I to say? 'Father save me from this hour?' No, it is for this that I came to this hour. . . . Father, glorify your name. . . . When I am lifted up from the earth I shall draw everything to myself. (John 12:20-24, 28, 32)

Jesus, at the last meal he will take with his friends, tells them to love one another; but he must go, and where he is going they cannot come (John 13:33-34). Peter and Thomas successively ask him where that may be. The first questioner receives this response: "If I go to prepare a place for you, I shall come again and take you to myself" (14:3). To the second, who has asked how, since the disciples do not know where Jesus is going, they can know the way, Jesus says: "I am the way, the truth, and the life" (v. 6). Philip is puzzled by Jesus' statement that no one comes to the Father except by him and challenges Jesus directly: "Lord, show us the Father; we ask no more." The answer comes: "Anyone who has seen me has seen the Father. . . . I am not myself the source of the words I speak to you. . . . It is the Father who dwells in me doing his own work. . . . I am in the Father and the Father is in me" (vv. 8-10).

This puzzlement, uncertainty, mystification among Jesus' intimate associates is the device John uses to elicit expositions of who Jesus is in relation to God and the work God has called him to do on behalf of, not his friends only, but all humanity. Three times more will John employ characters in his play to have Jesus speak the truth of who he is in the faith of the Church. The Roman prefect Pilate is the first of these. The evangelist makes him stand for the uncomprehending "world" that, having heard the message of the kingship of God that is at the heart of the Gospel, cannot accept it (John 18:28-38). Thomas once again plays the foil for Jesus with his demand to see the nail marks in Jesus' hands and wounds in his side before he can believe he lives (John 20:25). Thomas has been recalled as a doubter ever since, without any amendment to his role as an early believer in Jesus' risen state (v. 28). The evangelist John has created him in words as both.

Mary of Magdala's first appearance in this gospel was a mention of her standing near the cross with another Mary and Jesus' mother (John 19:25). She is a third major character in the play of his death and risen life. John has her come to the tomb in the darkness of early Sunday morning, finding the stone moved from the inner chamber and rushing back to the city to tell Simon Peter and the other disciple whom Jesus loved of the body's disappearance. Her naïve question upon her return to the site is addressed to a man she takes to be the custodian of the property, who asks why she is crying so and whom she is looking for. She blurts out: "If it is you, sir, who removed him, tell me where you have laid him and I will take him away" (John 20:15). A woman alone carrying the dead weight of a corpse is beyond imagining, but John needs her proposal for his story. At that, the risen Lord calls her by name. He reveals himself to the woman of Magdala for who he is, but with an admonition. She must release him from the grasp of amazed delight with which she holds him about the feet and ankles. He has not returned to the old life. She must tell his companions in the task of proclaiming the reign of God that she has experienced him alive and that he must be off to the God whose worship they have in common.

The miracle accounts in this gospel, the multiplication of bread and fish and walking on the sea apart, are unique to John. All but the first two signs reported on, the water into wine and the healing of the royal official's son, serve as the occasion for Jesus' words, sometimes brief but more often lengthy. The first of Jesus' signs, as the evangelist calls them, is symbolic, like all that Jesus says and does in this gospel (John 2:1-11). His mother's report that the host's supply of wine is depleted, sudden death to a Middle-Eastern wedding party, is met with a response baffling on two counts. No grown man of that culture would think of addressing his mother as "Woman," nor would he use the Semitic phrase placed on Jesus' lips that says literally: "What to me and to you?" The next phrase, "My hour has not yet come" provides the key to what is going on here. John has made Jesus' mother a symbol of womanhood like Eve in Genesis, the mother of all the living, and water for ceremonial washing into wine of the messianic era. He has also provided the first clue in the drama, since the "hour" of Jesus' death and resurrection is that to which the entire narrative leads. Surprisingly, no discourse follows this sign. It is identified, however, as a revelation of Jesus' glory and the beginning of his disciples' belief in him.

The healing described as Jesus' second sign is unusual in John for its resemblance to the many instantaneous cures reported in the Synoptic

Gospels (John 4:46-54). Jesus is summoned to the bedside of a dying youth. He utters a cryptic remark of rebuff to the distraught father, telling him that along with his people he requires a sign or wonder before he can believe in Jesus. This clear challenge of the evangelist John to his contemporaries is followed, nonetheless, as with Jesus' acquiescence to his mother's request, with a deed of power, this time effected at a distance. "Go home," he tells the man, "your son will live." And so it happens. The symbolism at work here is fairly evident. In the irony that marks this gospel, the politically powerless Jesus works a deed of power for a man who is employed in the court of the sole Jew in the area who thinks he has power.

In inland Cana six stone jars, notably not Israel's sacred number seven, were discovered to hold the best vintage that was normally served last. The finest wine that will flow freely in the age to come (Hos 14:8; Amos 9:13-14; or in the mythical banquet hall of the Persian Ahasuerus, see Esth 1:7-8) inevitably comes to mind. Here in the lakeshore town of Capernaum, likewise in Galilee, the boy whose fever disappears instantly is the son of a man in the court of the quasi-royal personage, Herod Antipas of Galilee and Perea that flanks the Jordan. The empire had stripped him and his brothers of the title king that their father held, naming them tetrarchs instead. But in the popular Galilean mind this petty kingship did for royalty. Not so with his half brother Archelaus who had forfeited the title ethnarch in Judaea and been replaced by a Roman functionary titled prefect. The story of the miraculous healing of the royal official's son would undoubtedly have reached the ears of Antipas in the royal court, but that is not the use John makes of it. He may, however, have meant to endow Jesus' oblique encounter with petty kingship with symbolic significance as prefiguring the title king that would lie at the heart of the exchange with Pilate. Although only John composes a colloquy between the two in which he makes Pilate's misunderstanding of the Hebrew title messiah connote a political uprising, each of the gospels records a placard over Jesus' head on the cross in charcoal on gypsum-painted wood. It read "King of Judaea [the Jews]," in slightly different wordings in each gospel, as the charge against him. John represents it as not so much Pilate's irony as his contempt for this people who have no king in Judaea, where he himself now wields power.

This healing at a distance is designated Jesus' second sign, as the Cana miracle had been called the first. After this John ceases to enumerate them. The miraculous signs prove to be four or five more depending on whether the loaves and fishes and walking on the Sea are reckoned as two or one. This would make Jesus' restoration of the dead Lazarus to life either the seventh sign or the sixth, leaving Jesus' upraising from the dead as the seventh and final sign. In any case, the sequence of events in the Lazarus story is as memorable as anything in this gospel (John 11:1-44). Jesus gets the word from Lazarus's adult sisters of the severe illness of a man whom Jesus loves. Their home is in one of two Bethanys in the land of Israel, this one on a road east of Jerusalem around the foot of the Mount of Olives. The gospel has Jesus hear of the gravely ill Lazarus while he is in the place where John first baptized, identified as the other Bethany (John 10:40; 1:28). He delays there, remaining two days so as to proceed back across the Jordan on the third. His disciples try to dissuade him from a return to Judaea where his enemies pose a threat but, knowing somehow that Lazarus is already dead, he insists on the foot journey.

The two sisters go out singly in succession to greet him as he approaches the village. Jesus arrives on the fourth day after Lazarus's death, when the body was already beginning to decompose. The gospel makes a familiar turn at that point, this time from a tragic human situation to a calm exposé by Jesus. He spells out the important difference between the expected rising of the just on the last day that he and the sisters entertain in common with Pharisee thought and the resurrection and life he represents or, in fact, is in his own person. Only then does it become clear why John has placed this miracle of resuscitation on the eve of Jesus' entry into Jerusalem. The crowd that accompanied him as he approached the city as a Passover pilgrim witness his calling Lazarus from the tomb alive. Such was the final witness to him in the series of testimonies recorded in this gospel. The Galileans' enthusiasm for him, however, only helped to tighten the noose of enmity around him. John writes that crowds of Jews, that is, Judeans since everyone in this gospel is an ethnic Jew, had come to Bethany to view Jesus and the resuscitated Lazarus. The chief priests, the custodians of the Temple, hatch a plot to kill Lazarus, no less mortal than before, because the miracle had as its chief result the belief of many Jerusalem Jews in Jesus (John 11:53; 12:10). The one thing despotic authority cannot let flourish is mass support for the leadership of another. The priesthood's fear of the strength of the Jesus movement was transmitted to civil authority, which not only could not abide it but could do something about it.

The Last Supper Discourse

The Gospel according to John then moves into another phase than the narrative that had characterized it. Not precisely, however, since there had been numerous brief discourses placed on Jesus' lips in exposition of the Church's faith in him. These and the four longer ones to follow could only have been framed by a believer who, like Jesus' own immediate disciples, could look back on his cryptic utterances through a lens that showed a man who had been raised from the dead and ascended to heavenly glory. Faith in this risen Christ and Lord is responsible for the four homilies attributed to him at the Passover supper with his friends.

The first of these is now the bulk of chapter 14 and concludes with the exhortation: "Get up. Let us go." The company may at that point have set out from where the meal in common was eaten. This did not keep the evangelist from appending two distinct commentaries on the original discourse, what are now chapters 15 and 16. Nor was this inspired homilizing yet at an end. The evangelist decided to tack on still another that had a fresh theme, Jesus as about to depart to the heavenly dwelling place he had spoken of to continue intercessory prayer—which is the essence of the priestly office—for his disciples: "Father, they are your gift to me; my desire is that they may be with me where I am, so that they may look upon my glory, which you have given me because you loved me before the world began" (John 17:24; see 2:22; 20:9; cf. Mark 9:9; Matt 8:31). It is not easy to render this Greek prose, which is an ever-upward spiral rather than the more familiar parallelism, but its repetitiveness and building of image upon image, phrase upon phrase, identifies it clearly as Semitic writing.

The final discourse is basically a farewell address that enjoins on Jesus' disciples mutual love in his absence. This must be the distinguishing characteristic of such discipleship (John 13:34-35). His having departed from those who believe in him is made very clear by the wording, making this a charge to the early Church. It is not the earthly Jesus who is central to this transcendental reflection but, rather, the mysterious intimacy and common life of the Son with the Father who is God. Yet the two are not alone in the infinite reaches of deity. Another is sent from the Father at the Son's request who cannot be a creature but is necessarily a participant in the fullness of godhead because originating from the Father through the Son (John 14:15-17). The gospel identifies this Holy Spirit by function, using the term "one summoned alongside" (*paráklētos*, in Latin *advocatus*, the word for a counselor at law in all the Romance languages). Jesus calls the Paraclete the Spirit of truth who will be with the disciples forever and not only with them but in them: "The Advocate, the Holy Spirit whom the Father will send in my name will teach you everything and remind you of all that I have told you" (John 14:26). In brief, the disciples are by no means bereft by Jesus' absence. A Vicar, or Stand-in, for him is the gift of God promised. The promise has been fulfilled by the indwelling Holy Spirit in the community of believers, the Church, ever since.

The mutual indwelling of Jesus and his disciples is illustrated by the grapevines found everywhere in the Middle East. The vine, or stock, and the branches that stem from it live the one life. A healthy vine bears grapes in plenty. So must disciples do in living lives of love, the divine love that has been imparted to them. Acting thus will be a fulfilling of the one commandment Jesus imposed lovingly upon his friends that will inevitably give glory to God. That phrase by no means has the creature supplying a need experienced by the Creator, which would be absurd. It describes testifying to the divine glory; the word in the Hebrew Bible, *kabhod*, is identical with deity itself. The word does not connote refulgence as might be expected but, surprisingly, is the word for "heavy." Hebrew is a graphic, pictorial language. All creation is light in weight relative to the massive weight of God. To glorify God is to acknowledge the sobering fact of the godliness of God. Loving each other with the love God bears to each and all is the only way the glory can be given. Once given it brings joy, not delight in the short term but another kind: "I have spoken thus to you, so that my joy may be in you, and your joy may be complete" (John 15:11).

The next homily, probably delivered often by its author before he committed it to writing, faithfully echoes the previous two. There had been a reminder of the resistance to Jesus and his message in many quarters: "If the world hates you, it hated me first, as you well know. If you belonged to the world, the world would love its own; but now I have chosen you, who do not belong to the world, and for that reason the world hates you" (John 15:18-19). Jesus' friends can expect nothing different, ever: banning from the weekly assembly by fellow Jews, death threats, the lot (John 15:18-19; 16:2). His disciples had had a taste of it while he was still with them. In his absence things will only get worse. They are plunged into grief at his sobering words that promise how it will be when he is no longer with them.

But have they forgotten his promise of the Advocate? Jesus' absence from the earthly scene had been made the condition of his sending that "Spirit of truth that issues from the Father" (John 15:26). The Spirit will continue to bear witness to Jesus and they must do the same, bear witness to him, against all odds. "When the Spirit of truth comes, he will guide you into all the truth; for he will not speak on his own authority, but will speak only what he hears . . . He will glorify me, for he will take what is mine and make it known to you." The Church has gone on that assurance ever since. It has not supposed that individuals should consult a book of words and let the Spirit teach them what to make of it but that a living voice speaking from the body whose head is Christ, should speak to and through them, and by their deeds of love, speak to the world.

The final homily in John's collection of four is in the form of a prayer of Jesus addressed to his Father. It sums up the christological faith of the Johannine church that the other first-century churches already professed in different words or, hearing John's, made his their own. The speaker Jesus is confident that he possessed the Father's glory with the Father before the world began. He says that now he can resume that glory because he has done the work the Father sent him to do. That work was to share with his friends, that is, everyone who has ever heard of him and all those who have not, the glory that is his in the measure that a limited humanity can receive it. Jesus speaks of all that he has taught the men and women whom the Father gave him as coming from the Father. None of the message is independently his; he is the agent who transmitted it. The message is a gift. John has been busy up to now calling the gift "life," *zōē*, the life of God, at times with the adjective *aiōnios*, the life of the final eon or age. What age is that? In the Jewish thought of Jesus' day it was the days of Messiah, an age that was to come, God alone knew when.

All the early preachers of the Gospel proclaimed the final age of human history as having begun with the resurrection of Jesus. The translation of *aiōnios* as "eternal" is very old, going back to the Latin of the third or fourth century. Eternity is a Greek concept meaning timelessness. There is no word like it in Hebrew or Aramaic, however, since all Semitic thought is linear, the before and after of Israel's or the world's history. This means that the phrase "eternal life" came to mean life with God after death, whereas for the evangelist John it was the reality of new life begun in the present life. He defines it as "knowing the only true God and Jesus Christ whom [God] has sent" (John 17:3). It is for the disciples' continued possession of this life that Jesus makes his prayer to the Father. This intercessory role, which is the work of a priest, has earned for this extended passage, chapter 17, the description "Jesus' high priestly prayer." It occurs in this Fourth Gospel as the introduction to his entry upon the work of heavenly sacrifice where he will be both victim and priest, "so that the love you had for me may be in them, and I in them" (John 17:17-26).

Chapter Five

Jesus' Death and Resurrection

A detailed account of the death of Yeshua, the Galilean from Nazareth, is first found in the Gospel according to Mark. There is a hypothesis that it was an edited version of a shorter narrative that was being transmitted orally and perhaps in writing but this cannot be proved. As the passion narrative appears in this gospel, the shortest of the four, it takes up two of what would later be fifteen chapters and is introductory to a final one of eight verses that speak of the discovery of the empty tomb of Jesus, buried there two days before (Mark 14:1–16:8). A young man in a white garment seated near the rolled-back stone at the mouth of the burial chamber speaks to three women who had gone at early dawn to anoint Jesus' body. The Sabbath had ended in darkness twelve hours before. "Do not be alarmed," he said to the trio, dumbstruck in his presence. "You are looking for Jesus of Nazareth, who was crucified. He has been raised; he is not here. See, there is the place where they laid him!" (Mark 16:6). In these few words there is announced the event unique in human history of a person alive again some forty hours after death and burial. Without this event, the corpse having lain there to decompose like any other, the world would almost certainly never have heard of Jesus in the long history of the Jewish people. Despite his teaching of how to live faithful to Israel's God and his reputation as a wonderworker, he might at most have merited the few lines awarded to him by the Jewish historian Flavius Josephus. The lines devoted to John the Baptist were more extensive but they were few enough (*Antiquities*, book XVIII, 63–64; 116–19). Jesus' arrest, vicious manhandling, and death on a cross are described in Mark's unelaborated prose as preliminary to the climactic event of his resurrection.

117

The Markan Passion Narrative as Basic to Matthew and Luke

This gospel speaks early of a plot by Pharisees and Herodians to put Jesus to death, without having provided reasons why that unlikely pair of conspirators should wish to do so. The first of these plotters were, so far as we can tell, zealous protagonists of the Oral Law that had been extracted creatively from Written Torah by their forebears of no more than a century before. These Pharisees, as they came to be called, had no record of violent behavior whatever. The Herodians, on the other hand, did. These were people largely out of power in Judaea, there being no son of Herod the Great incumbent there but only local disaffecteds or hangers on at the court of Herod Antipas in Galilee. That puppet king might well have wished to eliminate anyone whose popularity with crowds could be perceived as a threat to his power. We know that he did so with John the Baptist. The mention of a plot early in Jesus' public life is the storyteller's device of putting hearers of his chronicle on notice of what lay ahead. The summary of the sufferings, death, and resurrection of Jesus that he placed on Jesus' lips not once but three times were indications of how the narrative would end (Mark 8:31; 9:31; 10:33). As to the view Herod himself had of Jesus, Mark's only reference is a mention of Herod's superstitious fear that Jesus was John the Baptist—whom he had ordered beheaded—redivivus (Mark 6:16). This Herod is not named by Mark in Jesus' last hours. John's gospel does have Pilate referring Jesus to Herod Antipas on learning that he was a Galilean, therefore his political subject. The difference of detail is one of many that prove the impossibility of deriving a single, coherent sequence of events from the Scriptures. Their authors had access to different sources, contributed details of their own based on passages from the Scriptures, and in general were more interested in eliciting sympathy for this innocent sufferer than conveying a careful factual account.

Each of the four, however, possessed a few important factual data. There was certainly a remembered confrontation between Jesus and the men of commerce in the Temple's open court, a scuffle in which he overturned the money changers' tables. Mark has the leading priests' hearing of it as being confirmed in their resolve to find a way to put him to death. Jesus retreats to Bethany, the village that had been his stopping place on the way into the city, after the incident (11:15-19). From there Jesus' disciples followed his instructions to borrow a colt from its owner for Jesus' entry to Jerusalem as a Passover pilgrim. Mark has the priest custodians of Temple worship in league with the men of learning called scribes in a plot to eliminate Jesus (v. 18). This was presumably because of fear of Jesus' growing popularity, but it was triggered by his challenge to their venality in selling birds and beasts for sacrifice in Temple coinage only.

Following Jesus' vigorous action, he is described as returning from his base in Bethany to Jerusalem more than once to deliver some of his most provocative teaching. Pharisees and men of Herod's party try to entrap Jesus over whether Jews should pay taxes to the Roman emperor, leading to his request for a coin that bears the current Caesar's image and inscription. They have such a coin. He does not. He then gives the cryptic response: "Pay to Caesar what is Caesar's and to God what is God's," leaving them to figure out which is which (Mark 12:17). The Sadducees, who deny resurrection in the body, pose a bogus challenge by telling a tale of a woman successively married to seven brothers and outliving them all (Mark 12:20-23). Their question is: "At the resurrection whose wife will she be?" Jesus' answer has stood for the faith of the Church ever since that the resurrection bodies of the married will not be sexually engaged but will exist in an altered state. How this can be remains a mystery. Faith that there will be such a risen life, in part like the present life, meanwhile remains impervious to challenge.

Jesus then puts forward a teaching of his own, not in refutation of Sadducee tradition and not couched as a response to a challenge, although Matthew will make it such (Mark 12:35-37). It is undoubtedly the way the Markan church was proclaiming Jesus both as a descendant of David and as superior to that great one of Israel's past. God's Holy Spirit is assumed to be the author of a psalm sung at the enthronement of some king of Judah. It has Israel's God, the LORD, confirming the new sovereign, called "my lord," in power by having him take a seat at the LORD's mythical right hand. From there he will overcome all of Israel's enemies. The gospel's point is that Jesus, a Davidic offspring and as such the Messiah, must be far superior to David in that role if the king over Israel's twelve tribes can address him respectfully as his "lord." This was a title that the Caesar or emperor had adopted for himself (*Kýrios*). The early Church was already calling Jesus "Lord" in a much more than political sense and quoting a psalm to prove the correctness of the usage.

The teaching quoted by Mark as if spoken by Jesus of himself is not the last delivered in Jerusalem before his Passover supper with his friends and his arrest. The evangelist provides at this point what is for him a lengthy discourse in which Jesus is made to counsel his disciples on how to react if the Last Day should overtake them. The description of that chaotic time is clothed in words and phrases so close to an account of the actual events of the sack of Jerusalem forty years later that Mark has to have been familiar with those horrendous happenings.

"You see these great buildings? Not one stone will be left upon another; they will all be thrown down. . . . When you hear of wars and rumours of war, do not be alarmed. . . . The end is not yet. . . . When you see the desolating sacrilege set up where it ought not to be (reader, you will know it), then those who are in Judaea must take to the hills" (Mark 13:2, 7, 14). The frenzy of inhabitants of a city under siege goes on and on but the remembrance of things past is interlarded with dire warnings of cosmic catastrophe in days to come (Mark 13:24-25; Isa 13:10; Joel 2:10). With this as background the Son of Man will be seen coming in the clouds with great power and glory, summoning his chosen from the four corners of the earth. For this coming the chosen must always be watchful, alert. The day and time are known only to the Father, not even to the angels or the Son. "On guard! Keep watch!" Jesus teaches.

The scheme of chief priests and scribes to seize Jesus and put him to death is repeated, but any action is deferred out of fear of the crowds. As he sits at table in Bethany in the house of a leper (not Hansen's disease), an unnamed woman at the dinner pours precious ointment on Jesus' head, surely symbolic of his anointed status as Messiah (Matt 26:6). When some present complain at the waste, Judas stalks out of the house, makes a deal to betray Jesus for money, and begins to seek an opportunity to hand him over. In another gospel narrative the whole company passes around the bread that Jesus has blessed, broken, and said of it that this is his body; and they drink one of the four cups of wine traditional at a Passover meal, a cup that Jesus has called "my blood, the blood of the covenant, shed for the many" (Mark 14:24). Jesus then utters a vow not to drink of it again until he shall drink it new in the kingship of God. Why does Jesus speak of abstaining from wine, having shared it with others? He is portrayed as fasting until he shall enter on the new life that will be his after his death. The gathered company then departs the supper room, singing the Great Hallel that was traditional at the close of a Passover supper (Mark 14:26; Pss 114[115]–118[119]).

The Galileans who had come to Jerusalem for the feast were remembered by Jesus' disciples and their wives, plus some unattached women, to have welcomed him as he entered the city, as was the custom with pilgrims having come from all directions. The tradition of leafy branches spread on the road before the man on a donkey, identified as of palm only by John, is certainly a historical reminiscence. Matthew and Luke speak of people laying down their garments as well. The cry of Hosanna! (in Hebrew, *Hoshia nna*, Save we beseech you!) is found in one of the psalms that provides the messianic wording found in Mark and other gospels (Ps 118:25, 26-27; see Zech 9:9 for a king and savior who will come to Jerusalem meek and riding on the colt of an ass). Jesus' prayer in the place called Gethsemane would have been equally well remembered.

After that, the reminiscences so well recorded and transmitted would have been: Judas's betrayal of the Master, for what motive we shall never be sure; Jesus' arrest by a crowd of military thugs led by Judas to the place where Jesus prayed; his appearance before a Jewish court of some sort that turned him over to civil authority as guilty of "leading the people astray," that is, in revolt against the Roman Empire; an appearance before its representative Pontius Pilate who found him guilty on that charge and sentenced him along with two others; and, finally, death by crucifixion. That he was subjected to this mode of execution would have been well remembered by many Galileans in the crowd, just as the damning detail that all his disciples had fled the scene was known to his followers. Only his mother, some other women, and one male disciple especially beloved of Jesus were recorded by John to have stood somewhere close to the stake and crossbar that was his instrument of death. From this bare but essential set of recollections the first passion narrative was framed and, after it, the others. Some disciples may well have told again and again the dramatic exchange between Jesus and the handful of Temple police sent to arrest him.

Mark tells of an unnamed bystander making a lunge with the knife from his belt at a slave of the high priest and, in the scuffle, cutting off his ear (Mark 14:47). Could a friend of Jesus have succeeded at this against a member of an armed band? Yes, if he were brandishing it threateningly and had brought it close to the head of a member of the arresting party. John, who is more careful about details than the other three, gives the slave's name as Malchus (John 18:10; Mark 14:47; see Luke 22:51). It is Luke who says the ear was severed and has Jesus heal the injury on the spot.

Who, if any, among the disciples might have heard the questioning by members of the Temple priesthood is a doubtful matter. John does say, however, that a disciple known to the high priest accompanied Peter and gained entry to the courtyard with Jesus, leaving Peter at the gate outside until the disciple spoke to the gatekeeper and got him admitted.

This same gospel writer says that Jesus was led to Annas, the father-in-law of the high priest Caiaphas, first and then by him to Caiaphas himself (John 18:13). Matthew gives the high priest's name, as neither Mark nor Luke do. In the matter of which priestly authority questioned Jesus about his teaching, Mark reports it as the chief priests and the whole council (Mark 14:55-59; Luke 22:66). Matthew follows him in this, word for word, while Luke writes of the elders of the people and places the chief priests and scribes in apposition as those who led Jesus away to the council. They sought testimony against Jesus to have him executed, but it was false testimony and the witnesses did not agree.

Mark has used the intercalation or sandwich technique of telling a story within a story six times (of which 5:21-24 [25-34] 35-43 and 11:12-14 [15-19] 20-26 are perhaps the best known) before framing the inquest of the council (Sanhedrin) between Peter's vehement declaration that he would never deny Jesus and his later doing exactly that (14:54 [55-65] 66-72). Peter has followed Jesus at a distance into the high priest's courtyard and seats himself among the Temple guards warming himself at the fire. Since Mark has had the arresting party bring Jesus directly from Gethsemane to a hearing before the entire Sanhedrin, the impression clearly given is that there was a night session of a representative number of that body of seventy (Mark 14:29-31, 53-65, 66-72). Luke, who follows Mark in his narrative, if not as faithfully as Matthew, is alone in saying that a slave girl saw Peter by the light of the fire. This means that he assumes that there was a "night trial," as the centuries of gospel hearers have assumed ever since.

But Mark was writing a gospel, not a modern-style history. He is at all points proclaiming who Jesus is, an innocent sufferer, and that those who would be his followers must suffer with him. Peter has affirmed that he will endure even death in proof of his fidelity to Jesus. Moments later in a scenario composed by Mark we hear the probable cause of priestly antipathy: Jesus' preaching against the conduct of Temple worship, colored by the evangelist's knowledge that it already has been destroyed in the Roman siege of the year 70. Mark couples with it a statement of who Jesus is, for whose cause early believers will have to suffer. The high priest is thus given the lines describing Jesus in the eyes of later faith in him. He is "Messiah." He is "son of the Blessed One," the LORD who is the God of Israel (14:61). Jesus' acknowledgment, "I am" that one, is a faith statement of the early Church. As posed, it does not have the character of blasphemy that the high priest says he has just heard. For that offense there must be either a direct cursing of God or attack of some sort on the Blessed One. Probably at issue was the early proclamation of Jesus' sonship of God, a union so participative of divine power that the oneness of godhead was taken to be denied. In any case, Mark adds to Jesus' acquiescence in the high priest's charge the faith of believers in him that he is now seated at the right hand of the Power. This phrase had been merely figurative in a psalm (Ps 110:1) but is now taken to mean that Jesus as Son of Man or the Human One would come with the clouds of heaven (Dan 7:13). This was a vision from the age of the Maccabean revolt that foresaw a tiny Israel victorious under the Ancient of Days over all its enemies.

The Roman Legionaries and the Pilate Characterization

Mark has the entire assemblage decide that Jesus is guilty and deserves to die. He proceeds to recount the indignities Jesus suffered at the hands of "some" of them. They spit upon him, in the Middle East a sign of contempt, strike him while he is blindfolded, and taunt him with the demand that he "Prophesy!" Perhaps realizing how unbefitting such behavior is of leading figures, Mark has the guards standing by as the ones who shower Jesus with blows. This is the beginning of the variety of torment and torture Jesus is subjected to, as described in the four gospels. There is no overall agreement as to who did what. Luke adds to the core Markan narrative, "And so they went on heaping insults upon him" (22:65). The major acts of brutality are reserved in this gospel to the Roman legionaries after Jesus has been turned over to Pilate. The Sanhedrin in Mark had found him guilty of blasphemy, a religious charge in which the governor would have had no interest unless it were somehow seen to have a civil and criminal overtone. Pilate asks Jesus in a brief hearing if he is king of Judaea/the Jews and gets the noncommunicative answer, "You say so." In the other three gospels Pilate poses the same query and receives a similar response. Chief priests and elders are in on this scene and they pour accusations into Pilate's hearing. The governor was "amazed" at the magnitude of the charge, criminal revolt, which the claim of kingship would have constituted, and the silence of the accused on this matter in his defense. Pilate goes on to make an equally amazing offer to the festival crowd, the chance to release one prisoner of their choice. Will the crowd cry out for his release or that of Jesus? Mark presents amnesty as if it were a Passover pilgrimage custom on Rome's part. Jewish history, however, knows nothing of it. It is also contrary to anything we know of Pilate's conduct toward the subject

Jewish people of his ten years in office. Most amazing is the reason Mark gives for the imprisonment of Barabbas. He is described as an insurgent sentenced and incarcerated for the "uprising," again an event of which we know nothing in that decade. The final implausibility in the tale is the man's name. Barabbas quite simply means "son of the Father," with a final *sigma* added to *abba* because the gospel is written in Greek. No such Jewish name has ever been encountered, probably because every man is the son of some father known or unknown. But Jesus was, to faith, the unique son of a heavenly Father. Perhaps, then, the occurrence of the story in the four gospels is attributable to an early midrash or homiletic expansion on the Father-Son relation that saw innocence judged guilty and guilt set free. For Mark, Jesus' only crime was that he was in fact "King of the Jews" in a way Pilate could not be expected to fathom.

This is the point at which Pilate—noted in the only portrait we have of him from Jewish historian Josephus for his swift judgments against any resistance to imperial authority and his slaughter of many Jews[1]— begins to take Jesus' part. Pilate is puzzled by the crowd's outcry, "Crucify him!" and asks what crime Jesus has committed. Remembering that we have here a piece of religious writing rather than a historical account, we have to ask why Mark does this. Pilate's subsequent attempt to exercise clemency, in which Matthew and Luke follow him and which John develops at length, can only be the creation of a contrast between the behavior of a pagan and that of Jesus' own people. It is impossible to know the motivations of the evangelists in this matter, or it may be the motivation of the sources they drew upon. Some interpreters of the gospels have speculated that they used the passion narratives as a means of defense of the earliest Christians against harassment by imperial authorities. That is not likely since each of the gospels was intended for circulation within Christian circles only and probably never came to be known by political authority. In any case, a favorable view of one functionary would not have provided a protective shield. The man in question, Pontius Pilatus, was ultimately removed from office for a mishandling of several tense situations in Rome's government of the Judaean people.

The depiction of Pilate, faced with the prisoner Jesus, has to be accounted for on other grounds. The story of a dream Pilate's wife had on the previous night provides a clue (Matt 27:19). As there is no way for any Jewish disciple of Jesus to have known of such an exchange between

---

[1] *Jewish War*, book III, 169–77; *Antiquities*, book XVIII, 55–59, 62, 87–89.

spouses, it has to be a story devised to affirm Jesus' innocence: "Have nothing to do with that just man," she tells him. The pagan couple is made to realize what the Temple priesthood could not or did not: Jesus' justness, which is a Jewish, not a Roman, term for innocence. Pilate's protagonism of Jesus on the suspicion that he had done no wrong could only have been a result of Jewish shock at Jesus' death sentence, a shock that lasted for decades. How could there be, the early Church wondered, any members of their own people who would want Jesus dead? They set in stark contrast to this wish the judicious conduct of a pagan, one noted for his cruel repression of the Jewish people, as if he were as puzzled as they. The ironic reversal has escaped generations of Christians to this day who still read the story as literally true. There has even been a devotion to St. Procula, the name devised by legend for Pilate's wife in the Coptic Church.

John has situated the hearing before Pilate in early morning, that is, shortly after 6:00 a.m. when the whole city came alive. He has identified Jesus' trial and death as happening on the Preparation Day for Passover, rather than on the first day of the feast like the other evangelists, but also on a Friday. The Jews who might have had entry to Pilate's temporary headquarters stay outside to avoid ritual defilement, leaving them free to eat the Passover meal. Then, with Jesus inside the building, the gospel has the prefect come out, go in, then bring Jesus out to be mocked, come out again to address the crowd, and go in once more for an exchange with Jesus. The whole sequence is made a setting for a theological exposition of what exactly the kingship of Jesus consists in: not a rule of this world but over minds and hearts.

Returning to the brutality Jesus experienced at the hands of Roman soldiery, it is reported as having taken place in the *praetorium* or military garrison that Pilate used as his headquarters while in Jerusalem. We know that he hated the city for its heat and its turbulence, with intermittent riots directed against the occupying army and its empire. Normally he spent the year at Caesarea enjoying the cool breezes that come off the Mediterranean. But he did not stay there during the three pilgrimage feasts, of which Passover in the spring was the chief. For a long time archaeologists and guides of Christian pilgrims have thought that the fortress Antonia on the Via Dolorosa, north of the plaza behind the Second Temple as Jews call it, was the site of his headquarters. More recent archaeological work has settled on the ruins of a palace Herod built for himself, the foundation of which is still to be seen near what became fifteen centuries later the Jaffa gate of the old city. Jesus is led inside the palace, which also served as a military garrison, and there he is subjected to the brutal treatment normal for prisoners the world over and to this day. Mark has him decked out in a purple cloak, which Matthew will correct to scarlet, the military rather than the royal color, with a reed placed in his hand to simulate a scepter and a crown woven of buckthorns on his head. "Woven" or "plaited" is the Mark and Matthew word; Luke omits any verb whatever. But anyone familiar with the North American pyracantha, or firethorn, with its relatively short spikes, knows that you do not delicately weave a crown of it. If it happened as described, branches from a thornbush would have been beaten into Jesus' skull. There is every likelihood that his subjection to mockery of this sort was remembered by his disciples, especially if as John has it he was publicly exposed for display (John 19:5). This would have been a graphic lesson to the Jewish pilgrim crowd from Galilee, in particular, of the folly of attempting a revolt. The outcry, "Crucify him!" (Mark 15:14) could scarcely have come from Jewish throats applauding one more cruelty of the oppressor. If it was heard at all in that noisy mob scene it would have been, "Crucify *them*," directed not at Jesus but at the two who died with him. That is because the gospel word describing them is ambiguous and may mean bandits on the high roads who preyed on their own people. It is far more likely, however, to have described insurrectionists, Jewish patriots, whose crucifixion the pilgrimage crowds would scarcely have applauded.

The torture Jesus was subjected to in Mark's passion narrative is described succinctly in what are now five verses (15:16-20). That account has Jesus stripped of the cloak and given back his own clothes, which Matthew follows, if not in exact wording. Matthew adds to the Barabbas incident a gesture of Pilate. Once he has asked the crowd, "What evil has he done?" and has seen that his attempts to release Jesus are going nowhere, Pilate performs a characteristically Jewish gesture—one totally unlikely to have been done by a pagan Roman—washing his hands publicly as a sign of innocence of "this man's blood" (Matt 27:24). Mention of the practice is found several times in the Scriptures (Deut 21:6-7; Ps 26:6; for a declaration of innocence of bloodshed, Josh 2:19; Acts 20:26). When the people cry with one voice in response to Pilate's action, "His blood be on us and on our children," they use a phrase that is likewise a claim of innocence, meaning may our family suffer the consequences for generations if we are guilty of this crime. Nowhere in the Scriptures does it mean acknowledgement of guilt. (For attribution, see Jer 26:15; 51:35). Because a gentile Church has been ignorant of this as well as many other Semitic locutions, it has tragically misread its own biblical heritage. Matthew attributes the outcry to "the whole people," meaning the assembled crowd, but while he is at pains to implicate the Temple priesthood in Jesus' death he scarcely intends to say that the Jewish people are accepting the guilt of the death of one of their own for generations to come. But that is the way gentile Christians have understood it, to the pain and persecution of Jews at Christian hands for centuries. Matthew, like the other evangelists, is very much a Jew. He is familiar with the Roman oppression of his people in the land of Israel, even though he, like the others, does not write from there. He has no interest in multiplying their woes, hence, could not conceivably have created a shout calculated to accomplish it.

Some Touches Proper to Luke and John

John has one more act of brutality not found in the other gospels, a flogging of Jesus ordered by Pilate when he yields to the crowd's demand and release of Barabbas (John 19:1). At that point, all four narratives speak of Jesus as handed over to be crucified. Luke and John phrase it, "delivered to their wishes," without specifying whose. Mark has a man named Simon, a pilgrim from Africa Cyrenaica, modern Libya, dragooned into carrying the heavy crossbar to Golgotha, the little hill outside the city wall that was the site of public executions. Mark identifies it as "the skull place," from the Aramaic word for it. The earth formation probably accounted for the name but the skull of an occasional nameless victim might have come to the surface there in a heavy rain.

Simon of Cyrene must have been a well-known figure among early believers because he is identified by the names of his two sons. The crossbeam he carried would have been very heavy indeed and not of trimmed wood. It was designed to be lashed to an upright beam already solidly planted in the earth. John alone, who does not have the tradition of the Cyrenean, says that Jesus carried the cross himself. The three synoptic writers tell of a hastily made placard placed on the stake over Jesus' head identifying him as "the King of Judaea/the Jews." This is a claim he never made but the one on which he was condemned as a potential insurrectionist. John spells out the history of the title in a fairly lengthy narrative in which Pilate, having ordered it with the expanded wording to follow "Jesus the Nazorean," is challenged by the crowd to revise it to read: "This man said 'I am king of the Jews.'" Pilate is adamant, saying, "What I have written I have written" (John 19:19-22). This has become a watchword for the ages of standing firm on one's position, *Quod scripsi, scripsi.*

Luke provides a vignette proper to him alone in which great numbers of people follow Jesus and Simon to Calvary, the Greek *Kraníon*, in much later Latin *Calvus*, the Skull. Many women are among those who mourn Jesus in loud threnody. Jesus consoles the daughters of Jerusalem in their keening in words that echo a prophetic book: "They shall mourn for him as one mourns for an only son, a firstborn" (Zech 12:10, recalled in Luke 23:27). Their tears are misplaced, Jesus says. Those for whom their tears should be shed are their children and their children's children who in the future will "cry out to the mountains, 'Cover us,' and to the hills 'Fall upon us'" (Hos 10:8; see Isa 54:1). Hosea is quoting the lament of the women of the Northern Kingdom over the eighth-century invasion by Assyria, but Luke applies the instance of weeping and wailing to the sack of Jerusalem described earlier in his gospel at nearly chapter length. Jesus is made to foretell it here with the added proverbial statement of the green wood and the dry. The former is the present decade of the Jerusalem women's sorrow. It is as nothing compared to the indescribable grief that lies ahead for inhabitants of the city in its destruction, already known to Luke. The passage undoubtedly gave birth to the legend interpolated within a fourth- to fifth-century Latin *Gospel of Nicodemus* in which a certain compassionate Veronica along the way dried Jesus' face of blood and sweat, leaving his image on the cloth. Her name has been accounted for by the macaronic Latin and Greek for "true image," *vera icon*, but it probably originated long before that in the East when the name *Bereníkē* was awarded to the woman whom Jesus cured of hemorrhaging over a twelve-year period. Despite the legend's total unreliability it has had a place in Christian piety ever since.

Luke alone mentions that two bad actors (malfeasants, miscreants) were led off to be put to death with Jesus. The terms he uses are generic and leave us in the dark as to the nature of their crime. John leaves it at "two others" who were crucified with Jesus, while Mark and Matthew denominate them *lēstaí*, a term that can mean brigands or bandits but more likely in this case armed insurgents against Roman authority. If the word had the latter meaning only, we would have confirmation on why Pilate acted on all three, two for the actual crime of attempted revolt and Jesus on suspicion of it. Even without certitude as to the term's meaning, Pilate is much more likely to have punished in this drastic fashion fomenters of revolt than mere criminals against the public order.

The Crucifixion Proper

At the scene of his execution Jesus, according to Mark, is offered wine mixed with myrrh, thought to have a narcotic effect on the dying and rendered aromatic, perhaps to overcome nausea (see Prov 31:6). Jesus refuses the well-meant offer. Matthew reads the phrase in Mark and changes the potion to wine mixed with gall, either having in mind the metaphor of Psalm 69:22[21] or else an actual poison to bring Jesus' life to a quicker end. Mark does not say who divided Jesus' clothing among them, but Matthew and Luke name the means of decision. Casting lots could be by dice or the short straw or any other way. Only John names the soldiers as those who take the meager spoils, but he lingers on the action longer than the other three. Matthew makes the division occur after Jesus has been crucified. John does not say but speaks of a four-part division, one for each soldier. Ever the symbolist, John may wish it to stand for the empire's division of the land of Israel and trans-Jordan into four tetrarchies. He quotes a psalm in support of their act of dividing, saying that the verse of the lengthy poem about the harassment of an innocent Israelite by his enemies is fulfilled (see Ps 22:19). But John is much more interested in Jesus' seamless tunic. It is this, and not the four parceled-out parts of a garment, for which lots were cast. The symbolism is clearer here than in the act of division. The evangelists may have meant by the division nothing political but, rather, factional loyalties on the part of Jesus' spiritual heirs. Jesus' many phrases in John's Last Supper discourse about unity, a union as close as that between Father and Son, indicate his conviction that Jesus' heritage must be a company of followers undivided. It cannot be that the teaching Jesus has from his Father is symbolized by the seamless garment; that much can be taken for granted. It is a body of disciples unmarked by rivalries, antagonisms, or schisms who received from Jesus all the teaching he received from his Father: "No longer do I call you servants but friends . . . because I have disclosed to you everything that I heard from my Father" (John 15:15). They are friends not only to the now risen Lord but to each other, an undivided and, in ideal, an indivisible company of love.

Jesus, at the site of his execution, is lashed by his arms to the crossbar with huge spikes driven into his hands for good measure. The legionaries would then heave high his body and those of the other two, similarly affixed, onto the stakes in the ground that were rough-hewn trees. The soldiery was not unfamiliar with this mode of execution. We know from Roman writings who the victims were of this peculiarly cruel punishment that ended in death: deserters from the army (but not officers); bandits who murdered in the process; and, above all, revolutionaries against Roman rule. Pilate is known to have decreed death by crucifixion for many over his ten-year period in office. That Jesus, a village artisan whose only known public career was as a teacher of Torah, should have been chosen for it is credible only if he were suspect of the last of those crimes. If the two men who were executed on either side of him were guilty of conspiracy in mounting an uprising, Jesus may have been erroneously condemned for participating in the same plot. Pilate would not have been overly careful in soliciting evidence on the point. Accusation alone would have been sufficient. As to the Temple priesthood's wanting him eliminated, it could not have had anything to do with his public teaching on any matter except threats of the Temple's destruction. The priests had been a learned class centuries before but in Jesus' day simply were not. Their sole function was to engage in and oversee Temple worship. Such was the case even with the hundreds of humble men of priestly lineage like Zechariah, father of John the Baptizer. Jesus' fulminating in the very Temple court against the conduct of public cult was all that was needed to incur the chief priests' deep-seated hostility. He may have prophesied that this holy house of the people would one day be forsaken and desolate, or perhaps some disciples framed that as a prediction after it was fact. It does not matter (Matt 22:38; Luke 13:35). Whether it was a foretelling or not it was all of a piece with the supposition of an early Christian prophet that Caiaphas, in the prophetic role priests once exercised at sacred shrines, must have said to the Sanhedrin after the Lazarus miracle: "You do not grasp the situation at all; you cannot realize that it is more to your interest that one man die for the people than that the whole nation be destroyed" (John 11:49-50). This counsel of throwing a hostage to fortune may have done something to keep the imperial troops from demolishing the city for another forty years. It was in any case an unconscious prophecy of a much larger event, the redemption of the world, and meant to be such by the Johannine author.

And now the event itself was at hand. Mark places the crucifixion at nine in the morning, three hours after the council's decision to hand Jesus over to Pilate (Mark 15:25).[2] Mark later says it was noon when

[2] On details of this cruel method of execution and who was subjected to it, see Gerard S. Sloyan, *The Crucifixion of Jesus: History, Myth, Faith* (Minneapolis: Fortress Press, 1995), 1–44.

darkness fell over the whole land, which lasted until three. Matthew and Luke follow him in this (Mark 15:33; Matt 27:45; Luke 23:44). John provides the detail that the placard above Jesus' head giving the *titlos*, the crime or cause of the death penalty, was in Hebrew (undoubtedly Aramaic), Latin, and Greek (John 19:20). Galilean women were onlookers at the tragedy from a distance, five of them if Salome and the mother of James and John, Zebedee's sons, are a different person. John places Jesus' mother and her sister there as well as two of the others whom the Synoptics name. The disciple whom Jesus loved stands alongside Jesus' mother, and when Jesus sees them he calls out from the cross, "'Woman [the same address as at Cana], there is your son,' and to the disciple, 'There is your mother,'" followed by the injunction to take her into his house (John 19:26-27). This sounds like the normal concern of an adult son at the point of death, but nothing in John's gospel means as little as it says. The Church of East and West has always taken Jesus' commitment of his mother, almost certainly a widow because there is no mention of Joseph, to the care of a beloved friend as standing for the position of Mary in the life of the Church: motherhood not only of the apostolic company but of all "those who will believe in me through their word" (John 17:20). The two instructions together are Jesus' spoken last will and testament.

The absence from the cross of any other male disciple as Jesus breathed his last is noteworthy. Two of the synoptic authors have them all turning tail and running as Jesus is apprehended at prayer in Gethsemane, the place of "the olive press." Mark does more. He adds the flight of a fearful young man, in such haste that he leaves behind the linen cloth in which his body is wrapped and runs off naked. Strangely light clothing even for a warm spring night in Roman Palestine. But Mark, who is himself an accomplished symbolist, places a young man in a white robe at the right side of the entry to the tomb to proclaim its emptiness. This is surely the rehabilitation of a disciple in his cowardice, just as the story of Peter's threefold protestation of his love for Jesus is a symbol of the repentance of all the disciples (John 21:15-17).

The elevation and affixing of Jesus to a cross is spoken of in a single sentence in each of the gospels, despite the duration of Jesus' agony while hanging there. The gospels devote more words to the continuation of his torment and taunting from the previous night of his captivity. The mockery is not the normal vilification of three criminals who might be supposed by Passover pilgrims to be guilty of mugging, robbery, and murder on the roads. It is placed on the lips, not of ordinary onlookers—

the crowd drawn to all public executions—but of antagonists aware of the "false testimony" against Jesus that maintained he had said, "I will pull down this temple, made with human hands, and in three days I will build another, not made with human hands" (Mark 15:29; 14:58-59). Mark has the chief priests and scribes joining in this chorus of scoffers as part of his determination to make them the villains of the piece. "He saved others but he cannot save himself. Let [him] come down now from the cross. If we see that, we shall believe" (Mark 15:31-32). What we probably hear in these taunts is the skepticism that the earliest proclaimers of a crucified and risen Messiah met with, and on its very terms. Mark and the others were proclaiming the Gospel based on two basic events, death and resurrection, rather than providing an exact chronicle of happenings or verbal exchanges. The latter they composed for their apologetic, theological purposes and as Jews would have called Jesus, "King of Israel," rather than the gentile Pilate's, "King of Judaea/the Jews." The same is true of the reviling of Jesus by the two criminals crucified with him, which Luke alone expands from a mere mention to a memorable dialogue. One of the two hanging there demands that Jesus who "saved others" save himself and them if he is Israel's Messiah. The other shouts over the din of the crowd to his fellow lawbreaker: "Have you no fear of God? You are under the same sentence as he is. . . . We after all are paying the price for our crimes but this man has done no wrong." And then he utters the plea that has merited him the title "the Good Thief," or the legendary St. Dismas: "Jesus, remember me when you come into your kingdom," a phrase redolent of the prayer Jesus taught. To it Jesus replied, "Truly I tell you, this day you will be with me in Paradise" (Luke 23:43). This Persian word for a garden, taken over into Hebrew, occurs elsewhere in the New Testament, as it does in some non-canonical Hebrew scriptures, to describe a transcendent place of blessedness, the Paradise of God (see 2 Cor 12:4; Rev 2:7). In transliterated Arabic in the Holy Qurʾan it has become the term for the bliss of heaven.

This utterance of Jesus, along with his words to his mother and a disciple, are two of Jesus' seven last words culled from the four gospels. The others are: "My God, my God, why have you forsaken me?" (Mark 15:34; Matt 27:46; Ps 22:2[1]); "Father, forgive them, for they know not what they do" (Luke 22:34; see Acts 7:60; 3:17); "I thirst!" (John 19:28; Ps 69:22[21]); "It is accomplished" (v. 30); and "Father, into your hands I commit my spirit" (Luke 23:46). The last of these is meant to affirm Jesus' death as voluntary, not coerced, while the one before it is a succinct form of "I have finished the work that you gave me to do" (John 17:4).

The words given first in transliterated Aramaic, *Eloi, Eloi,* then Greek, are the opening words of a psalm that ends in total trust in the LORD. Jesus' prayer of forgiveness of his executioners does not occur in any early manuscript and was probably taken from Stephen's prayer for those stoning him to death (Acts 7:60). Each of the seven is in some sense the fulfillment of some place in Scripture in the rabbinic manner, chiefly of the just Jew as innocent sufferer even though only one word from the cross is cited as such, namely, John in one place (see John 19:28; Pss 22 and 69, among others; Wis 2:10–3:9).

All Other References to Jesus' Death Unlike These Playbooks

The most remarkable thing about the four passion narratives is the verbal restraint that marks them. Each evangelist has written a passion play, not a history of Jesus' last days and hours in the modern manner. All four are good drama in their economy of words and settings, their succession of short scenes and shifts of scene, and the climax with which each concludes. The plethora of realistic passion plays that began to be staged in the second millennium in the Catholic West are all of them bad drama. The histrionics of Judas, Peter, the chief priests, and Mary of Magdala—the latter very early confused with a woman of the streets—are desperately bad drama. This is equally true of the production that has run each decade for 350 years at Oberammergau and Mel Gibson's epic movie in ruddy gore, *The Passion of the Christ.* Aside from vastly inferior playbooks with bogus dialogue devised for a variety of characters in bathrobes, there is the basically incorrect theological assumption that the human race was redeemed from sin from Adam to Christ and forever after by the bludgeoning and physical pain of a member of the human race. From St. Paul's authentic letters, those of his disciples written after his death, and the other canonical New Testament writings that date from 70 to 135, it is clear that all written proclamations of human redemption in Christ and the Spirit confined themselves to one-word references to the first stage in that one act of God: Jesus' "death," his "blood," his "sufferings," or his "obedience," with no elaboration of detail whatever.

Only once outside the gospels and Luke's book of Acts is there mention of anyone who figured in Jesus' last days. It occurs in a late first-century deutero-Pauline letter and speaks of Pontius Pilate, "before whom Jesus Christ made that noble confession in testimony. . . . In the presence of God" (1 Tim 6:13). Saint Paul's authentic correspondence can be dated at least a decade before Mark was written, but that does not explain the total silence regarding passion narrative details in the other first-century writings. It is that, while the gospels narrated Jesus' life, teachings, death, and resurrection as the acts of a human being whom God chose to achieve redemption or a new life for the human race, other apostolic teachers chose modes of proclaiming it in almost laconic phrasing. They characteristically employed a single word: "life," "sufferings," "death," "upraising," "glorification," to stand for the entire divine-human act. Saint Paul does not normally let emotion color the phrasing of his references to God's redemptive deed, but in one place he does write in open-mouthed admiration and gratitude to the Son of God "who loved me and gave himself up for me" (Gal 2:20). The erroneously named Hebrews likewise departs once from its sustained argument that Christ is behind the veil of the heavens acting as humanity's great high priest when it appeals to the emotions of the hearer or reader: "In the course of his earthly life he offered up prayers and petitions, with loud cries and tears, to God who was able to deliver him from death. Because of his devotion his prayer was heard; son though he was, he learned obedience through his sufferings" (Heb 5:7-9). The passage goes on: "and once perfected, he became the source of salvation for all who obey him."

The observations in the paragraph above are not meant to call into question the part Jesus' sufferings had in the world's salvation. They are only a caution against falsely supposing that his patient endurance of humiliation and pain is what, alone, accomplished humanity's victory over sin and death. There has even been a badly flawed theological supposition that the torments he endured that ended in death should have been visited on us in our sins, not on him the sinless one. The watchword "Christ in our place" means nothing of the sort. Correctly understood, it means that there was one thoroughly obedient human being who lived and died before God as all of us ought and was raised up from the dead as all of us hope to be. God accepted this obedience as the purchase price, so to say, of a sinful humanity released from its captivity to sin. Redemption, reconciliation, justification, sanctification, and salvation on the Last Day are all figures of speech for a global, even cosmic reality. If humanity, which alone can give tongue to the cosmos, accepts the gift held out to it (first having heard of it, in response to the missionary command) and lives humanly as it ought, meaning humanity at its best, then every good thing will be given in this life and a life with God besides. The fullness, the consummation of this gift as experienced in the life of the man Jesus has yet to be spoken of at length in these pages.

The Resurrection of Jesus that Changed Everything

The writer known as Mark has apprised those who first heard his gospel not once but three times as to how Jesus' earthly life will end. He will be rejected and handed over to the power of men who will deliver him up to the gentiles, who will mock him, spit upon him, flog him, and then kill him; but three days later he will rise from the dead. Mark's hearers did not need to be told that God would raise Jesus up on the third day. They already believed it because they had heard and accepted the apostolic preaching. But they might well have been surprised not only at the brevity of the risen life account but also at the odd way their teacher Mark has brought his narrative to its culminating point. He may have shared with them many times orally any of the several narratives of Jesus' risen life that were circulating in the mid-first century. But, assuming that he had, it is clear that he had another purpose in mind for the gospel he composed. It was to impel early believers to *share* the good news of the risen Christ, not to be dissuaded from doing so by anything or anyone, least of all by fear of reprisal for charging Jewish or gentile authority with a gross miscarriage of justice. The known associates of criminals are often rounded up and subjected to grim punishments. This can happen even to those as innocent as the person convicted. In any case, Mark's main message is, "You must fear no one. Spread the word!"

He goes about it by first bringing women disciples of Jesus to the burial site very early on what is today's Sun Day morning, the *Dies Solis* of the Roman but not the Jewish calendar, where it was Yom Aleph, First Day. Their purpose was to anoint the body in customary fashion. Most peoples of the world bury their dead on the day of death. Embalming is by no means a globally widespread practice. If a body is kept overnight it receives the customary care, but after a thorough washing aromatic spices are placed all around it to overcome the stench of early decomposition. It is a commonplace in countries like Italy to enter a church and see a body lying reposefully in death as if on a narrow bed (not a coffin) in an antechamber near the door of entry. The person's body is sure to be buried that night or at the latest early the next morning. The aroma of the chamber's flowers is pleasing to the nostrils of the visitor or passerby.

Thus did Mark transmit the tradition of three women known by name, two Marys and a Salome, who went to perform this task when the Sabbath's twenty-four hours were over and it was daylight. On their way they wondered how they could have access to the body, knowing that the mouth of the rock tomb would have been closed by rolling or dragging a rock the size of a huge millstone to cover the opening. Their well-founded suspicion on finding the stone rolled aside was that the body might have been stolen. In any case, they viewed the empty tomb in shock and surprise. Seated alongside it was a young man, probably the one who had fled naked two nights before, whose message was more important to the evangelist than the removal of the stone. The basic, flat statement came first, "He has been raised; he is not here," followed by the invitation to peer further in to see the place where two men friends had laid him. Then the youth, now splendidly dressed in a white garment, gives the command that explains the entire gospel passage. The first words of the young man as the women looked on dumbfounded had been: "Do not be alarmed." Now he says, "Go and tell his disciples and Peter, 'He is going ahead of you into Galilee; there you will see him, as he told you.'" Did they immediately go scurrying back to the city to impart this stupendous message? Not for a minute. "Then they went out and ran away from the tomb, trembling with amazement. They said nothing to anyone, for they were afraid" (Mark 16:8). Mark uses an unusual construction in his last sentence to make his hearers hang in midair, ". . . they were afraid, for . . ."

Early in the history of the Gospel according to Mark some pious persons who believed in it as publicly proclaimed thought there must be some mistake. No gospel should end this abruptly, least of all with the failure of three early women friends of Jesus to convey a message as important as this one. Out of fear? Fear of what or of whom? Their not having done as instructed, many supposed, was simply incredible.[3] Or

---

[3] Three endings to Mark's gospel by early Christians who thought that no gospel should end that way have survived. One, "The Longer Ending," has for all the centuries been considered a part of canonical Scripture, while the other two have not. It is printed in all Bibles as the lengthy continuation of v. 8 and then 9-20 of chap. 16. The ending is an anthology of verses taken from the following places in the New Testament: (9) John 20:16; Luke 8:2; (10) the Magdalene bringing news to the Eleven, John 20:18; (11) the disciples' unwillingness to believe her report, John 20: 19-29; (12) Jesus' self-disclosure to two disciples walking toward Emmaus, Luke 24:13-32; (13) they bring news to the others, who in Mark disbelieve them, Luke 24: 33-35; (14) Jesus appears to the Eleven at table, scolding them for their disbelief, Luke 24:36-40; (15) the missionary command, Matt 28:19-20; (16) the necessity of baptism, Matt 28:19; (17) the signs that will accompany the spread of the Gospel, Acts 2:4; 28:5; Mark 6:13; 9:38; Rom 15:19; (19) the ascension of Jesus, Acts 2:33; (20) a summary of the spread of the Gospel as reported chiefly in Acts. The "shorter ending," so-called, appears in four seventh- to ninth-century Greek manuscripts. It follows v. 8 and goes: "And they reported all the instructions briefly to Peter's companions. Afterwards Jesus himself,

so it would be if Mark were engaging in straight historical narrative, as he is in saying, "It was nine in the morning when they crucified him." But there were certain touches in the story up to this point to indicate that something more was going on than the recall of actual events. There is the calculated confusion between "Eloi" in a mixture of Hebrew and Aramaic with the name of Elijah. There is the rending of the Temple curtain at the exact moment of Jesus' last loud outcry. Finally, there is Pilate's agreement to let a member of the council have Jesus' body taken down from the cross. All this was a symbolism devised after the fact to account for Jesus' unique place in the life of his people Israel. There should be no surprise, then, that Mark should have used the conclusion of his narrative as a teaching moment for people who already had faith in its central event. They had known for several decades the reason why the tomb was found empty. They and later believers needed to hear again and again what to do about it. They had to proclaim that the Jesus they believed in, the man upraised from death and the tomb, was the Christ and sovereign Lord.

Three Non-Markan Ways of Bringing the Story to an End

The only two first-century writers that we have record of who edit Mark's ending are Matthew and Luke. As we might expect, each did so intelligently. Matthew reduces Mark's trio of women by eliminating Salome. But there, in his rhetorical style that magnifies the divine power at every turn, he has an earthquake as the women reach the tomb. He has an angel, not a youth, be the one to roll away the stone and promptly sit upon it. Matthew also has guards placed by the tomb to see that the

---

through them, sent forth from east to west the sacred and imperishable proclamation of eternal salvation. Amen." Everything about the wording betrays a later, literalist hand. Finally there is the fourth- to fifth-century ending known as the "Freer Logion" from its place in the Codex Washingtonensis in a gallery of the Smithsonian Institute. It occurs after v. 14 and runs: "And they excused themselves saying, 'This age of lawlessness and unbelief is under Satan, who does not allow the truth and power of God to prevail over the unclean things dominated by the spirits [or, does not allow the unclean things dominated by the spirits to grasp the truth and power of God]. Therefore, reveal your righteousness now.' They spoke to Christ. And Christ responded to them, 'The limit of the years of Satan's power is completed, but other terrible things draw near. And for those who sinned I was handed over to death, that they might return to the Truth and no longer sin, in order that they might inherit the spiritual and incorruptible heavenly glory of righteousness. But . . .'" This and the other two elaborations show what leaden prose later learned Christians were capable of in their anti-heretical zeal.

body is not stolen. These tremble and become as dead men, struck by the angel's bright clothing and overall appearance as of lightning. The address to the women is in the exact wording of Mark, but their departure from the tomb is in fulfillment of the instruction, with fear to be sure but also great joy as they "run to tell the disciples." Luke at this point has neither one young man nor one angel at the tomb but two men in dazzling garments. In providing the names of the "the women who had come from Galilee with him" he includes two of the familiar Marys and Joanna, whom he had mentioned earlier along with the Magdalene and Susanna as having supported the itinerant company out of their means (Matt 27:60; Mark 15:43-46; Luke 23:50-53; see Luke 8:2-3). The women arrive at the tomb very early on the first day of the week, find the stone rolled away, go inside, and do not find the body. Utterly at a loss, they are confronted by the men who say, "Why search among the dead for one who is alive? Remember how he told you while he was still in Galilee, that the Son of Man must be given over to the power of sinful men and be crucified, and must rise again on the third day" (Luke 24:5-6). Then they recalled Jesus' words. Returning from the tomb, they reported everything to the eleven and the others. But the apostles considered the story to be nonsense and did not believe the women. This sounds like an echo of the widespread skepticism the early proclaimers of the resurrected Christ must have encountered. Like any detail in these narratives, it is there for a purpose. In this case it serves as a lead in to the stories of Jesus in his risen state that establish the reality of his bodily upraising. It should not be taken as male resistance to a statement by women prone to be emotionally overwrought. The statement that Jesus lived again would have strained credulity no matter who made it, which is its meaning in the context of the gospel.

Matthew meanwhile, himself no mean master of the rhetorical elaboration Jews call *midrash*, has the women disciples fleeing the tomb to give the word to the others as instructed. They are caught up short by meeting Jesus on the road. Jesus greets them calmly in the Greek manner, *Chaírete*, "The grace of God be yours." Jesus would, of course, have said, "Shalom!" But how could they be at peace at the sight of him? In the turbulence of their emotions they bowed low and grasped him at the ankles in a sign not only of devotion but of adoration. Matthew then adds to this totally believable account the midrashic addendum spoken of above. Like Luke, Matthew has an abbreviated account of Mark's story of a member of the Sanhedrin, whom he describes rather as a wealthy disciple named Joseph of Arimathea, who has asked Pilate for Jesus' body and been given it for burial "in his own new tomb." Matthew also leaves the two Marys seated opposite the sepulcher rather than merely viewing it before leaving the site (Matt 27:60; Mark 15:43-46; Luke 23:50-53). Matthew continues the story with an incident that he alone has. On the Sabbath, the day after Jesus' execution, he has chief priests and Pharisees gather before Pilate to ask him to order that a guard be set over the sealed tomb until the third day, lest Jesus' disciples steal the body and claim that Jesus has been raised from the dead to validate his remembered prediction. Pilate acquiesces, requiring that the grave be made secure (Matt 27:62-66; 28:11-15). All this is preliminary to the reason for which the supposed precaution was taken. For while the women are on their way to deliver the angel's message the guards, who had been felled by the earthquake and the sight of the angel who rolled away the stone, have gone into the city to report everything to the chief priests. Those worthies offer the soldiers a substantial bribe to say that the corpse was stolen, and that is the story "that is current in Judaean circles to this day." If this rumor is still circulating as Matthew writes, he has composed his complex tale to demonstrate its utter falsehood.

His account of the two Marys standing in Jesus' path as they joyously depart the tomb is one of two narratives of the risen Jesus. Matthew concludes his gospel with the other. The disciples have made their way back to Galilee and are assembled at the unnamed mountain designated by Jesus as their last meeting place. Upon seeing Jesus they kneel in worship before him "but some are doubtful." This seems to describe the early Church in which some are still unsure in faith after several decades. Jesus approaches the eleven—no one has yet been chosen to replace Judas—and instead of engaging in a tearful leave taking they are given a solemn charge. Jesus tells them that, in virtue of the full authority that has been given to him in heaven on earth, they are commanded not simply to teach but to make disciples, either of all the gentile peoples or all the peoples of the earth including Israel. The word *ĕthnē* that Matthew uses, *goyim* in Aramaic, could mean either, in this context. The latter is more likely, as an amplification of Jesus' previous injunctions to his Jewish disciples to confine their evangelizing efforts to the house of Israel (Matt 28:19; 10:6; 15:24). The scope of his sending them forth is without limit. Their message is to be what God the Father of all peoples has done for them through the Son and in the Holy Spirit. The sign of acceptance of this message in faith is a bath in water in the threefold name of the one God. The phrase claiming "full authority" is an early Church statement of who the risen Jesus is, not simply Messiah, the Anointed of God for his own people, but Lord of all peoples under the Father who constituted him as such by upraising him from the dead. The missionary command is at the same time a statement of the Church's christological, ecclesiological, and sacramental faith. It represents the realization of early believers that God, in raising Jesus up from the dead, had done something not for his own people only but for the whole world.

Mark has no stories of appearances of the risen Jesus to his friends and Matthew has the two we have just reviewed. What, if any, are reported in Luke and John? Because Luke tells of two encounters that are intimately personal and John three that are the same, they are well remembered and repeated over the ages for different reasons than the concluding appearance in the Church-centered Matthew. Luke's statement that the tale of the women seemed to be nonsense to the unbelieving apostles was a prelude to the two appearance stories that immediately follow. In the first of these a pair who presumably knew Jesus well encounter him on the road to Emmaus but do not recognize him (Luke 24:13-35). The point of this story has to be Jesus' altered condition upon his resurrection. This was no resuscitation by God's power such as he had achieved for the daughter of Jairus, the widow's son in Nain, and Lazarus. All three returned to their old life. Not so Jesus. He was the same person after as before but evidently launched on a new life in another sphere. In spite of this he could still be present to people as in his former circumstances and in theirs. Luke the skilled storyteller reports the sorrow of the two men as they left Jerusalem at what might have been. "We had hoped that he was to be the liberator of Israel," is the way they express their dashed hopes (Luke 24:21). At that point Jesus deplores their dullness of heart and slowness to believe. Always the teacher, he begins to instruct them on the way all the Scriptures speak of him. The evangelists are ever at pains to convey right faith in Jesus, often placing it on his own lips. The men press Jesus to stay with them; he accepts and is soon seated at table with them. There they recognize him in "the breaking of bread." That was common practice at the start of a Jewish meal, but the phrase early came to designate the Lord's Supper or Eucharist. Luke uses it to identify the ritual act of the community in which the risen Jesus will best be known.

Upon their return to Jerusalem to share their adventure, the couple learns that the assembled disciples already know that Jesus has appeared to Simon. Almost on cue, "there he was, standing among them. Startled and terrified, they thought they were seeing a ghost" (v. 37). He was no wraith but one whose flesh could be touched and who, moreover, was hungry. Jesus asked them for something to eat. This tells us nothing of the condition of his glorified body. It does tell us that in Luke's day some in the community could be challenged: "Why do doubts arise in your minds?" Jesus' display of his hands and feet and eating a piece of cooked fish was a strong affirmation that his life in the body was real (Luke 24:36-43). This passage and that of the disciple Thomas in John's gospel may be speaking to early gnostic believers in the Gospel who have settled to their satisfaction on a spirit-only, heavenly Christ, not a flesh-and-blood human, either before or after Jesus' earthly lifetime.

John's account of the risen Christ occurs in two parts, the first in chapter 20 meant to be final (vv. 30-31) and the second in chapter 21, an addition in the spirit of the gospel by a disciple of "the one whom Jesus loved" who may have served as editor of the whole. This evangelist has shown a penchant for attaching individual's names to incidents as part of his narrative technique: Philip three times, Andrew twice, Mary of Bethany, Caiaphas, and Thomas twice before the doubting incident. At the same time John lets the mother of Jesus, the woman of Samaria, the man born blind, and the disciple Jesus loved go unnamed. He chooses one woman of the four or perhaps five who are named as the holy women from Galilee, Mary the Magdalene, as coming to the tomb alone (John 20:1) and Thomas, which means twin (as does *Didymos* in Greek), for a less-heroic role than his previous expression of bravado, "Let us, too, go and die with him" (John 11:16; 20:24-29). In any case, that one Mary has survived in memory as if only she had brought the news of Jesus Christ risen to the disciples, while Matthew credits her and "the other Mary" as having done it. Luke, speaking of the "apostles" rather than "disciples," says that Mary of Magdala was one of a larger company of women that reported the announcement of the two men, unpersuasive as it happened. The story of her standing near the empty tomb weeping, followed by Jesus' self-disclosure of his identity to her, resulted in her reporting to his "brothers," as he told her to, that he was ascending to their common Father (John 20:2, 17). The transmission of this message led to her being called in Christian tradition "the apostle of the apostles" and having the Creed recited on her feast day Mass in the Roman calendar, which is normally confined to apostles and martyrs.

But John's gospel has another tale to tell before it finishes that one. Simon Peter and the ever-anonymous "other disciple, the one whom Jesus loved," upon receiving Mary's message, "They have taken the Lord out of the tomb and we do not know where they have laid him," rush out to the site to see for themselves (John 20:3-9). The evangelist has referred to the one especially beloved of Jesus twice before (John 13:23; 19:26), but he also knows that Jesus had made the impetuous Peter the leader of the Twelve. He crafts a brief tale to credit each of the two with discovery but in distinct ways. The other disciple runs faster and gets to the tomb first, peers in and sees the grave cloths lying there but does not go in. Peter catches up with him, enters the chamber, and views the linen wrappings neatly folded with the cloth that had been around Jesus' head set apart. The other disciple then goes in, sees, and believes.

That not-quite relay race of the two has nothing to do with the beloved as the younger, swifter man, as has so often been depicted in realistic-type art. It is the evangelist's careful way of crediting Peter as first among the Twelve, while naming the other disciple as the first to believe what the linen winding cloths signified. In their neat array it is clear to him that this was no hasty grave robbery of a still-wrapped corpse but that Jesus' body was no longer there by an act of God. The special attention to the head cloth is John's way of describing the veneration with which Joseph and Nicodemus had prepared the body for entombment (John 19:38-40).

With that important distinction made between the first among the disciples and the other who for the evangelist was really the first, the story returns to Mary who has stayed at the tomb as the men leave (20:11). She peers into the tomb—Peter and the other disciples are by this time nowhere in sight—and is asked by the angels at either end of the empty stone slab why she is crying. She turns around and encounters a stranger who asks the same question. Just as with Luke's travelers on foot to Emmaus, she who knew Jesus well is made by the story not to recognize him. This evangelist, like the other, is making the point that the risen Lord is different in appearance, recognizable by the sound of his voice but not by sight. Jesus speaks her name and the contrived confusion in her mind with the one who tends the nearby olive garden is immediately removed. She exclaims, "My Teacher!" and does what any Oriental woman might do, lunges at his feet in loving embrace. The gospel then provides the clue to what this narrative is about: not an outpouring of affection, although there is that, but chiefly the difference between the man Jesus in his resurrected state and in his relatively brief life on earth. "Let me go," he says (not the erroneous "Do not touch me" of the Latin Bible's translation), "for I have not yet ascended to the Father," and then the message to the others as above. The meaning has to be that it is truly the Jesus of the Magdalene's amazement and affection but that he is fated shortly to leave her and all his other friends.

They cannot resume a life in common on the old terms. He must ascend to the Father.

The absence of Jesus from the earthly scene was something early proclaimers of his resurrection had to explain constantly. The mystery of his glorification by God that the Last Supper discourse spoke of in so many phrases, the upraising and ascent heavenward, was in fact one mystery not two. But there were evidently multiple appearances to former disciples remembered as well as the one to Saul of Tarsus a few years later, the main outlines of which entered into the tradition in stories that three of the gospels retained.

Two more need to be reported on and with that the gospel accounts of Jesus crucified and risen will be at an end. There are no others, only fanciful, legendary theological romances that began to be written a century and a half later.

The evangelist John tells of Jesus' self-disclosure to more than one disciple as having happened late that same day, the first day of the week. A "tale" in this context means simply a narrative, not a fiction. It was very much a reality for those to whom it happened, a remembered faith experience but now told in story form. The male disciples are assembled but behind locked doors for fear of the *Ioudaîoi*, in this gospel those Jews antagonistic to the Jesus-believing Jews of the evangelist's day. Jesus appears in their midst instantaneously to give them a gift. In a very few lines this is John's missionary command, quite unlike Matthew's account in wording, but Jesus' gift of the Spirit to forgive and withhold forgiveness resembles Matthew's binding and loosing texts. There is very little resemblance to Luke's Pentecost scene in the book of Acts. Jesus breathes on the assembled company—the word for breath and wind and spirit is the one word in Hebrew and Greek—and then gives the gift of deity in its fullness, which his breath had symbolized, the Holy Spirit, to fearful, threatened men and women who would need all the divine assistance they were capable of receiving in the work Jesus had for them (John 20:19-23). It was to preach the forgiveness of sins at the hands of a merciful Father and to be themselves a community of mutual forgiveness. That tiny band would expand shortly into a community that called itself the Church, the Greek word for Jews who believed in Jesus' resurrection, in distinction from the Jews who used another Greek word to designate themselves "the Synagogue." The Church has been faithful to the first part of the one command, preaching God who is willing at every turn to forgive human waywardness. It has not done very well at the second part, mutual forgiveness. The holding back of forgiveness in Jesus' words can only be of those who persist in evil ways and wish no forgiveness. Failure to forgive is another matter. The Church over the centuries has not distinguished itself in the eyes of others by consistently forgiving those who trespass (offend, injure, sin) against them, the condition Jesus put for being forgiven by a Father in heaven. Committed to clemency and the remission of others' sins, its members have time and again paid back injuries in kind, the very opposite of forgiveness.

John's gospel has a little more to do about Jesus risen from the dead. He hypothesizes an absentee from the circle of those who had experienced in immediacy the presence of the risen Lord. Thomas is the designated skeptic standing for many more, like all the named and unnamed characters in this series of one-act plays. Like Matthew's "but some were doubtful" even on seeing Jesus in his valedictory appearance, some believers known to John must still be saying they "hae their doots." An ancient proverb in all the world's languages says that seeing is believing, but it is not true. Seeing is seeing. Believing is believing. The one may lead to the other, but the two are not the same. Thomas as absent says he will trust only the evidence of his senses. Seeing and touching Jesus' wounds one week later, he then believes (John 19:24-29). He need not have believed. We are such strange creatures that we can doubt the evidence of our senses and manufacture explanations in support of our persistent doubt. John's story of Jesus' restoration of sight to the man blind from birth is instructive here (John 9). Jesus commends Thomas for believing after seeing, as he need not have done. The evangelist provides the reason for the presence of the incident in the gospel tradition: "Because you have seen me you have found faith. Happy are those who find faith without seeing me" (John 19:29). This is a watchword for the Christian ages. It describes trust in God who speaks a word through a living Church, a word that has been passed on since the first disciples saw and believed: the reality of the resurrected Jesus.

Do we know what prompted an anonymous disciple in what has been termed the Johannine circle to write a complete short gospel, now chapter 21, in the spirit of the longer one? More than that, how much influence must he have had to get his work appended to the longer writing? He himself supplies the probable answer to that question of his influence. He speaks of the same disciple as the one immediately referred to above by Peter, "the disciple whom Jesus loved." It is he who "vouches for what has been written here. He it is who wrote it and we know that his testimony is true" (John 21:24). That does not mean that the beloved disciple did the writing in his own person, but it has to mean he is the dependable source not only for the short chapter 21 but for the whole gospel besides. If this forever nameless person is "another disciple" who was known to Caiaphas the high priest and who gained for Peter entry into the latter's courtyard, much would be explained about details in John's narrative about Jesus while on pilgrimage in Judaea. The one who was loved would have to have been highly placed in Jerusalem society, not a Galilean like the others, and one whose anonymity was guaranteed for whatever reason by the gospel author.

Does he place himself in the last story of an appearance of the risen Jesus to his friends? Yes, but only obliquely. The real reason for the addendum or epilogue must first be taken care of. Mark has told the women that Jesus is going ahead of the disciples and Peter to Galilee where they will see him. That was the essence of the undelivered message. Matthew follows Mark in this as in other matters but has the women telling the men that Jesus was raised from the dead as they were told to do, with the result that the disciples have gone to Galilee and the mountain Jesus designated. Hence the basic tradition that the Good News or Gospel of what God had done in Christ and the Spirit originated in the northern province and went out from there. Luke's gospel and Acts, on the other hand, have the early Church coming to birth in Jerusalem and spread out from there as center. There is no certainty that the Gospel was as yet circulating when John wrote, even though he seems to have available to him some touches of tradition about Jesus found in Luke and Mark. John's chapter 20, which has all the air of finality about it, ends with the disciples in a locked room in Jerusalem. The writer of chapter 21 seems to know that the apostolic band fanned out from Galilee down to Judea and beyond, so he makes that correction by situating Jesus' disciples on the lakeshore. The emperor Tiberius had renamed Lake Kinnereth for himself in Jesus' adult years. The writer has a second purpose, the rehabilitation of Simon Peter who, when last heard of in the gospel, had denied to slaves in the high priest's court that he was a disciple. "Did I not see you in the garden?" This time a relative of the man whose ear Peter had cut off put the question. Peter had denied the allegation hotly, not once but three times. Three times Jesus elicits a protestation of love for him from this Rock who had become shattered stones in a crisis (John 21:15-19). Three times he was rehabilitated. The four gospels that proclaim the one Gospel come from four churches of the one Church. This could not have happened as it did if Peter had gone the Judas route. He had to have been restored to his leadership role.

Chapter Six

Jesus in Late New Testament Epistles and Second-Century Writings

Jesus is spoken of as "Christ Jesus" and "Christ Jesus our Lord" in the first of the three Pastoral Epistles, as they are traditionally called.[1] This is no surprise since the two letters to Timothy and one to Titus, along with Ephesians, are based on letters written by St. Paul. Appended to the first of the titles, which is repeated in its initial appearance, Jesus is called "our hope," a usage also found, but indirectly, in the epistle to Titus. It speaks of our awaiting "the happy fulfillment of our hope, when the splendor of the great God and of our savior Jesus Christ will appear" (Titus 2:13). The references to Jesus in Paul's letter to Philemon are peppered with those titles as with the others of his authorship, hence their appearance in the deutero-Pauline epistles.[2]

Jesus is "the Lord Jesus Christ" in the opening verse of James and again as the second chapter opens (Jas 1:1; 2:1) but is not mentioned again until and unless it is he and not Israel's LORD who is referred to as "the Lord" who will come as "Judge" (Jas 5:7, 9). That is because before and after the passage 5:7-8 "the LORD" refers to the God of Israel. There is an apparent return to Jesus as "the Lord" in whose name the presbyters/

---

[1] 1 Tim 1:1-2; see also 1:12; 2:5; 4:6; 5:11, 21; 6:3, 13 [with its mention of Pontius Pilate]; the same titles accompany the name of Jesus in 2 Tim 1:1, 9, 13; 2:1, 3, 8; 3:12, 15; 4:1; and Titus 1:1, 4, where he is called "our Savior," as also in 2:13 and 3:6.

[2] See Phlm 1, 3, 23, 25, plus "Lord" alone (16, 20) and "Christ" alone (8, 20).

elders of the Church are instructed to anoint a sick person (Jas 5:14-15). Martin Luther's dismissal of James as "an epistle of straw" for not having "driven home Christ" undoubtedly meant its silence on righteousness by faith alone, a phrase found in James alone at 2:24, who denies its exclusive effectiveness.

The First Letter of Peter, which has been identified by many as in part or whole an early baptismal homily, is so Pauline in spirit that numbers of New Testament scholars see in it the hand of a disciple of Paul. The reason for the attribution according to the theory was to divert attention from Paul who was ill thought of in the Jerusalem church, as he himself acknowledged, by crediting its champion Peter with authorship (see Gal 2:12-14; Phil 3:2-4; 2 Cor 11:13, 26). In any case, the epistle contains the titles Lord and Christ in various combinations but never the name Jesus alone, as found in the gospels and in rare epistle references.[3]

The Second Letter of Peter in its opening verse speaks of "the righteousness of our God and Savior Jesus Christ," but the later use of "our Lord and Savior" referring to Christ in two places suggests that the better English rendering of the Greek of the first verse is "of our God and of the Savior Jesus Christ," not "of our God and Savior Jesus Christ."

Jude (in Greek Judas), to whom a brief letter of twenty-five verses is attributed, may well be one of the "brothers of Jesus" of Matthew 6:3, hence "the brother of the Lord" whom St. Paul speaks of along with Cephas in 1 Corinthians 9:5; or again, Paul may have the James in mind who is frequently identified that way. The context is that these apostles were accompanied by their wives in their travels. Jude is described as "a brother of James" in the heading of the epistle that bears his name and as "a slave of Jesus Christ." The latter honorific title follows the name of Jesus four times more with "Lord" appended, but in the first instance he is also called "our only Master" (*despótēs*). That title is often used of Israel's God. It is not to be understood here, however, as an attribution of deity to Jesus, since it was the ordinary word for a sovereign lord in secular Greek. The last verse of Jude calls the One who can "set you in the presence of his glory . . . the only God our Savior." This is an indication of the way the phrase in 2 Peter 1:1; 2:20; 3:18 may be read.

The second and third epistles of John are letters in the true sense, while the first, the longest of the three, is a treatise in exposition of ideas in the gospel that bears his name. They originate from the Johannine

---

[3] 2 Cor 4:10-11; 11:4; see 1 Pet 1:2, 3, 7, 13; 2:5; 3:15; Christ alone 1:11, 19; 2:21; 3:16, 18; 4:1, 13, 14; 5:10.

school, or circle, which means that the references to Jesus in them should be expected to resemble closely those in the gospel. That writing is chiefly concerned to identify Jesus as Messiah and Son of God. The gospel refers to him as "the Word" in its opening verse but not again in the remaining twenty-one chapters. As was indicated above in the discussion of Jesus' titles in Revelation, Jesus is called "the Word of God" there in the only other place in the New Testament than John's gospel (see Rev 19:13). In 1 John "the Word of/that gives, life" seems to be "the message that we have heard from him and proclaimed to you" (1 John 1:5). The "life" spoken of here is "the eternal life that was with the Father and was made visible to us." It could well be intended as an echo of the life "that came to be through him" (John 1:3b), hence eternal godhead enfleshed in Jesus. Whatever the case, "the blood of [God's] Son Jesus" is the first designation in the epistle of the unique divine sonship that is primary in the gospel and is preceded and followed by the same usage in sixteen other verses. Once, it should be noted, the term for sonship is "begotten of God" (1 John 1:7; 1:3; 2:22, 23; 3:23; 4:2, 9, 10, 15; 5:1). The term "Christ" attached to Jesus in combination with "Lord Jesus" or "Christ" standing alone, is interesting in that in 1 John this Greek translation of Anointed is always used, whereas the gospel employs Messiah without exception, with a final letter *sigma* supplied to accord with Greek usage (see 1 John 1:3; 2:1, 22; 3:23; 4:20; 5:1, 6, 20). Aside from the two major titles "Son" and "Christ," Jesus is once called "an Advocate with the Father" in 1 John, echoing the "other Advocate" of John 14:16, who is presumably Jesus, and in apposition to that title, "the just one" (1 John 2:1). In another place he is "the Son whom the Father has sent as savior of the world" (1 John 4:14; cf. John 4:42, the new faith in Jesus under that title of the townsmen of Sychar).

As to other titles, "expiation (*hilasmós*) for our sins" occurs twice as a description of Jesus stemming from his work (1 John 2:2; 4:10; cf. the cognate *hilastērion* for expiation in Rom 3:25). In his person Jesus is the instrument, or agent, of restoring humanity to friendship with God. The one who denies that Jesus is the Christ is called a liar in this letter, while the guarantee of possessing the Father is confessing Jesus to be the Son (1 John 2:22; the origin of the term "antichrist" occurs here and at 4:3). These statements and similar ones that demand faith in the Son seem to be a polemic against groups known to the writer that deny Jesus' Messiahship, a human title of a member of the Jewish people, or call into question his origin from God as Son, as bespeaking deity in its fullness (see 1 John 2:24; 3:23; 4:9, 14, 15; 5:6-12, 20). All these passages appear to show that

1 John is a treatise in christology but that it is that only secondarily. Its main point is that as a result of who Jesus is, both a sinless human being and the hoped-for Messiah of Israel who is at the same time uniquely Son of God, believers in him and in the Spirit's action have become God's children in a new way (1 John 3:5; 4:2; 5:6-7 on the three who testify including Jesus' blood; 3:2; 4:4 and "begotten by God" and the address "Children" throughout). Like all the New Testament writings, the emphasis is on the lives of the baptized more than on the Father who has given them these gifts through Jesus Christ in the Holy Spirit. The divine activity is taken for granted. It is its effect that is stressed.

The fairly exhaustive account in the present and a previous chapter of the ways in which Jesus is featured in New Testament writings other than the four gospels has shown him to be the risen Christ and Lord now at the right hand of the Father. He is active there as intercessor with God on behalf of sinful humanity but at the same time present on earth in his body the Church through the indwelling Spirit. The only references to his earthly existence are two: Paul's mention in Galatians 4:4 of Jesus' having been born of a woman and subject to Mosaic Law, and 1 Timothy 6:13-14 where mention is made of his noble confession in his testimony before Pontius Pilate. Hebrews does have a few scattered phrases about his sufferings in his last hours and gives the impression that the Temple still stands while the book is being written, but the text does nothing to confirm or disconfirm this with certainty.

Jesus in the Extra-Canonical Writings: 1 Clement

Thus did the various writers of the apostolic age other than the four evangelists present Jesus, always as Israel's Messiah or Christ, Son of God, Lord of the Church, never as the Galilean teacher, wonderworker, and exorcist. The only way he was portrayed in his brief earthly life was in his last hours of suffering and death. In the case of Paul's authentic letters, by the time he wrote his last preserved epistle the four gospels did not yet exist. Dating the other non-gospel materials is nearly impossible except in several cases, after Paul's death. Even if portions of what came to be incorporated into the gospels were circulating among the infant churches, the early writers felt no need to share what they knew of Jesus' public career. That he had been raised up from the dead three days after death in ignominious circumstances was enough for them. From this absolute *novum* in human history they deduced all the rest about what God must have meant by it. Failing this event, his disciples in life, male and female, would have lived with the memory of his holiness, his teaching, and his share in divine power but nothing more. They would have gone to their graves after lifetimes of spreading his teaching, wondering what his meteoric life had meant. They would have wondered how the good God let one who had been gifted so much above the ordinary die as a condemned criminal.

In the event, they were not left with the problem. Experiencing him alive again in the flesh—in the profoundly altered flesh of glory—answered the question with which they were not faced, while posing a myriad of others. We know from the writings of the apostolic age, that is, the years 30 to roughly 135, what they made of the one mystery of his death and resurrection. Did they bring to light anything more that was known about Jesus than was found in the writings that came to be identified by around the year 200 as canonical Scripture?

We might suppose that simple curiosity about Jesus' earthly life would have resulted in the further development of the traditions behind the gospels. It does not seem to be the case. Nor do any of the many apocryphal gospels, so important to the imaginative writers about "the early Church," come from the period of the first and early second centuries. We have from the years roughly 100–180 only three writings that show any interest in Jesus' life. Some of these writings, it should be noted, were still being described as inspired but not canonical Scripture as late as the fourteenth century. The earliest of these is a lengthy letter by an anonymous writer of the Roman church to the church at Corinth, datable about the year 95. It has long been considered the work of someone there acting as a kind of foreign secretary, later identified as Clement, the second after Linus in the order of bishops following the martyrdoms of Peter and Paul. Early in the letter there is mention of Christ's words and his suffering as having been stored up in Corinthian hearts, but none of these is specified in that place (1 Clem 2.1). Following God's precepts should keep the people behaving in a way worthy of Christ, the letter says. That they are not doing so is the burden of this entire, severe piece of correspondence.

Specifically, some young Church members have fallen victims to rivalry and envy and wish to force the older leaders out of places of authority. The first half of the letter is a tissue of citations from the Scriptures giving examples of disharmony but also of harmony. The legend of the phoenix who rises from his ashes is recounted, with the comment that there should be no surprise that the Creator has promised to raise up those who serve him in holiness (1 Clem 25–26). When Jesus begins to be spoken of with frequency he is always "Christ," "Jesus Christ," or the "Lord Jesus Christ." He is to be reverenced as the one "whose blood was given for us" (1 Clem 21.6). "The Master continually points out to us that there will be a future resurrection. Of this he made the Lord Jesus Christ the first fruits by raising him from the dead" (1 Clem 24.1).

There are echoes of New Testament places that speak of the Lord Jesus as a descendant of Jacob "so far as his human nature goes"; as Jesus Christ who "by God's will called us to be justified not of ourselves" but "by that faith by which Almighty God has justified all from the very beginning"; and as "our salvation, Jesus Christ, the high priest of our offerings, the protector and helper of our weakness" (1 Clem 32.2, 4; 36.1). This treatise has a descending-order hierarchy of God, Christ, and apostles that resembles 1 Corinthians 15:23, leading down to the apostles who "went out in the confidence of the Holy Spirit to preach the good news that God's Kingdom was about to come" (1 Clem 42.3). The office and importance of the title bishop and strife among men who hold that office was already foreseen by the apostles, thanks to Jesus Christ, a matter spelled out more clearly here than in the Pastoral Epistles. They are described as ministering to the flock of Christ and "offering the sacrifices with innocence and holiness" (1 Clem 44.1-6). "Do we not have one God, one Christ, one Spirit of Grace which was poured out on us? And is there not one calling in Christ?" 1 Clement asks, immediately afterward quoting Jesus' saying: "Woe to the man who causes scandal to one of my chosen ones" (46.6-8; cf. Matt 26:24; Luke 17:1, 2 and parallels). In one place the Lord Jesus Christ is called "the scepter of God's majesty who came not with pomp or pride of arrogance but in humility, just as the Holy Spirit said of him" (1 Clem 16.2; in Isa 53:1-12, which follows in full). Clearly Jesus continues to be viewed at the turn of the second century as one through whom God holds out the gift of salvation in the power of the Holy Spirit and as the teacher of the way of life that leads to it. The latter role occupies a secondary if important place.

Jesus in the Didachē

Jesus as teacher surfaces in the second century in a brief treatise that exists in two distinct parts, the first being a collection of moral maxims or principles largely from scriptural sources under the headings "the way of life" and "the way of death." The second part is a manual on the proper way of celebrating baptism and the Lord's Supper, with some suitable suggestions about community conduct appended. This short work came to light only in 1875 and is entitled *The Teaching [Didachē] of the Twelve Apostles.* Two of Jesus' several quoted sayings are from Matthew's Sermon on the Mount, paralleled in Luke's discourse on the plain; another ten come from Matthew. Only one is from Luke only. Further individual sayings resemble a place or two in the Psalms (37:11), Exodus (20:13-17), Isaiah (66:2), or 1 Peter (2:11). What all this says is that the writer probably does not possess a complete gospel or biblical book but is well armed with collections of the aphorisms of Jesus and of an earlier prophet teacher. Like any writer of the period he may have dozens, even hundreds of Jesus' sayings or Old Testament passages committed to memory, rather than having access to complete biblical books on papyrus or parchment. In any case, he provides a quite thorough moral catechesis for adults. Live this way, says the *Didachē.* See that you do not live that way.

There is a charming sensitivity shown to the difficulties pagan candidates would have in adopting this disciplined way of life: "If you can bear the Lord's full yoke you will be perfect. If not, do what you can." Jews new to life in the Church would not need this gentle mitigation of demand, since their forebears had been living this morality since Ezra's day in the return from the exile. Similarly, baptism in water as a sign of repentance and new life would have been well familiar to Jews in their various rites of purification and to gentiles as a natural sign of cleansing.

Jesus appears in the baptismal formula as the eternal Son of God in the words familiar to later centuries, "in the name of the Father and of the Son and of the Holy Spirit," while water from a running stream or river is being poured on a person's head (chap. 7). Did the *Didachē* get those sacramental words of commitment to the triune God from St. Matthew's gospel? More likely both quoted them from Catholic practice in their area, which is thought to be Syrian Antioch from indications given by that gospel and later writings from the locale. "'Pray as follows' as the Lord bade us in his gospel," comes next, a clear indication that the writer knows the Matthean formula. "Our Father in heaven" occurs in the wording of that gospel, not Luke, concluding not with "Amen" but "for yours is the power and the glory forever" (8.2). This ending, along with the word "kingdom," is found in later manuscripts of Matthew's gospel, not the earliest, suggesting that some fifth-century scribes knew it from the *Didachē* or from liturgical practice where they labored.

The wording of the *Didachē*'s Eucharist (Greek for prayer of thanks) calls Jesus "your child" (*paîs,* servant/slave) in its address to God. It goes on: "We thank you, our Father, for the life and knowledge you have revealed through Jesus your child." That prayer (chaps. 9–10) is spoken over wine first, called poetically "the holy vine of David," meaning Jesus, and bread, called a fragment, *klásma*. In later writings as mentioned above, *klásis*, the word for breaking, was used to refer not only to the bread but to describe the whole ritual meal. Interesting in the instruction on how to perform the two basic Christian rites is the use of "Jesus" unadorned by title, although in a sentence that follows he is twice called "the Lord." Shortly thereafter in a prayer of grace after the meal God is addressed: "Almighty Master, . . . to us you have given spiritual food and drink and eternal life through Jesus your child." This moves easily into a prayer to the LORD for "your Church" to be saved from all evil, made holy, and be gathered into "your Kingdom." Abruptly, then, "Let Grace come and let this world pass away," in which "Grace" is surely Jesus, God's gift (*Cháris*) whose coming is expected at the end. "Our Lord, come" (*Maran atha*), the prayer in Aramaic St. Paul uttered in 1 Corinthians at 16:22, then follows.

Every apostle, indeed everyone who comes to the community, must be welcomed as if he were the Lord, but travelers who stay more than three days must be sent packing (11.4; 12.1, 5). They are "trading on Christ." The first day of the week—"every Lord's day of the Lord"—is called his special day for assembly "to break bread," which is there twice called "your sacrifice" (14.1, 3). Had the sixteenth-century Reformers reckoned any writings outside the canonical twenty-seven books to be sacred Scripture as did the early Church, they would not have polemicized so vigorously against the Mass as a sacrifice. In the remainder of the treatise Jesus is called "the Lord" four times and "the Christ" and "the Truth" once each, in a context of his glorious return. The mysterious denomination "the Curse himself" also refers to him, as having undergone an accursed form of execution (16.5; see Gal 3:13; Deut 21:23).

The Letters of the Great Ignatius, Martyr

Saint Ignatius of Antioch in Syria calls himself "the God-inspired" in the heading of six of his seven letters written from shipboard to six churches in western Asia Minor and one each to Bishop Polycarp of Smyrna and to the church at Rome. He is being transported to his martyrdom there sometime around 109–110. Normally he writes of Jesus Christ, at times Christ Jesus, but also with an intense devotion to the person of Jesus in his sufferings, in a way not found in the Pastoral Epistles or 1 Clement. Ignatius calls Jesus our Teacher and Savior (Ephesians 15.1; 1.1). Notable too is his departure from New Testament usage in speaking of Jesus Christ as "our God," "God's blood," and once even using the phrase "the Christ God" (Smyrnaeans 10.1). He calls Jesus "the New Man" (Ephesians 20.1) and frequently stresses the incarnation by speaking of Jesus "in the flesh" and as "a real human being . . . even after the resurrection" (Smyrnaeans 3.1-2; see Magnesians 13.2). Once he calls him whose resurrection occurred when Pontius Pilate was governor "our Hope" (Magnesians 11) and another time "the door to the Father" (Philadelphians 9.1).

Summing up, we find the bishop from Syria holding fast to the apostolic teaching of Jesus' divinity and humanity, which the Council of Nicaea would reaffirm two centuries later, specifically in opposition to Arius's teaching that the Son was the first of God's creatures and not eternal deity. One hundred years after that at Ephesus, Ignatius's fellow Antiochenes found a lack of strong support for Jesus' full humanity in Mary's defined title "the God bearer," which neither Nestorius nor any Antiochene theologian denied. Eutyches, an influential Alexandrian monk, and his many disciples were teaching that Jesus' humanity was thoroughly subsumed by his divinity in one nature. A council at Chalcedon in 451, twenty years after Ephesus, again taught the perfection of each of Jesus' persons, which the New Testament did, if not in fifth-century philosophical language.

Jesus in the Second-Century Apologists

Saint Justin wrote in the mid-second century at Rome a defense of the Church in the form of a vigorous denial that it taught any absurdities of the sort found in pagan myths along with the worship of the emperor as a god. His longer *First Apology* of two did not devise any new titles for Jesus but did speak of him in a distinctly new way. Since Plato had had a theory that the architectonic principle of design in the cosmos should be called Reason or the Word (*Logos*), Justin concluded that the change of formless matter into an ordered universe by the successive "Then God said" in Genesis was a borrowing by Plato "from our teachers" of the concept of a creative Word. Justin thus understood Moses, the presumed author of Genesis, and all the writers of accounts of biblical theophanies to be describing activities of God's Word before it took flesh in Jesus.[4] Justin seldom attends to Jesus' human soul but he does

---

[4] *1 Apology* 59: "So by God's word the whole universe was made out of this substrate (*tohu vabohu*, formless matter), as expounded by Moses and Plato and those who agree with him"; cf. Ps 33:6: "By the Lord's word the heavens were made, by the breath of his mouth all the host of heaven [planets and stars] was formed."

speak of him as crucified, surrendering his spirit and his feelings in the face of his passion (*Dialogue with Trypho* 105.5; 103.7).

The other second-century apologists write in a similar vein to Justin of Jesus' God-manhood, but they show little interest in the Jesus of the gospels. Aristides of Athens, for example, was a philosopher who stated that "this Son of the most high God descended from heaven in (or as) holy spirit and took flesh from a virgin" (*Apology* 15.1), while Tatian, a pupil of Justin in Rome who later turned founder of a rigorous, gnostic-tending sect (*Encratites*, i.e., the self-controlled, the ascetic) described Jesus as "God in the form of a man" (*Address to the Greeks* 21.1). Melito was bishop of Sardis, not far from ancient Smyrna, who was very prolific literarily. His poetic homily *On the Pasch* (*Passover*) has been criticized roundly for its biblical typology that makes the Jewish people responsible for the death of Jesus. That major flaw apart, his late second-century christology and soteriology are orthodox and quite familiar: "Born as Son, / led like a lamb, / sacrificed like a sheep, / buried as a man, / he rises from the dead as God, being by nature both God and man" (*Perì Páscha* 8). And so in many passages.

Jesus in the Lengthy Treatise of a Missionary Bishop

Saint Irenaeus of Lyon was the Greek bishop of that busy Roman city (Lugdunum) who had come there as a missionary, stopping off at Rome and at some point returning there for a visit (ca. 177). He wrote an apologia, *The Refutation and Overthrow of Gnōsis Falsely So Called*, in five books. It can be dated sometime after 190 from the death of the most recent bishop of Rome whom he mentions. He later composed a compendium of it in one hundred brief chapters, *Demonstration of the Apostolic Preaching*. Irenaeus is remembered especially for his typological version of Christ as the second Adam, developed from Paul's parallelism in Galatians, who summed up in himself the whole human race, sanctifying it and becoming the first figure in a new, redeemed humanity. He made Eve a virgin in the garden, since the disobedience of the pair preceded their parenthood in the tale (and of their being "like gods knowing good and evil," a probable reference to their exercise of sexuality), and a type of Mary. This had been done before him in the Letter to Diognetus[5] and in Justin, later in Tertullian, but not spelled out so explicitly as Irenaeus does. His consistent stress on Jesus' corporeal nature as part of his

---

[5] Especially if the anonymous author of ch. 11 was Quadratus writing ca. 129; *Dialogue with Trypho*, 100; *On the Flesh of Christ*, 17.

ongoing polemic against gnostic spiritism or Jesus' merely seeming human (Docetism) is not our main concern in the current chapter. How he dealt with Jesus in any way other than as Word made flesh who was God's agent in the power of the Spirit in redeeming the human creature, is. With that exposition we shall conclude the citation of second-century writings.

While Justin had drawn on the gospels sparingly in making the case for the culmination of Israel's story and the hope of all the prophets fulfilled in him, Irenaeus draws more copiously on the gospels and epistles for his portrait of the person of Jesus and not simply of his work. He is, of course, concerned to show that the sharing of the eternal Word with every aspect of human life was necessary if the redemption were to be accomplished. For this reason the phrases "truly God" and "truly man" occur with great frequency. Early in this book-length treatise there is a creed that resembles the Roman Creed on which the much later Apostles' Creed is based. It speaks of the following dispensations of God: "the comings [visitations], the birth of a virgin, the suffering, the resurrection from the dead and the bodily reception into the heavens of Christ Jesus our Lord, and his coming from the heavens in the glory of the Father to restore all things, to raise up all flesh . . ." (*Adversus Haereses*, X.1 [title of extant Latin translation]). In discussing the variant forms of gnostic baptisms Irenaeus tells of the attempts to distinguish between a baptism of the perfect and that of John for repentance that the Church has adopted (I.21.3). As part of this discussion several gnostic baptismal formulas are provided that feature "the Power of the Father," "the good Spirit," "Life," "the Name hidden from all godhead," "Christ who lives for angelic redemption," and "the Name of Restoration." This ethereal vocabulary accompanied a baptism achieved by anointing with balsam or by repeated pourings of oil and water on the candidates' heads "in the name of the ineffable Greatness," "the incorrupt Wisdom, who is in the Father," "who is in the Mother of your mother, for it was a female made of a female who made you" (for all the above see I.21.4-5). In general the Gnostic Christians of Irenaeus's Roman acquaintance—and his knowledge of their teachings was thorough—were well aware of the gospel narratives but were at pains to dematerialize or reformulate them. They could see in a savior nothing so crude as the son of a human mother. The mother of Jesus had to be the symbol of the mother god of a disembodied Christ. *Gnōsis* retained the spirit vocabulary of Christianity and jettisoned anything that smacked of matter.

Irenaeus operated at ease as the inheritor of a tradition that came from the age of the apostles. He claimed to have known when he was a small boy Polycarp, bishop of Smyrna who, in turn, he linked with John, son of Zebedee. He held a number of positions on the composition of the gospels that Eusebius transmits in his *Church History* of 335, which critical scholarship, beginning in 1800, did not leave standing. His sense of the importance of human tradition in matters of Christian faith is, however, unimpeachable and served to anchor the Gospel of Jesus Christ to the earth, not letting it float off to some gnostic heaven, as it threatened to do at the turn of the third century. This faith was further rescued by the martyrs under Decius in 250, who testified to its historicity with their blood. Providentially, the Church of East and West possessed in Irenaeus's five books the story of the tradition in the terminology that went back to the apostolic age, earthly yet filled with spirit, but by no means the spirit language that exorcised all terms descriptive of life on earth:

> What God was it who sent John, the forerunner who bore witness of the light? Was he not the one whose messenger was Gabriel who brought the good news of his birth, who also promised that he would send his messenger before the face of his Son and that he would prepare his way . . . in the spirit and power of Elijah? So how could John who was sent by the Creator and Fashioner of this world testify to that light which descended from things that are unimaginable and invisible? (III.11.4)

Irenaeus's rhetorical question is a challenge to the gnostic claim that the rogue creator of a world of matter, the so-called Demiurge or Populist Worker, was ignorant of the power above him. The son of Zechariah appeared as witness to Jesus and anyone who pointed him out, so he must have been knowable. Thus did Irenaeus take on, point by point, the illogic of gnostic teaching on the total unknowability of deity.

Or take the materiality of the Gospel, which Gnostic Christianity was at pains to deny, although it had no problem with the power of miracle:

> It was a good thing that was made by God's creation in the vineyard and was first drunk as wine. None of those who drank it spoke ill of it, and the Lord partook of some of it. But better wine was that which was made by the Word directly and simply out of water for those invited to the wedding. . . . Taking loaves that came from the earth and giving thanks, and making water into wine, he satisfied those who reclined to eat and he gave drink to the wedding guests. Thus he showed that God, who made the earth and commanded it to bring forth fruit . . . and in these last times through his Son gives to the human race the blessing of food and the favor of drink,

conveys the incomprehensible through the comprehensible and the invisible through the visible, since there is none beyond him and he is in the bosom of the Father. (V.5)

The polemic against "'the knowledge' falsely so-called" is relentless in the five books, always in a wordy narrative style. Irenaeus consistently illustrates the Catholic conviction, as opposed to the Gnostic, of a creator God of all that is good, with stories from Jesus' public life as told in the gospels. By this device he demolishes that cosmic mischief-maker the Demiurge (an *ergon* imposed on the *demos*, an evil work foisted on the people) by proclaiming the Creator spirit who is responsible for the material universe and above whom no divine principle can conceivably be.

Late Apocryphal Gospels, Some Orthodox, Some Gnostic in Intent

The one through whom God brought into existence all that is, is the Word who became the human being Jesus, a man born of a woman. By employing copiously Jesus' deeds and words, the bishop from Syria is the first one of record after the New Testament to employ the Jesus of history as the one in whose name salvation was proclaimed, rather than Jesus the risen Christ and Lord. That is exactly what each evangelist meant to do in his gospel. Irenaeus may have been preceded by the author of a semi-fictitious gospel or two, like the *Proto-Gospel of James*, which focuses on Jesus' mother Mary, and the *Infancy Gospel of Thomas*, the *Gospel of Peter*, the *Gospel of Mary*, or the *Epistle of the Apostles* (a gospel). These mid- to late-second-century gospels were based on the canonical four and were written to satisfy a natural curiosity about Jesus' early years. They do not supply dependable information. From the first of these one learns the names of Mary's parents, how she was brought to the Temple as a small child to be raised by the priests, and how the aged Joseph, the father of sons, was chosen to be her protector when his rod alone of the many deposited with the chief priest sprouted a dove that rested on his head. The second of these is replete with tales of Jesus' miraculous power in early boyhood, sometimes exercised to resuscitate the dead or heal a stricken person but at other times, in childhood anger or petulance, withering one child or striking another dead who irritated him. These gospels were mostly romances, but they occasionally had a cruel twist as indicated.

In the third century the *Gospel of Peter*, the *Gospel of Mary*, and the *Epistle of the Apostles* were written to make the case for Gnostic Christianity. It is these that report that Jesus loved Mary of Magdala above all women as part of a description of her outsmarting Jesus' male disciples in wisdom. Some recent popular writing has failed to feature the late date of these gnostic writings, giving the false impression that they contain authentic reminiscences that come from the apostolic age. In fact there was no recorded suppression of women's voices in the apostolic era other than the passage in 1 Timothy 2:11-12, later inserted into 1 Corinthians at 14:34-35, but there *was* a rejection of these gnostic-oriented gospels for their heretical content. The same was true of the teaching of Montanus and his colleagues in prophecy, Maximilla and Prisca, who predicted that the heavenly Jerusalem would shortly descend on the Phrygian mountains of Asia Minor.

These are the ways some second-century writers whose works have been preserved speak of Jesus: always in the manner of the New Testament books including the four gospels, that is, in terms of the deed of God achieved through him in the power of the Holy Spirit, the redemption of Israel, and salvation of the human race. Only late in the century was there an extensive treatment of Jesus' words and acts as reported by Mark, Matthew, Luke, and John. This was the work of Irenaeus of Lyon, sometimes called the Church's first (pastoral) theologian. The lateness of his resort to the public teaching and deeds of power of Jesus in telling the story of salvation may be accounted for by his first having access to all four gospels at this date but even more by his proving the Gnostics wrong by his insistence on redemption as achieved through an enfleshed or corporeal Word, not by a spirit Christ only. God's revelation to the Jews who became the earliest Church was an axis whose two poles were the teaching *of* Jesus and the teaching *about* Jesus, Lord and Christ, sent by the Father in the power of the Holy Spirit.

Chapter Seven

Jesus at the Center of
Doctrinal-Political Argument

There has been much irresponsible writing about Jesus in the last twenty-five years. Some nineteenth-century rationalists maintained that he never existed, that the gospels portrayed an ideal Jew who never was. A clutch of German and British writers was capable of that historical nonsense, some of which has resurfaced. It would be easier to establish that there never was an emperor Nerva, a name invented to fill the gap of ignorance of the years between Domitian and Trajan. In fact, we know more of Jesus from his reported teachings and of what was believed of him than any person, Jew or pagan, of his time: twenty-seven "books" plus a sprinkling of writings from the turn of the next century.

Some authors are currently explaining at book length how Jesus was promoted from the status of Mediterranean peasant to Godlike human being, even making it to full membership in the triad of the one, all-holy God. Remarkable social progress! Another subject of a spate of recent writings is the supposed suppression by chauvinist males of the total equality of women with men in the liturgical leadership and governance that had marked the early Christian communities. To make this claim those who do so must identify some Gnostic Christian writings of the third century as coming from the apostolic age. Some encounter between the Gospel and *Gnōsis*, a full-blown religion from the East, seems however to be an undeniable reality of the late first century. A few phrases in the secondary Pauline corpus suggest as much: "Stop drinking water only.

Take a little wine for the good of your stomach," may be more than a friendly health tip (1 Tim 5:23). What are the dangerous "myths" and endless genealogies that are being warned against in the same letter? They probably are not Jewish since they are described as "profane and silly" (1 Tim 4:2, 7) and "cleverly devised" (2 Pet 1:16). Who would be forbidding marriage and promoting abstinence from "God-given foods" (1 Tim 4:3) if not gnostic teachers who "do not believe everything created by God" (1 Tim 4:4) to be good? Again, the profane babbling and the absurdities of so-called knowledge (1 Tim 6:20) warned against seem more like the gnostic teachings that Irenaeus of Lyon (d. ca. 190) denounced than anything Jewish, some practices of which tradition also come in for the epistle's censure. Few and vague as the above admonitions are, they sound like a curtain raising to the full-scale threat to the Gospel that the religion that termed itself *Gnōsis* (knowledge) would later pose.

Some other challenges to right faith and conduct as they touched on a preexistent Christ came from within. Saint Paul and other writers speak of the Lord's twofold order of being, one according to spirit, his deity, and the other according to flesh, his humanity. As a person Christ was always conceived as individually one; but some early writers in the Catholic stream, like Justin (d. ca. 165), accuse others of Jewish stock whom they know as Ebionites, Aramaic for "the Poor," of an incorrect faith in Jesus that fails to acknowledge his deity (Justin, *Dialogue with Trypho* 47). Eusebius as late as 325 reports in his *History of the Church* that a Palestinian Jew of the second century named Hegesippus, as a Christian, wrote five books against the Gnostics in which he accused seven groups of fellow ethnic Jews of having no faith in Christ or possessing a faith that was inadequate (4.22.2). Another group termed Nazoreans was said to have correct faith in him while retaining Jewish ritual practices. Ignatius of Antioch (d. ca. 110), spoken of at length above, records the Catholic tradition that held the line against the gnostic incursion of Roman intellectuals, namely, that Jesus was the one Christ and Lord, at once human and divine, flesh and spirit. Some early spirit christologies, however, held that God's Son as Holy Spirit became flesh of the virgin Mary.[1] Melito, bishop of Sardis, could speak of Jesus' two substances, meaning human and divine, using the word *ousíai*, which later would

---

[1] See J.N.D. Kelly, *Early Christian Doctrines* (New York: Continuum, 2000), 142–45, who reports on Callistus, Hippolytus, Melito, and Tertullian as holding such a Holy Spirit christology.

be replaced by natures (*physeîs*). The Greek vocabulary used by native speakers of that language to describe the reality of Jesus Christ was fluid and would later be the cause of much confusion. But then, all human words intended to capture the mystery of deity are bound to fall short.

Thus, there emerged a number of teachers around the year 200 so convinced of the unity of godhood and the divinity of Christ, whose positions we know of only from their orthodox opponents, that they were tagged Monarchians, the "one divine origin party." For them, Christ as divine had to be somehow enfolded within the one God. This position resulted in a number of modalist christologies, meaning modes, or ways in which the one God took shape as self-revealed in the world. Tertullian accused a certain Praxeas of holding that Father and Son were one identical person.[2] A more sophisticated teacher, Sabellius, had the one divine Monad expressing itself in three operations on the analogy of the sun that gives forth heat and light.[3]

The Vocabulary of Debate and Its Major Topic

The third century was marked by any number of treatises, debates, charges, and countercharges on the correct language with which to speak of the mystery of Jesus Christ and the triune God. Most of it was carried on in Greek but a little in Latin, as by Tertullian, a learned layman, and Cyprian, bishop of Carthage. The vocabulary of argument was largely derived from the New Testament, while some came from the Septuagint, the Old Testament in Greek translation (but of the Hebrew books other than the version much later standardized by the Rabbis called Masoretes). A few nonbiblical terms, such as those for nature, person, essence, and subsistence (in Latin substance) were taken from philosophy. All were inserted into the debates in the interest of clarity, but this was not always the result. Such was the case when, for instance, *ousía* sometimes represented essence or nature and at other times person, a distinct person of the deity. The heated christological and trinitarian debates were carried on largely by men of goodwill but not always. There was the intellectually keen Hippolytus who coveted the bishopric of Rome but saw it awarded by vote of the presbyters to the less-gifted Callistus, a Latin speaker; Hippolytus managed to achieve the role of antipope. Both of them died in Sardinian exile, victims of imperial persecution.

---

[2] Ibid., 121.
[3] Ibid., 122.

The politics of ethnicity was very much a factor in the fourth- and fifth-century struggle between the Alexandrian party led by their bishop Cyril and the Antiochene party led by Nestorius, Patriarch of Constantinople. The latter and his former teacher, Theodore bishop of Mopsuestia, were Syrians who therefore had the edge of knowledge of a Semitic tongue in their exploration of both Testaments but not always of rhetorical and philosophical skill, which Cyril held over Nestorius.

The Catholic, or orthodox, position on the mystery of Christ and of Father, Son, and Holy Spirit had for the most part prevailed over a variety of modalisms by the year 300, although all heresies have an afterlife of sorts. By 312 Constantine, son of Constantius I Chlorus and his repudiated Catholic wife Helena, had become the first western emperor and sole emperor in 324. He was in early youth devoted to the god known by its symbol the Unconquerable Sun but was enrolled as a catechumen at some point in his adulthood. This means that he lived as a Christian believer but deferred baptism to the approach of his death in 337. The Church had endured bloody persecution during the brief reign of Maximinus in 235–38 and again under Decius in 249–51.[4] A presbyter of the Roman church, Novatian, acted as a spokesman for the Church during the latter bleak period of fourteen months. When the violence ceased and the Roman clergy chose Cornelius as bishop, Novatian was immediately voted to the papal office by his partisans and served as shadow pope for eight years. Paradoxically, Novatian resembled Hippolytus in being a better theologian than the true pope. His treatise on the mystery of the triune God netted him the title founder of Roman theology. The election of Cornelius over him was a case of an influential Roman family able to place in office Novatian's fellow presbyter of greater administrative ability.

For the moment, it is Novatian's position on Jesus that detains us, rather than his leadership of a schism (Tertullian, *On the Flesh of Christ* 17f). Novatian's was the christology of the North African rhetorician Tertullian (d. ca. 225), who had maintained firmly the two natures (his Latin term was substances) in Christ: the Word, a distinct Person from the Father, and the man Jesus who could accomplish his work on humanity's behalf only as a man. Novatian declared Jesus Christ to be both God and man, using the figures of the Word's joining himself to the human Jesus as a husband joins himself to his bride, or the Word's putting on of

---

[4] See J.N.D. Kelly, *The Oxford Dictionary of Popes* (Oxford: Oxford University Press, 1986), 16–17, under the entries Anterus, Fabian, and Cornelius.

humanity as a garment. Obviously both theological thinkers were struggling to employ language that would avoid any incorrect expression of the union of two natures in one person that derived from the Church's apostolic tradition, if not in that wording. There, both Testaments were seen to record that Jesus from his conception was truly human and at the same time truly divine. Up to the year 300 or so, the stress of most writers was on Jesus' full possession of the divine spirit, his humanity being taken for granted. An exception was when some argued forcefully against those who held he was material only in appearance that he truly took on flesh, for example, became human through birth of a human mother. This was not by passing through her as a mere channel, like water through a tube, the position of some of the later gnostic Valentinians. It was a real birth from a real human being.

The Heretical Teaching of Arius

In 313, Constantine, already favorably inclined to the faith of the growing Christian population, published an edict granting toleration to all religions but with the Catholic body chiefly in view. A religious dispute in Alexandria on the Nile Delta in 318 may not have come immediately to his attention. It had, however, reached such proportions by 325 that he called a council to settle the matter. The chosen site was Nicaea, across the Bosporus from his new capital Constantinople, the Byzantium that he had renamed for himself or his father. Bishop Alexander of that city had learned that a member of his presbyterate, one Arius, was very effectively putting forth unfamiliar teaching. It was that the Word who became flesh was not eternally begotten of God, the familiar Catholic teaching, but was begotten in the only sense Arius thought that word could have, namely, created, or brought into being. This persuasive preacher acknowledged the truth of all that was said of Jesus in the tradition and the Scriptures, that he is the Word made flesh whom God had used, in the Holy Spirit, as instrument or agent of the world's redemption. The starting point of Arius's theological construct was the term "firstborn of all creation" found in a hymn in Colossians 1:15 and elsewhere in other New Testament contexts. Arius was a biblical literalist like many before and after him who preferred his interpretation of a word or phrase, in this case firstborn, to centuries of Catholic tradition. He took the Word who, in figure, was begotten of or came forth from the Father to have come into existence as Word as human infants do at birth. Arius's thought was so molded by monarchy that he could say in a letter to his bishop, that God is alone "ingenerate," that is, not brought into existence, is alone without beginning, true, all sovereign, and all wise. A corollary of God's total uniqueness was therefore that the divine indivisibility could not in any way be shared or communicated, least of all with another like the Word who was believed to participate fully in the mystery of deity. Arius had in mind the Son as full possessor of the divine nature, and he denied it.

Alexander, at the time bishop of Alexandria, told Arius to desist from his teaching that made of the Word a creature and not eternal God. He refused and at the council spoken of above was declared excommunicated by the assembled bishops. This is not a lifetime exclusion from the Church's sacramental life but a temporary debarring from sharing the Eucharist with all other bishops until he should repent his error. Upon such public repentance the ban is lifted, usually in a rite of reconciliation. Arius would have none of it. His false teaching did not wither and die at the promulgation of a Catholic creed at that council. Rather, it flourished and spread, chiefly when some bishops espoused it in a political rebuff to Constantinople's patriarchal office. Not until the year 600 or thereabouts did the widely scattered and numerous Arian heretics return to Catholic unity. The popular appeal of the heresy was rooted in the fact that it was preached in such subtle theological language that the people could not distinguish it from Catholic faith upon a hearing, and that some rulers of Arian persuasion were sponsoring the ordination to the episcopal order of those priests only who thought their way. This was not an exclusively religious struggle by any means. It was profoundly political, as is the case in the progress made by all heresies.

The brief creed drawn up at Nicaea, with Ossius of Cordoba in the chair representing the emperor and only two Western bishops standing in for Pope Sylvester I, was based on an even shorter creed that Eusebius, bishop of Caesarea (modern Kayseri in Turkey), had proposed for adoption. That one was not accepted because, although perfectly orthodox, it did not face the Arian challenge head-on. The Creed of Nicaea reads as follows:

> We believe in one God the Father All-sovereign, maker of all things visible and invisible;
> And in one Lord, Jesus Christ, the Son of God, begotten of the Father, God of God, Light of Light, true God of true God, that is, of the [same] substance (*homooúsion*) of the Father, through whom all things were made, things in heaven and things on the earth; who for us humans (*anthrōpous*, not *andres*, males) and for our salvation

came down and was made flesh, and became man, and rose on the third day, ascended into the heavens, is coming to judge living and dead.

And in the Holy Spirit.

And those who say "There was when he was not,"
   and "Before he was begotten he was not,"
   and that, "He came into being from what-is-not,"
   Or [those who allege] that the son of God is
      "of another substance (*hypostaseos*) or essence (*ousías*)"
      or "created" (*ktiston*);
      or "changeable" (*trepton*)
      or "alterable" (*alloiōton*),
   these the Catholic and Apostolic Church anathematizes.[5]

The creed proper ends with "and in the Holy Spirit." The statements that come after are obviously false, being a series of propositions that the Arian party affirmed and Catholic faith denied. Note that the Creed has no word for person or nature. *Ousía*, "being" or "essence," comes closest to the latter. In debates of a later era the distinct divine persons will most often be designated *hypóstaseîs*, literally "subsistences," the Greek word that will yield in Latin to *personae* (which is really a translation of the Greek *prósōpa*, an alternate term used for *hypóstaseîs*). The three nouns immediately above do not occur in the New Testament. Readers familiar with the singing or reciting at the Sunday Eucharist of what is erroneously termed the Nicene Creed will miss a number of phrases that were inserted at the First Constantinopolitan Council of 380–81 to cope with new heretical beliefs about the human and divine Christ who is one person: "begotten not made"; "was conceived of the virgin Mary"; "was crucified, died, and was buried"; "will come in glory and his kingdom will have no end." All the phrases that describe the inspiration of the prophets and the "goods of salvation" attributed to the Holy Spirit were added at I Constantinople to refute the denial of distinct personhood to, and work of, the Spirit.

Basil's Defense of the Holy Spirit as a Divine Person

Some fourth-century Christians whose chief spokesman was a certain Eustathius were called Spirit-fighters because of their view that "the

---

[5] *Documents of the Christian Church*, ed. Henry Bettenson and Chris Maunder (Oxford: Oxford University Press, 1999), 27–28.

Spirit" described the Father and the Son at work in the world, not a personal agent responsible for such action. Basil, the bishop of Caesarea, provided the argument that prevailed at the council. He said that the Matthean baptismal formula long in use, which named the Holy Spirit on a par with the Father and the Son, showed that "we believe he is not alien to the divine nature, accomplishing until then what they accomplished."[6] He knew it was absurd for the baptized to dedicate themselves to two divine persons and to a power they exercised in common.

It is true that every act of God is performed by the Father through the Son in the Holy Spirit, not by any one alone. Each possesses deity in its entirety. Since deity is infinite, indivisible, and immeasurable there cannot be any question of a numerical three. Similarly, if division, separation, or addition is impossible in God, any division, separation, or addition in Christ, who is Word infinite and human son of a human mother must also be inadmissible. Every act of Jesus in his lifetime must have been theandric, that is, a deed of his unified Godmanhood. This gives the lie to what used to be said in works of piety (past tense, it is to be hoped)—that Jesus did this in his divinity, multiplied bread and fish, for example, and that in his humanity, endured physical pain and mental anguish. The Jesus the Church believes in did and does all that we know and believe of him as one person, not two. How his complete humanity and complete divinity are conjoined in the one person we cannot know, only that they are. The christological, pneumatological, and trinitarian debates of the second through the sixth centuries give the impression that theologians of the time thought they knew. They "explained" the inner life of God and Christ as if both were available to human knowledge by virtue of the revelation of the death and upraising of Jesus and the descent of the Holy Spirit.

It is not so. When we speak of unfathomable mystery we know just enough not to get the words wrong by remaining true to the Church's tradition in the biblical deliverance. Some even to this day speak of divine revelation so confidently that they need to be challenged, "How *did* God convey to finite humanity the 'truths of faith' that you write about nonstop?" It is not an easy question to answer. Saint Paul's answer was, "By living those truths." A theology of divine mystery can be arrived at only by such living, to which is joined the speculation on what is said in Scripture and the Church's liturgy in many languages, both of which are

---

[6] Kelly, *Early Christian Doctrines*, citing Basil's Epistle, 159.2, 261; and Gregory of Nazianzus reporting the reason that marked his teaching, 260.

the theologians' proper business. But, whereas discerning the meaning of language as it speaks of things earthly is what the wise and the learned are about, all human language about God and God's work in the world is a matter of analogy, figure, and metaphor. We can never be sure how closely it approximates the divine reality. Least of all can we know how persuasive the arguments carried on in Greek were to all those native Aramaic, Syriac, and Coptic speakers who possessed it as a second language. The same can be asked of what sense the outcome of these debates means to intelligent catechists of adults whose first language is a Melanesian or Polynesian tongue, for example, when they are told that Jesus had a human nature but was not a human person, and whether the statement is true as stated in any language.

This brings us to the years of the fourth century that followed Nicaea and, seventy years later, I Constantinople. The Arians and the Spirit-fighters (erroneously called Macedonians after a bishop of Constantinople of that name who had little to do with it) were hardly satisfied with the decision that they did not hold the Church's faith. In the first case, a strange position arose called that of the semi-Arians, something like a partial pregnancy, since the Word is either uncreated God or creature of God with no middle term possible. The *Homoioúsion* party (of like substance to the Father), not of the same substance (the *Homooúsios*; in Latin the word is *consubstantialis*) as the Father, flourished for a while but only as a Catholic description of persistent Arians. That Arian-Catholic struggle was carried on largely between theologians who were native speakers of Greek. The next two, more bitter, debates were complicated by differences in language and culture, the Alexandrian party of intellectual Greek thought from west in the empire and the Antiochene or Syrian party from farther east. The emerging Latin language intellectuals of North Africa and Italy identified themselves with the latter position chiefly, in the way the human Jesus was spoken of in a context of faith in him.

The Christological Teaching that Prevailed After Nicaea

An anti-Arian reaction set in after Nicaea in the East and West, which stressed Jesus' divinity in popular preaching and teaching, with a complementary de-emphasis on his humanity. One feature of the realization that infinite deity and finite humanity are totally incommensurate was that Jesus' role as great high priest and intercessor with God on behalf of fellow humans was diminished in favor of his wholesale divine powers described graphically in a new one-word title, *Pantokratōr*, the All-Powerful.

Saint Ignatius of Antioch had written of "our Christ God" in his epistles, which became a common form of address in the liturgical prayers that come from that period. Another result of faith in Christ as the eternal Word of God was the less frequent calling on him as Lord and Christ as the agent of God's mercy for us. Into that near vacuum in the Church's prayer life stepped Mary. She was a fellow human and, unlike her Son, nothing more. Thus, the Church's praise of her as new Eve, in which Justin and especially Irenaeus and later Tertullian had placed her in parallel to the mother of all the living, saw her cult grow rapidly in the post-Nicaean era. Impetratory prayer to the martyrs also contributed to her role, providing as it did numerous intermediaries with Christ. But she by any reckoning was the chief.

The Creed and the anathemas of 325 and the emperor's espousal of them as the faith of Christians in the empire did not bring the religious peace intended. The official condemnation of Arius did nothing to subdue his partisans. The man had powerful friends and was a master of manipulating public opinion. He went on maintaining that "Son of God," "the Word," and even "God" were courtesy titles applied to Christ and not to be taken to connote the fullness of deity. Anti-Nicene coalitions were formed, the exiled Arians returned to their towns and bishoprics, and the close relation of the Catholic party with the emperor was attacked. By 380, with its First Council of Constantinople that dealt with several other matters, including the addition to its creed of the chief works of the Holy Spirit, the Nicaean faith had begun to prevail over the Arian. Pope Damasus I (366–84), the son of a priest of Rome, had done much to consolidate papal power and repress heresy, at times brutally. This was a time when trinitarian theology took a large step forward, chiefly through the writings of the brothers Basil of Caesarea and Gregory of Nazianz, joined by their close friends Gregory of Nyssa and the monk Evagrius of Pontus. Augustine of Hippo, Hilary of Poitiers who preceded him (reputedly the last married bishop of the West), and Pope Leo I of Rome brought Latin theology to the fore as it had not been since the early writings of the apologists Minucius Felix and Lactantius.

But after the relative calm of the one hundred years that spanned the fourth and fifth centuries, a theological storm broke out over who exactly Jesus Christ was that he could be called "the savior of the world" (John 4:42), a question that the creeds of Nicaea and Constantinople had not settled to everyone's satisfaction. These theologians, after all, were creatures of passion as well as intellect, with strong ethnic and political loyalties.

Nestorius's Defense of the Humanity of Christ

Nestorius was a man of Antioch and a former student of Theodore, bishop of Mopsuestia. Both stressed Jesus' human status in a way that was not characteristic of most Alexandrian christologies. Quite early in Nestorius's accession to the patriarchal chair of Constantinople he was asked to have an opinion of the suitability of the title *Theotókos* for Mary. He was being baited and he knew it because the title, seemingly about her motherhood, was actually about the Son she bore. Nestorius responded that it was correct to call Mary "the God-bearer" provided the second title *anthrōpotókos*, "the human being-bearer," was added. Not leaving well enough alone and detecting that the term was meant to demolish the Arian view of the Word as a creature, he went on to maintain that a more fitting title still would be *Christotókos*, since it traditionally described one who was both divine and human, not divine only. That was the response that Cyril of Alexandria hoped for. He reported to Celestine I, bishop of Rome, that this promoter of Antiochene theology denied the divinity of Christ. He secured condemnations of Nestorius by synods at Rome and Alexandria and appended to a letter to Constantinople Twelve Anathemas.[7] He made this a part of his charge that Nestorius believed in two persons in Christ, a human and a divine, who were united in a moral union only, not a personal one. His word for person was *hypóstasis*, and since Christ could be only one person that person had to be divine. What of the Jewish son born of Mary? She could only have borne a human nature that, at Jesus' conception in her womb, was joined to Jesus' divine person and nature. The divine person, the Word of God, was more than capable of standing in for the nonexistent human person Jesus, who nonetheless from birth had a complete human nature. This was a case of more than adequate substitution. Cyril described the conjoining of human nature to a divine in the one individual as *katà hypóstasin*, "according to person," hence forever after the term "*hypostatic union.*" It is still being taught in theological faculties as if it were the faith of the Church, even though at the Council of Chalcedon twenty years later the Church did not adopt it as its faith. If there is a better theory it is at least not as flawed as Cyril's, which was open to the charge of a suffering eternal *Logos* on the cross. He came around to seeing two natures in Christ but never two persons, a theory he was convinced Nestorius

---

[7] The letter was approved with Anathemas at the Council of Ephesus, 431. See Bettenson and Maunder, *Documents of the Christian Church*, 50–51, for full text.

held, which he did not. Cyril was a Word-flesh believer, not a Word-man believer, a tag he attached to the Antiochene school generally.

Nestorius grew weary of attacks on his orthodoxy and asked the emperor Theodosius I to call a council that would clear him. It did the opposite. Pope Celestine, on the advice of the monk John Cassian, found his position erroneous at the Roman synod mentioned above that Celestine summoned in 430. He called on the patriarch Nestorius to recant within ten days or stand excommunicate. Cyril, no mean strategist, assembled a synod of sixty bishops of his own persuasion in June of 431. At it he drew up Twelve Anathemas (false propositions) that he demanded Nestorius sign in repudiation. Thus predisposed to antagonism, the two parties of bishops met in the tiny church at Ephesus, the foundation stones of which are still there in the tall grass. A second church of the same size was built later facing the first and attached to it.

Nestorius was the first to arrive with his attendants. The Antiochene bishops came late with John of Antioch as their leader. When they assembled on June 26 they learned that Nestorius had been excommunicated four days before. In response they deposed Cyril and the local bishop of Ephesus and rejected the Twelve Anathemas. Such were the opening salvos. In November, however, by virtue of long and hard debate each side began to see a certain merit to the other side's case—for the Antiochenes, the full and complete humanity of Jesus as distinct from the divine person to which it was united, and for the Alexandrians, the unique godhead from which the Word, a distinct *hypóstasis*, eternally originated without effecting any change or confusion of the two natures in Christ. In the end, Cyril's anathemas were not adopted and Nestorius's views were not condemned. Pope Celestine died one year later and the new pope, Xystus III, like him a presbyter of Rome, showed an immediate desire for peace between East and West. He oversaw a Symbol, that is, a creed, of Union drawn up by Theodoret, bishop of Cyrus, an Antiochene, which Cyril surprisingly accepted. It confessed a Christ

> consubstantial with the Father in respect of his divinity and consubstantial with us in manhood. A union (*hénōsis*) of two natures has been accomplished. Hence, we confess one Christ, one Son, one Lord . . . [and] the holy Virgin as *Theotókos* because the divine Word became flesh and was made man and from the very conception united to himself the Temple taken from her.[8]

---

[8] The Symbol of Union of which this an excerpt was contained in a letter of John to Cyril. It is given in full in Kelly, *Early Christian Doctrines*, 328–29.

The Twelve Anathemas had been dropped, the Antiochenes were convinced they should abandon Nestorius for the sake of a settlement and he was condemned, the divine Word made man was the subject of the union of natures, and *Theotókos* was admitted as orthodox. Despite the prevalence of Antiochene language Cyril acknowledged himself satisfied. But not for long.

Each side began to register unhappiness with the Symbol of Union drafted after the council, Alexandrians especially for its acceptance of the Two-Natures doctrine when Cyril had stood so long for the one person and nature of the divine Logos. Nestorius was banished to exile and from there two decades later wrote *The Bazaar of Heracleides*, discovered only early in the twentieth century, in which he declared agreement with the settlement of Chalcedon (451) and proved that he had never taught that there were two persons in Christ.

Eutyches and the Chalcedonian Settlement

Cyril died in 444 but not before certain right-wing Alexandrians had pressed the phrase, "one person, one nature" from early in his polemical career to the limit. Toward the end of his life he had come to see its heretical possibilities. At his death the opponents of the Two-Natures doctrine enunciated after Ephesus rallied their forces. Cyril's successor as bishop of Alexandria, Dioscorus, thought Cyril had given in on one nature out of weakness, while the repudiation of Nestorius still rankled with the Syrian party. In 448 an aged monk of Alexandria, one Eutyches, who was head of a huge monastery there, was denounced as a heretic for his opposition to the Symbol. Flavian, Nestorius's successor in the see of Constantinople, read out a formula that he assumed to be orthodox but that was being interpreted otherwise by a new generation of monophysites (the One-Nature people): "We confess that Christ is of two natures after the incarnation, confessing one Christ, one Son, one *hypóstasis* and one *prósōpon* [literally "face"]." Each of the two nouns had at times signified a person and by using both Flavian prepared the way for Chalcedon. He meant by the phrase "of two natures" to be the union in Christ that dated from his human conception, but Eutyches and company took it for victory: only one nature eternally but of two natures after a certain point. Eutyches, who was evidently not too keen intellectually, when pressed by envoys of the Synod Flavian had assembled (at which he refused to appear), said, "After the birth of our Lord Jesus Christ I worship one nature, that is, of God made flesh and become man." He had no difficulty acknowledging that Christ was perfect God and perfect man by virtue of his human birth and that Mary was consubstantial with us. It was the idea that Christ also was consubstantial with us that he balked at, having always thought of the body of Christ as the body of God. He said, however, when he finally appeared before the Synod that if the bishops who were pressing him required it he would agree to such consubstantiality but only because they required it. "I admit that our Lord was of two natures before the union, but after the union one nature. . . . In this I follow the doctrine of the blessed Cyril and the holy fathers and the holy Athanasius." Eutyches is unfortunately on record as having maintained that the humanity of Christ is swallowed up in the divinity like a drop of honey in the ocean. The Synod condemned him, at which point he appealed to Leo I, bishop of Rome, who upheld Flavian's adverse judgment. Eutyches was deposed from his position as archimandrite and made an example of propounding this heresy at its worst, even though there was a far more extreme monophysite teaching abroad than his. This included a Docetism with respect to Jesus' humanity, namely, that he gave the appearance of being human but was not so in fact, that his body in life had been ethereal.

Western theologians up to this point had stayed out of the debates based on Greek subtlety in speech, contenting themselves with the forthright commitment of Tertullian to duality in unity based on the teaching of Origen. There had begun to be good writing on christology by Ambrose of Milan, Hilary of Poitiers, and Augustine of Hippo. Pope Leo I had framed a Dogmatic Letter, or Tome, based on Augustine's voluminous writings that he sent to the Patriarch Flavian in 449. His purpose was to indicate strong opposition to the One-Nature doctrine. It was intended to contribute to Eutyches's condemnation but it did not have that effect. Theodosius II, who was inclined to the monophysite view, held a synod at Ephesus in 449, which Leo called a hijacking or grand theft (*latrocinium*) in its vindication of Eutyches and anathematization of the Patriarch Flavian and the entire Two-Natures party. But Leo's Tome was to have a lively subsequent history, for when the new emperor Marcian convoked a council at Chalcedon in 451 (Theodosius had died the previous year in a fall from a horse), the five hundred assembled bishops were ready to bury all disputed and heretical christologies of the previous two centuries. The imperial commissioners present knew that the council would have to agree on a dogmatic formula that all would sign, making it mandatory for the empire's bishops and people. Leo, in his dozen years as bishop, had increased the respect and authority accorded to the Roman

See, which helped make his carefully crafted, if far from original, Tome the basic document for discussion.

The assembled fathers first approved the creeds of Nicaea and Constantinople (in which the latter said among other things that the Holy Spirit proceeds from the Father); then canonized Cyril's two letters, a move that made Nestorianism a heresy for any who held Cyril's view of that teaching; and, by and large, approved Leo's Tome. As a formal confession of faith its terms will be familiar to Catholics of the West who sing or recite it at each Sunday's liturgy. Asking representative numbers of those enrolled in an academic course to do so in chorus, slowly and antiphonally—one side of the room, then the other—should provide the basis for discussion of the Creed's most sensitive phrases. What can "light from light" mean in the text? Why the need for "true God of true God" after "God from God" has been said? And why does "one in being with the Father" make a faith statement about Jesus Christ that leaving the Latin word "consubstantial with" does not do in the ordinary English ear? The Creed insists that the only Son of God is no creature ("begotten, not made"). Both phrases are ways of saying in succinct fifth-century language that the Word is identical in substance, essence, or nature with God who is Father. At the same time, the statement that the Lord Jesus Christ "took flesh of the virgin Mary" (a baby formed in the womb) "by the Holy Spirit" and, more starkly, "became a human" is the only meaning *caro*, translating the earlier *sarx*, can have in the context of all the disputes.

The Confession of Faith framed at Chalcedon on the basis of the *Tomus Leonis*, the pope's little book, went beyond approving the Nicaeno-Constantinopolitan Creed just quoted. It tackled a number of positions that had been held on the mystery of the enfleshment of the Word by speaking of:

> One and the same Son, our Lord Jesus Christ, at once complete in godhead and complete in manhood, truly God and truly man, the latter [*auton*] of a rational [*logikē*] soul and body, of one substance [*homooúsios*] with the Father as regards his godhead and at the same time of one substance with us as regards his manhood; like us in all respects, sin alone excepted.[9]

---

[9] The Greek via a collection of conciliar pronouncements begun by J.D. Mansi in 1759, updated to 1927; helpfully translated to English in Bettenson and Maunder, *Documents of the Christian Church*, 56–57. Note that the suffix "head" means "hood," as in motherhood, and has nothing to do with the word head. Thus, godhead means deity or divinity and has no special reference to God's headship of all creation or the Father's headship of the Son.

Then, because the relation of the two natures of the one Christ—human and divine—to each other had been featured so much in rancorous debate, it went on to say of him that

> before the ages as regards his godhead, begotten of the Father but, as regards his manhood, for us and for our salvation, of Mary the Virgin, the Godbearer, one and the same Christ, Son, Lord, Only-begotten, recognized in two natures unconfusedly, undividedly, unchangedly, unseparatedly, the distinction of natures being in no way annulled by the union [*hénōsis*] but, rather, the characteristics of each nature being preserved and coming together to form one person and subsistence [*hypóstasis*], not as parted or separated into two persons, but one and the same Son and Only-begotten God, the Word, Lord Jesus Christ.

The definition was a marvel of balance and genius in what it did not say as much as in what it did say. One need not be too clever to deduce that each side was convinced it had won out over the other. The one matter that could lead to endless debate is how the two natures are joined in one person. Cyril thought he knew. The Chalcedonian fathers abstained. What they accomplished for the Church of East and West was to say in other words who the gospels and the epistles and the other biblical writings say Jesus is.

Why, then, are not the biblical words sufficient? Some Christians say, "We have no creeds," as if this were a boast, not a defect. Other Christians say to them, "You are living perilously," or perhaps better, "You are living on the spiritual capital of your forebears, which you would do well to acknowledge." For the mystery of Christ is so far above human comprehension that erroneous conceptions of him lurk behind all attempts to capture him in thought or word.

The proof of this is perhaps what followed in the two centuries after Chalcedon: the Second Council of Constantinople in 553, a bit of a disgrace; and the Third Council of Constantinople in 680-81, which delivered an important corrective.

What can be disgraceful about a Church council, the first seven of which the East and West count ecumenical, meaning Church-wide? It deserves that name even if its acts, disguised as orthodoxy, are vindictive. Such was the case with the condemnation by that council of "Three Chapters," portions of writings of three Syrian theologians who had taken on Cyril, or the One-Nature party, a century before what led up to Chalcedon. The men were Ibas of Edessa, Theodoret of Cyrus, and Theodore of Mopsuestia. None of the three was committed to heresy. All were committed to Nestorius's attempt, and the Antiochene follow-up, to keep the human Jesus fully in view when theorizing about his natures, the relation between them, and how his humanity was related to the Word. The acts of the Second Council of Constantinople have gone down in the history of the Church as if they were a triumph of christological orthodoxy. They were no such thing. A better description might be a dancing on an honest theologian's grave. An actor in that drama was the emperor Justinian, a man full of zeal but not skilled in theology. He listened to the anti-Antiochene council and signed off on the condemnation of three long-dead thinkers of another persuasion.

The seventh-century occurrence was a further echo of Chalcedon but involved a genuinely erroneous position. Beginning in the 630s some highly placed figures began to teach that, although Jesus' humanity was complete, his conformity to the divine will was so total that he had no need of a human will. It can be seen as a corollary, perhaps, of his having a human nature without being a human person, God infinite filling in the gap with ease in both cases. This is not heresy in the strict sense, but a pious insistence on the divine in Jesus that Arius had denied. The patriarch of Alexandria, a certain Carus, not surprisingly held this view. So did Sergius, patriarch of Constantinople. The major defenders of Jesus' possession of a human will were a certain Sophronius, a native of Damascus who became bishop of Jerusalem, and St. Maximus the Confessor, the outstanding Greek theologian of the seventh century. Sergius wrote a letter to Pope Honorius I in 634 telling him how successful the formula "two distinct natures but one operation" had been in winning over disaffected monophysites. What he meant by the formula was that the same Son was the subject of every operation, human and divine. Honorius was no theologian though an outstanding executor of the papal office. He bought the package and wrote several letters to his fellow patriarchs in support of their erroneous position. He was dead by the time the emperor Heraclius in 638 wrote a position paper—more a decree—saying that monotheletism (One Will) described Jesus' free choice best. At the Third Council of Constantinople of 680 this theory was anathematized as thoroughly erroneous. But it did not die. When the Christians in the Lebanon mountain range who venerated St. Maron as their founder came into communion with the Roman See in the sixteenth century it came to light that in their isolation they had long held the monothelete position, although the rite itself maintains that it had been uninterruptedly orthodox.

The conclusion to be drawn from all that was said in this chapter is that Chalcedon is the last word of the whole Church until now on who

Jesus Christ is for the Church. It professes a strong faith in the divinity of Christ and equally strong faith in his full humanity—which, in preaching and teaching, has not been nearly so strong. Theologians can be censured for not speaking of the divine in Jesus every time they mention him, but not for failing to feature his humanity with equal emphasis. Speaking or writing of his birth in Bethlehem or his passion and death on the cross constitute the exceptions.

Epilogue

There is more known about Jesus of Nazareth in Galilee than of any other historical figure of the ancient world, pagan or Jewish. The portrait that emerges from the written sources that speak of him has been discounted in some quarters as biased, hence non-dependable, because they are the work of religious believers in him. By this test, what we know of Moses the Lawgiver, Gautama the Buddha, Muhammad the Prophet, or any figure of the distant religious past is equally inadmissible since all are recalled orally or in writing only by believers in them. Christian canonical Scripture, that is, the twenty-seven books of the New Testament, is distinguished by its recording of the many who did *not* believe in him in his lifetime or in the mission of his disciples after his lifetime. The Qur'an does something similar in writing of the resistance to Islam in its earliest decades but without nearly so many specifics.

A late eighteenth-century scholar of Semitic languages, Hermann Samuel Reimarus, wrote that Jesus' disciples were so disappointed by his death by crucifixion that they devised the tale of his resurrection to keep the memory of his teaching alive, then spun the stories of his words and deeds that became the four gospels. Another German religious thinker Bruno Bauer, who lived through most of the nineteenth century, credited the Gospel in its entirely to the imagination of one man writing in the lifetime of the emperor Hadrian (d. 138) and the epistles of Paul to another in Marcus Aurelius's day (d. 180). At the turn of the eighteenth century John Toland in England, joined later by Matthew Tindal, denied the possibility of the miraculous and anything supernatural about the mysteries of the incarnation, the Holy Trinity, and the redemption. Bauer was followed by a German or two who denied that Jesus had ever lived and affirmed that the gospels were a pastiche of biblical hero types and teaching formed in the image and likeness of a single person. This fantasizing was traceable in part to the skepticism of David Hume, a Scot. Weary of this fantasizing, Richard Whately, an English clergyman who later became the Church of Ireland archbishop of Dublin, wrote the serious spoof *Historic Doubts Relative to Napoleon Bonaparte* two years before the little corporal's death in exile, calling his existence into question. Not long after, Ludwig Andreas Feuerbach and David Friedrich Strauss came on the scene with theories of a mythicization process that produced the image of both God and Jesus.

If Jesus is not a figure of human history, no one is. A human figure he was and a great one in the history of our race. Yet in the first written source through which anyone outside the boundaries of Roman Palestine heard of him, Jesus was being proclaimed a true human and more than human, the innocent victim of Roman "justice" in whom the Son of the God of Israel had taken flesh. The title Son of God, at least in a generic sense, could be attributed to any Israelite true to the covenant and the demands of Torah. Unique in Jesus' case was the claim that eternal God dwelled in him as in no human before or after.

The earliest written words about Jesus that managed to be saved are the epistles of St. Paul's authentic authorship. They come from the decade of the 50s. With the exception of Revelation, the other non-Pauline writings are largely undatable, although the three epistles that claim to be written by him came after his death and others conceivably before. The gospels can safely be dated from 65 to 125 or 135, while Revelation gives evidence of authorship in Domitian's reign (d. 96) or perhaps Hadrian's (d. 117). Saint Paul in his extant letters tells nothing of Jesus' public career, only that he was a Jew born under the Law, and identifies some few of Jesus' teachings as from "the Lord." Paul confines mention of him to the sufferings he endured in his final days and hours. These references are invariably consolidated under the single word "the cross," and his crucifixion normally as "his death." Paul uses the word "resurrection" more than once to describe Jesus' upraising by the power of God but also, in the future, the resurrection of the faithful or the just on the "day of Christ." It can be shown from his earliest written letter to the church at Thessalonika, which he founded, that he considers Jesus to be unequivocally human and unequivocally divine, whatever divinity may connote to the limited human intellect. Why Paul and other writers like the authors of the letters that were attributed to apostles at an early date—those of James, John, Jude, Paul himself, and Hebrews and Revelation—told nothing of Jesus' teaching or wonderworking is a mystery. The closest anyone can come to a solution is that the earliest Church deduced Jesus' resurrection and bodily ascent to have given meaning to the sufferings and death that preceded it and the upraising in glory that followed. These were the primary matters that needed to be proclaimed, not Jesus' brief career as a teacher and worker of miraculous deeds.

Saul/Paul and to some extent all the others saw in Jesus as glorified his importance in the two-millennia-long history of his people. Believing as his people did in the revelation in him of God whom they called LORD, substituting it for his proper name HWHY (read right to left), which out of awe they did not speak, they searched their Scriptures for clues to him that they had not recognized as such. Their expectation that the Messiah would go from victory to victory had to give place to the picture in Psalm 22 and the books of Isaiah and Wisdom of a beleaguered person who would be the subject of popular contempt, in Zechariah of a man entering Jerusalem not proudly on a stallion but on the foal of an ass, and the many conflicting images in other psalms of a tortured and humiliated human who would at the same time be foreshadowed by the huzzahs that rang in the ears of the kings of Judah at their enthronement. These were signs in most cases of the unfulfilled hopes of the people. But whether the descriptions were of a suffering and dying or a gloriously reigning figure, if they were in any sense Davidic they were seen as pointing to Jesus.

The late first century came to know much more of Jesus than in the claim that biblical prophecy was fulfilled in the events of his last three days and what followed. Four skilled researcher-writers satisfied the curiosity of people who believed in his resurrection as to what Jesus had been like as a teacher, wonderworker, and revealer of the Father. Jesus did not in any way reform the shape of the religion of Israel but only the way the lives of the people and their leaders should be reformed in their living it. The composers of gospels wrote from four locations outside the land of Israel. All four wrote in their native Greek. All quoted their people's Scriptures liberally in the Greek translation of another Hebrew text than the one much later fixed by the Rabbis. Called the Septuagint (because seventy was thought to be the number of pagan peoples of the Jewish Diaspora), it served the evangelists' purposes admirably. Occasionally one or other gave evidence of rendering a snatch on his own from memory or from another Hebrew text or the Aramaic paraphrases (Targums). It is impossible to know the locale in which any one of the four was operating. The near Diaspora is the best guess, that is to say Syria, or what is now Lebanon. The evidence that Mark wrote in Rome and John in Ephesus is late and seems to be thin. From their writing styles they appear to be ethnic Jews or if not that, in one or other case a gentile Godfearer. They are working from sources, oral and written, which in the latter case appear to be a matter of interdependence, Matthew deriving heavily from Mark, Luke less so, and both depending on a written source that has never come to light. This is a sayings collection containing Jesus' teaching in near verbatim form in some fifty-three cases and partial wording in another twenty-two. John's gospel betrays a knowledge of incidents and teachings in Jesus' public life that he always reports on in quite different fashion than the other three, omitting much but also supplying much that they do not contain.

Mark, Matthew, and Luke give ample evidence of having access to compiled collections of Jesus' proverbial sayings, his illustrative short tales called parables, his miracles of healing and a few of the control of inanimate nature, and instant cures of what were thought to be demonic possession. In editing all of these and placing them in new settings in Jesus' public life, each evangelist acted, not as a cataloguer or compiler with respect to, but as a literary creator of narrative. Each acted freely in creating contexts other than the other two or three of the same material. All had in common the purpose of weaving a persuasive homiletic product that would confirm the believers in the faith they already held— namely, that God had used Jesus, who at all points had acted freely to live a life of obedience to the divine will, to show all humans what living humanly meant. Moreover, by faith, that is to say, trust in this deed of God in him and its meaning, they would be empowered to live in a way that seemed beyond human capacity. Jesus not only provided an example of how to live but, in the power of God's Spirit, was the effecter of such a life in others.

There has been a serious scholarly effort over the past fifty years to arrive at a picture of "the historical Jesus." It tries to identify that teaching of Jesus in the form of sayings chiefly but also parables and, lastly, certain brief narratives that will disclose who Jesus was before he was believed in as someone sent by God. Because there is no exploration in the search of how belief in Jesus as raised up from the dead influenced everything about the way the evangelists put this compiled material to use, the impression is given that this is all there was to Jesus: a teacher of a way of life based on the expectation of a divine inbreaking in Israel's future in which God would reign over a people who would submit to this rule as it never had before.

The net effect of arriving at the Jesus of history, as it is called, is therefore a kind of reductionism. Such is not the intention of all engaged in the search, but the inquiry cannot arrive at the Jesus believed in by the Church, who is the only actual "historical Jesus." It was his upraising from death in a rock tomb by the power of God that alone enabled his friends and disciples to know who he was, as the gospels and Acts observe more than once (see Mark 9:9-10; 16:14; Matt 17:9; John 20:8-9; Acts 1:22; 2:32; 3:15). The search is certainly not to no purpose. It simply does not end in the triumphant disclosure that some claim for it. Having dismissed the Jesus of the Church's faith as a theological but not a historical matter, it discloses not Jesus' earliest teaching but the earliest historical compilation of some of his teaching by believers in him as risen from the dead.

That is why this book has proceeded as it has, by starting with the Jesus the Church believed him to be from its earliest days. Only later did it go on to the earliest compiling of Jesus' teaching and acts placed in a narrative context, as if there were another way to know him than by the received proclamation of his life, death, and resurrection. Much more is known of how and why he was first venerated, and literally adored, before efforts were made to recall and transmit his sublime teaching about the Law of God (*Torah*) and the Reign of God (*Malkuth*).

This in particular was known: that those who accepted the gift of faith in him engaged in a ritual washing they called baptism, which they viewed as the gateway to life in a community of Jews and gentiles they called, from the start, the Church, or the Life of the Final Eon, and some the Way. They regularly celebrated a ritual meal in bread and wine in which the power of God responded to the prayer of the community by transforming these gifts into his body and blood. This meal was early called the Eucharist (Thanks) and the Eulogy (Praise). The former came to prevail. It is correct to say that the Eucharist both makes and constantly renews the Church, the Body of Christ, who is the Jesus of heavenly glory in the world.

Further Reading

Bettenson, Henry, and Chris Maunder, eds. *Documents of the Christian Church.* 3rd ed. Oxford: Oxford University Press, 1999.

Brown, Raymond E. *An Introduction to the New Testament.* New York: Doubleday, 1997.

Garcia-Martinez, Florentino. *The Dead Sea Scrolls Translated: The Qumrân Texts in English.* Translated by Wilfrid G.E. Watson. 2nd ed. Leiden/Grand Rapids: E.J. Brill/William B. Eerdmans, 1996.

Guillamont, A., H.-Ch. Puech, G. Quispel, W. Till, and Yassah ʿAbd al Massiḥ, trans. *The Gospel According to Thomas.* San Francisco: Harper & Row, 1959.

The Harper Collins Study Bible. Revised Standard Version. San Francisco: Harper Collins, 1989. (Useful for introductions, notes, maps, and tables.)

Hurtado, Larry W. *Lord Jesus Christ: Devotion to Jesus in Earliest Christianity.* Grand Rapids: William B. Eerdmans, 2003.

Jeremias, Joachim. *The Parables of Jesus.* New York: Charles Scribner's Sons, 1963.

Johnson, Luke Timothy. *The Writings of the New Testament: An Interpretation.* rev. ed. Minneapolis: Fortress, 1999.

Kelly, J.N.D. *Early Christian Doctrines.* New York: Continuum, 2000.

———. *The Oxford Dictionary of Popes.* Oxford: Oxford University Press, 1986.

Lambrecht, Jan. *Once More Astonished: The Parables of Jesus.* New York: Crossroad, 1981.

Metzger, Bruce M. *The Canon of the New Testament: Its Origin, Development, and Significance.* Oxford: Clarendon, 1987.

The New American Bible. New York: Catholic Book Publishing, 1991. (Useful for introductions, notes, maps, and tables. The 1970 New Testament translation is that employed in the four-volume *Liturgy of the Hours* and reads more smoothly.)

Perkins, Pheme. *Gnosticism and the New Testament.* Minneapolis: Fortress Press, 1993.

The Revised English Bible with 1 and 2 Esdras and the Deuterocanonical Books. Oxford: Oxford University Press/Cambridge University Press, 1989.

Richardson, Cyril C., ed. *Early Christian Fathers*. New York: Touchstone, 1996.

Sanders, E.P. *Jesus and Judaism*. Minneapolis: Fortress, 1985.

Schoonenberg, Piet. *The Christ: A Study of the God-man in Relationship in the Whole Creation and in Jesus Christ*. New York: Seabury, 1971.

Sloyan, Gerard S. *John: A Bible Commentary for Teaching and Preaching*. Louisville: Westminster John Knox, 1988.

———. *The Crucifixion of Jesus: History, Myth, Faith*. Minneapolis: Fortress, 1995.

———. *Jesus on Trial: A Study of the Gospels*. 2nd ed. Minneapolis: Fortress, 2006.

———. *Preaching from the Lectionary: An Exegetical Commentary*. Minneapolis: Fortress, 2004. (Exegesis of Sunday and Feast Day Lections of Lectionary for Mass and Revised Common Lectionary if they differ.)

Index of Scripture and Ancient Texts

Index of Subjects and Persons